WIRTSCHAFTSINFORMATIK

Herausgegeben von Prof. Dr. Dietrich Seibt, Köln, Prof. Dr. Hans-Georg Kemper, Stuttgart, Prof. Dr. Georg Herzwurm, Stuttgart, Prof. Dr. Dirk Stelzer, Ilmenau, und Prof. Dr. Detlef Schoder, Köln

Band 68
Michael Röthlin
Management of Data Quality in Enterprise Resource Planning Systems
Lohmar – Köln 2010 ✦ 332 S. ✦ € 63,- (D) ✦ ISBN 978-3-89936-963-2

Band 69
Ludwig Fuchs
Methodology for Hybrid Role Development
Lohmar – Köln 2010 ✦ 272 S. ✦ € 58,- (D) ✦ ISBN 978-3-89936-978-6

Band 70
Andreas Helferich
Software Mass Customization
Lohmar – Köln 2010 ✦ 380 S. ✦ € 65,- (D) ✦ ISBN 978-3-8441-0006-8

Band 71
Tyge-F. Kummer
Akzeptanz von Ambient Intelligence in Krankenhäusern – Ein Ländervergleich zwischen Deutschland und Australien am Beispiel der Medikationsunterstützung
Lohmar – Köln 2010 ✦ 320 S. ✦ € 62,- (D) ✦ ISBN 978-3-8441-0008-2

Band 72
Stephan Wildner
Problemorientiertes Wissensmanagement – Eine Neukonzeption des Wissensmanagements aus konstruktivistischer Sicht
Lohmar – Köln 2011 ✦ 384 S. ✦ € 65,- (D) ✦ ISBN 978-3-8441-0043-3

Band 73
Rolf Schillinger
Semantic Service Oriented Architectures in Research and Practice
Lohmar – Köln 2011 ✦ 304 S. ✦ € 59,- (D) ✦ ISBN 978-3-8441-0062-4

Semantic Service Oriented Architectures in Research and Practice

Dissertation zur Erlangung des Grades eines
Doktors der Wirtschaftswissenschaft

eingereicht an der Wirtschaftswissenschaftlichen
Fakultät der Universität Regensburg

vorgelegt von: Rolf Schillinger

Berichterstatter: Prof. Dr. Günther Pernul

                           Prof. Dr. Hannes Federrath

Tag der Disputation: 23.11.2010

Reihe: Wirtschaftsinformatik · Band 73

Herausgegeben von Prof. Dr. Dietrich Seibt, Köln, Prof. Dr. Hans-Georg Kemper, Stuttgart, Prof. Dr. Georg Herzwurm, Stuttgart, Prof. Dr. Dirk Stelzer, Ilmenau, und Prof. Dr. Detlef Schoder, Köln

Dr. Rolf Schillinger

Semantic Service Oriented Architectures in Research and Practice

With a Foreword by Prof. Dr. Günther Pernul, University of Regensburg

Bibliografische Information der Deutschen Nationalbibliothek

Die Deutsche Nationalbibliothek verzeichnet diese Publikation in der Deutschen Nationalbibliografie; detaillierte bibliografische Daten sind im Internet über <http://dnb.d-nb.de> abrufbar.

Dissertation, Universität Regensburg, 2010

ISBN 978-3-8441-0062-4
1. Auflage Juli 2011

JOSEF EUL VERLAG GmbH
Brandsberg 6
53797 Lohmar
Tel.: 0 22 05 / 90 10 6-6
Fax: 0 22 05 / 90 10 6-88
E-Mail: info@eul-verlag.de
http://www.eul-verlag.de

Bei der Herstellung unserer Bücher möchten wir die Umwelt schonen. Dieses Buch ist daher auf säurefreiem, 100% chlorfrei gebleichtem, alterungsbeständigem Papier nach DIN 6738 gedruckt.

Foreword

Although they have gained tremendous interest recently Service-Oriented-Architectures (SOA) are not a new finding. If one wants to go back in the history of distributed computing the use of DCOM or the ORB based on the CORBA specification may be regarded as early SOA because in their widest sense they were mainly invented to enable services to communicate with each other.

It was only six to eight years ago when the SOA hype was on its peak and vendors promised to solve just every problem that enterprises faced with SOA. Whether it was interoperability of systems, scalability, asset reuse, or business agility - SOA was going to solve it all. Indeed, the enterprise IT world had the "SOA fever". Recently, however, there has been a very noticeable drop in the hype around SOA. For example, technology analyst Gartner once one of the first who pushed SOA had to acknowledge that many organizations have either dropped or postponed plans to adopt SOA. So is SOA being abandoned?

This book is constructed around this central question and benefiting from the authors participation in two European funded research projects, FP6 Access-eGov and FP7 Spike, both focusing on research and development of a large-scale service brokering infrastructure. Proposed in the book are an enriched semantic SOA and a generic architecture model for which Access-eGov as well as Spike are instances of. In the context of a research group working on these two competitive projects the author investigates questions like what is a proper design for the infrastructure, how will an implementation look like, are standard security services applicable to a semantic SOA, and more general are semantic SOA already usable and are they able to introduce value added?

In addition to its original contribution to new knowledge, this book also covers the state-of-the-art and recent developments in software architectural styles, security in different architectural styles, knowledge-based technologies and semantic web service frameworks. Whether you are a member of a technical staff concerned with SOA development who must address semantic technologies or security, a student, or a researcher, this book is highly recommended for study because it will provide you with a comprehensive treatment of the major challenges involved.

Prof. Dr. Günther Pernul
Department of Information Systems
University of Regensburg, Germany

Acknowledgements

While researchers often work in quiet, sparsely lit offices during the later hours of the day, the perception of a solitary researcher is wrong. Using today's communication technologies, researchers can discuss their thoughts with colleagues and friends all over the world in an instant. The resulting network of peers involved to a greater or lesser extent in a research effort is accordingly large and does not leave room for naming all these individuals personally. Of all the individuals in my network of peers some stood out, however. They have to be mentioned individually.

First of all, I would like to thank my advisor Prof. Dr. Günther Pernul for giving me the opportunity to work in two large, interesting, and challenging research projects while always giving me the freedom to solve the posed challenges in innovative ways. Frequent occasions for discussing my ideas on scientific conferences and project meetings are especially worthy of mentioning in these times of tight public budgets.

I also thank my co-advisor, Prof. Dr. Hannes Federrath, for the precious feedback and valuable input.

My current and former colleagues at the Department of Information Systems at the University of Regensburg were always open for fruitful discussions and were a frequent source of rejoice. I would like to especially thank Dr. Jan Kolter and Stefan Dürbeck for countless hours spent on discussing Access-eGov's architecture and security subsystem, Oliver Gmelch for an almost equal amount of hours spent as lector on this thesis, and the remaining members of the core SPIKE team, namely Christian Broser and Christoph Fritsch (already a graduand on Access-eGov). Sabine Schubert (for keeping in shape the IT infrastructure) and Christine Handl (for knowing and thus tackling many peculiarities of large public bodies) must not be forgotten in this context.

Members of the Technical University of Kosice also played an important role in the success of this thesis. Especially Peter Bednár and Marek Skokan contributed massively to many of the discussed topics.

Finally, I have to thank our students at the Department of Information Systems who, through term papers, diploma and master's theses, and projects, were frequent and important contributors.

This thesis would not have been successful without all these help.

Rolf Schillinger, Laberweinting, Germany, May 2010

Contents

IV. Application Cases   211

List of Figures

List of Tables

List of Abbreviations

AAI   Authorization and Authentication Infrastructure

ABAC   Attribute-Based Access Control

ADL   Architecture Description Language

AI   Artificial Intelligence

ASM   Abstract State Machine

AT   Access-eGov Annotation Tool

ATAM   Architecture Tradeoff Analysis Method

B2B   Business to Business

BPEL   Business Process Execution Language

BPM   Business Process Management

BPMN   Business Process Modeling Notation

CMS   Content Management Systems

CRM   Customer Relationship Management

CRUD   Create, Retrieve, Update, Delete

DDoS   Distributed Denial of Service

DNS   Domain Name System

DoS   Denial of Service

DRM   Digital Rights Management

EAI   Enterprise Application Integration

ERP   Enterprise Resource Planning

ESB   Enterprise Service Bus

GENSOA   Generic Semantic Service-Oriented Architecture

GUI   Graphical User Interface

HTTP   Hypertext Transfer Protocol

HTTPS   HTTP Secure

IDE   Integrated Development Environment

IdM   Identity Management

IEEE1471 IEEE/ISO Standard 1471

IOPE   Input, Output, Preconditions, and Effects

IRI   Internationalized Resource Identifier

IS   Information System

IT   Information Technology

JPA   Java Persistence API

JSF   Java Server Faces

KBT   Knowledge-Based Technologies

MAC   Message Authentication Code

MEP   Message Exchange Patterns

NFP   Non-Functional Properties

NLSRS   Natural Language Software Requirements Specification

OOP   Object-Oriented Programming

ORM   Object Relational Mapper

OS   Operating System

OWL   Web Ontology Language

P2P   Peer-to-Peer

P3P   Platform for Privacy Preferences

PAC   Personal Assistant Client

PAP   Policy Administration Point

PDP   Policy Decision Point

PEP   Policy Enforcement Point

PIP   Policy Information Point

PKI   Public Key Infrastructure

PPC   Production Planning and Control

RAD   Rapid Application Development

RBAC   Role-Based Access Control

RDBMS   Relational Database Management System

RDF   Resource Description Framework

REST   Representational State Transfer

RIF   Rule Interchange Format

RPC   Remote Procedure Call

RUP   Rational Unified Process

SAML   Security Assertion Markup Language

SAMR   SPIKE Administration, Monitoring & Reporting

SEC   GENSOA Security Architecture

SIAT   Security Information Administration Tool

SLOC   Source Lines of Code

SME   Small to medium-sized Enterprise

SOAP   Simple Object Access Protocol

SOA-RM OASIS SOA Reference Model

SOA   Service Oriented Architecture

SPI   SPIKE Portal Instance

SRS   Software Requirements Specification

SSB   SPIKE Service Bus

SSC   SPIKE System Core

SSOA   Semantic Service-Oriented Architecture

SSO   Single Sign On

SVN   Subversion

UML   Unified Modeling Language

URI   Uniform Resource Locator

WSDL   Web Service Description Language

WSML   Web Service Modeling Language

WSMO   Web Service Modeling Ontology

WWW   World Wide Web

XACML   eXtensible Access Control Markup Language

XSLT   eXtensible Stylesheet Language Transformations

XML   eXtensible Markup Language

1. Overview

1.1. Motivation

Complexity - The challenge

Information Technology (IT) has been positioned as the magic bullet for solving a wide range of problems within and between organizations. Paperless offices (1990s), ubiquitous computing (late 1990s), or cloud computing (late 2000s) are just some of the so-called[1] novelties that have entered IT and adjacent fields and left more or less visible traces. One thing is common to all those paradigms: None managed to significantly decrease complexity, neither in the software systems used nor in the attached processes. Quite to the contrary, usually these paradigms have the tendency to ever increase complexity. The paperless office ultimately leads to a need for huge and complex archival solutions, ubiquitous computing requires a whole new framework of technical and organizational changes [LY02], and cloud computing delivers on some of its promises but also increases overall complexity of the software systems [AFG+09].

In addition to this system-inherent complexity, IT structures within organizations have reached new heights of complexity as well. In today's enterprises it is very common to have Enterprise Resource Planning (ERP), Production Planning and Control (PPC), and Customer Relationship Management (CRM) systems alongside Content Management Systems (CMS) and usually a plethora of "quick and dirty" applications in all possible forms ranging from Microsoft Access based standalone applications to Intranet sites developed in scripting languages. The problem: All of these software systems are based on the same underlying real world objects (Customers, Products, Quotes, ...), but with many different representations of the same entities[2].

---

[1] Often these terms are nothing more than a repackaged set of technologies that have been in use in different contexts for a considerable amount of time.

[2] In the worst case, each of the existing applications has its own data store with an own data representation.

On the business process side of running an enterprise, the situation is equally intricate. The multitude of systems often causes interruptions in workflows as current state data attached to a running business process cannot easily be exchanged between systems. Commencing a workflow on one system and continuing its execution on another is even more unrealistic.

In order to master these problems, the IT sector regularly presents a new attempt at a solution.

SOA - The answer?

The most persistent and far-reaching of the aforementioned solution attempts is the service orientation which, in the form of the Service Oriented Architecture (SOA), was initially introduced by Gartner[3], an IT analyst, as early as in 1996 [SN96]. It however failed to gain widespread usage until the mid 2000s. If one of Gartner's publications so far had equally far-reaching press echo, it was the Gartner Hype Cycle that explains technology adoption in five phases[4]:

- Technology trigger
  An event that brings the technology in question into the (IT-)public view.

- Peak of inflated expectation
  The actual hype phase where only a tiny fraction of projects involving the technology are successful as opposed to the vast majority of cases where that specific technology fails.

- Trough of disillusionment
  The technology is put to rest in the media after the failures in the previous phase seemed to indicate its impracticability.

- Slope of enlightenment
  Some strongholds of the technology still exist and continue to use and evolve it, albeit silently.

- Plateau of productivity
  Later generations of the technology see increased usage in real-world scenarios after having been turned into stable and productive applications.

In a curious exception to this rule, SOAs so far did not seem to follow the Hype Cycle but rather were protected against crossing the "Peak of Inflated Expectation"

---

[3]http://www.gartner.com
[4]http://www.gartner.com/pages/story.php.id.8795.s.8.jsp

although certain signs are now implying that the hype finally begins to slowly cease: After projecting in 2003 that with a 0.7 probability by 2008 SOAs will be "prevailing software engineering practice, ending the 40-year domination of monolithic software architecture"[5], Gartner initially kept to that prediction: "SOA Will Be Used in More Than 50 Percent of New Mission-Critical Operational Applications and Business Processes Designed in 2007"[6]. Recently, however, Gartner had to acknowledge[7] that many organizations have either dropped or postponed plans to adopt SOAs. Lack of skills and expertise is cited to be one of the contributing factors as well as – even more interestingly – a lack of viable business cases. Whether this is for reasons connected to the economic downturn caused by the financial crisis starting in 2008 or is a generic or structural problem of SOAs is left for the reader to decide.

The hype surrounding SOAs is all the more inexplicable since SOA, as theoretically defined and practically implemented today, lacks key differentiators to other technologies. Section 3.3.5, by detailing the inner workings of the technology, gives an implicit explanation for the hiatus SOAs entered from their first description in 1996 on: it did not offer enough advantages over customary and - even in 1996 already - proven technologies like object orientation and the accompanying usage of interfaces.

It took the addition of another key technology, namely the Web Service, to develop enough competitive edge to ignite and sustain the hype. SOAs are still missing other functionalities like automated composition and orchestration of Web Services[8], however.

Especially in the context of these missing key features, another topic of IT should not go unmentioned: the increasing complexity. Above mentioned problems SOA adoption currently is seeing can at least be partially explained by the fact that SOAs add several layers of indirection and with them, more complexity and more resource consumption. It is hard to justify those additional expenses and possible problems when other solutions exist, especially if they are proven, effective, and in wide-spread usage.

At this point, it is important to notice that SOAs do have their areas of application, largely in connection with integration efforts. Enterprise Application Integration (EAI) often is cited as the key driver for SOAs and, as a special case, SOAs enriched with an Enterprise Service Bus (ESB).

---

[5]http://www.gartner.com/pages/story.php.id.3586.s.8.jsp
[6]http://www.gartner.com/it/page.jsp?id=503864
[7]http://www.cio.com/article/461015/Big_Drop_in_Plans_to_Adopt_SOA_Gartner_Survey
[8]Detailed in Section 3.3.6

The addition of a mix of Knowledge-Based Technologies (KBT) results in a largely improved SOA, called the Semantic Service-Oriented Architecture (SSOA) which finally features automatic composition and orchestration facilities and other very interesting features that will be explained in due course. SSOAs aim at taking architectural styles to a new level – and succeed.

1.2. Research methodology

1.2.1. Methodology Selection

Computer Sciences and Information Systems research are two different but closely related disciplines. Computer Science, looking at its curriculum, is more focused at the details of IT-based systems on a microscopic level, like the protocols, the algorithms, and data structures. Information Systems research on the other hand is concerned with the same systems, but on a macroscopic level, involving architectures, protocol interoperability or knowledge representation[9].

Oriented towards Information Systems research, this thesis looks at SSOAs from a macroscopic level accordingly. Wilde et al. are a first stop for a quantitative overview of often-used research methodologies in Information Systems research [WH07] but the publication is not thoroughly useful for conducting a thesis. Punctual, short-term research efforts[10] are the common sources for most of the introduced methodologies. Classifying or even guiding large, coherent nonetheless wide-ranging research does not fit well within Wilde's characterizations. Hevner et al. describe on the highest level two distinct approaches to Information Systems research, namely behavioral and design science [HMPR04], allowing to ground the research effort presented in this thesis more broadly.

Behavioral Science is rooted in the natural sciences, where its main application is seeking to explain or forecast "organizational and human" phenomena with regards to the Information System lifecycle. Contrary to that, Design science evolved as a methodology built around the task of problem solving, but problem solving through innovative usage of already existing theories and other applicable pieces of knowledge.

Vaishnavi et al. talk about Design Research as an alias to Improvement Research [VK04]. An adjacent view is presented in [HMPR04] where the authors regard improvement as key component of Design Research with an end result of solving

---

[9]The exemplary aspects do justice to neither of the disciplines but only serve as examples.
[10]The classical research paper publication.

a problem. Both views perfectly fit this thesis' previously mentioned main goal of improving SOAs by evolving them through the usage of KBTs, finally resulting in a SSOA. Thus, Design Research is the research method implemented in this thesis.

1.2.2. Design Research

Since selection of Design Research as predominant research pattern was based on theoretical merits, a crosscheck of Design Research feasibility in this context needs to build on descriptions of applied Design Research. Rather than defining a step-by-step process model as partially laid out by Vaishnavi et al. in [VK04], [HMPR04] establishes the following guidelines that describe the requirements of an effective Design Research effort:

1. Design as an artifact
   An artifact is one of the results of Design Research. Effective description is important in order to assure that it can be (re-)used across specific application domains. A clear definition of what defines an artifact in the Design Research sense is nowhere to be found, typical types of artifacts according to the authors, however, include innovative architectures of the proposed Information System (IS).

2. Problem relevance
   Business problems often are the triggers for research efforts, but in the Design Research case, a relevant business problem is the mandatory starting point for the research.

3. Design evaluation
   Evaluation is an essential phase and optimally is done in a feedback loop with the design phase as both tasks are iterative.

4. Research contribution
   The research contribution is always the most important measure of research success. Design Research produces measurable contributions in three different forms, namely either as an artifact, as additions to the theoretical and practical foundations of the topic, or as a methodology.

5. Research rigor
   Positioning the research effort in a system of relevance and rigor measures is problematic. High requirements for rigor are a potential threat to the relevance of the research. Design Research, at least according to Hevner et al.,

tends towards a pragmatic understanding of rigor [HMPR04]. Even without measures such as correctness proofs, the resulting information sytsems can be regarded as suitable if only "rigorous methods" have been used in design and evaluation.

6. Design as a search process
   Again, this guideline is rather pragmatic, diminishing the burden of finding all possible solutions to a given problem to the task of finding "satisfactory" solutions.

7. Communication of research
   Design Research output is targeted at both a technical crowd as well as upper management levels. Any communication of the research output has to satisfy the requirements of both target groups.

Takeda et al. introduced a "General Design Cycle" [TVTY90] much earlier, which is often used to describe the process a Design Research effort follows. Without the guidelines of [HMPR04], however, this process is not defined precisely enough. Figure 1.1 depicts the different phases of Takeda's process in the form proposed by [VK04]. After describing these steps, they are subsequently translated into the context of this thesis.

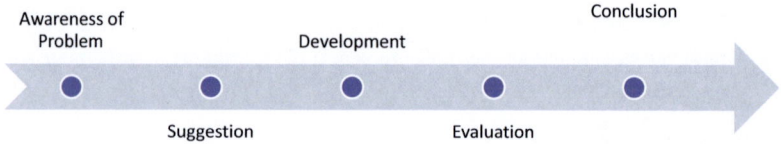

Figure 1.1.: Phases of the General Design Cycle ([TVTY90])

Phase 0: Awareness of problem

Finding interesting problems generally is easy in the field of IT. However, some constraints do exist that filter out a number of problems from the outset. Guideline "Problem Relevance" postulates for instance that the problem has to be relevant to business. The Motivation section of this chapter already showed that this thesis' main topic, the SSOA, is of utmost importance to overcome the shortfalls of traditional SOAs.

Phase 1: Suggestion

A set of suggestions for solving the problem at hand is collected in this step. This step usually involves finding and examining the key technologies in the specific problem domain as well as an overview of already existing solutions.

Phase 2: Development

In this step, the actual research contribution is created. In line with Guideline 4, the research contribution usually is either an artifact or a methodology and in this case is the Generic Semantic Service-Oriented Architecture (GENSOA).

Phase 3: Evaluation

All generated artifacts have to be carefully evaluated according to latest evaluation standards and methodologies.

Phase 4: Conclusion

Wrapping up the research effort, the priority of Phase 4 depends on the number of artifacts created in Phase 2. If only one artifact exists, the conclusion is trivial: Barring a veto from the evaluation process, the created artifact is selected as solution to the problem posed. When more than one artifact is evaluated, this phase compares the evaluations and chooses the best match.

1.2.3. Research Process

The research effort of which this thesis is the result extended this "General Design Cycle": Work in two large-scale research projects (Access-eGov and SPIKE)[11] has been carried out to support the design and evaluation phases as can be seen in Figure 1.2. Access-eGov in this context was simultaneously developed to the Generic Semantic Service-Oriented Architecture (GENSOA) architecture (cf. Section 11.3). Both tasks could mutually benefit in a number of ways, including:

- Continuous feedback of the Access-eGov project team regarding GENSOA concepts

- Backflow of GENSOA ideas into the Access-eGov system architecture and vice versa

---

[11] Access-eGov and SPIKE both are EU co-funded projects with more than 300 person months each.

7

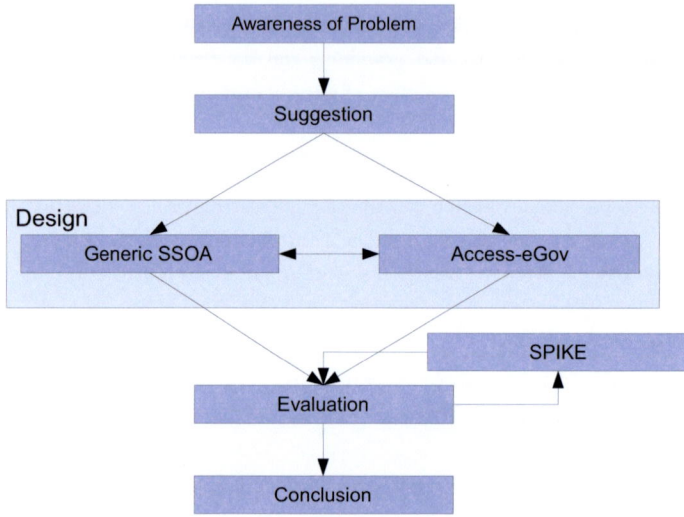

Figure 1.2.: Design Research Process Used in this Thesis (Adopted from [TVTY90])

- Independent[12] feedback on GENSOA concepts

- Having a full infrastructure at hand to demonstrate the advanced security component of the GENSOA

SPIKE, which has not been completely implemented[13] at the time of this writing also has an influence on this thesis in several ways:

- Second evaluation of the GENSOA

- Use case for an Enterprise Service Bus (ESB) and especially a semantically enriched ESB

- A very concise set of requirements for inter-organizational collaboration, all in all much more complex than Access-eGov and therefore better suited for evaluation tasks.

---

[12]i.e. Project partners not directly contributing to the architecture.

[13]As opposed to Access-eGov, which was successfully finished in March 2009.

1.2.4. Research Questions

Building software systems or architectures from scratch is not necessarily research. Design Research and routine design (system building) have to be discerned according to [HMPR04]. Research questions are a good way to prohibit neglecting the research in favor of routine design. In this thesis, the following research questions were initially posed in the context of a research group working on a large-scale service brokering infrastructure for e-government applications:

- What is a possible design for a large scale, extensible, service brokering infrastructure like the Access-eGov system?

  In order to build the best possible architecture for Semantic Service-Oriented Architecture (SSOA)s, a generic process model and reference architecture also spanning Access-eGov were developed. This reference architecture already contains concepts like an ESB, which are not needed and therefore not used in Access-eGov. Nonetheless, the need for these added components was anticipated quite early and the GENSOA could later be verified in another EU project called SPIKE[14] which was funded in the seventh Framework Programme[15].

- Are standard security services applicable in a SSOA? If not, can they be modified?

  Thorough analysis of standard security services and their application in important architectural styles is used to answer this question in Chapter 5.

- Based on a eXtensible Access Control Markup Language (XACML) architecture, can a flexible placement of a Policy Decision Point (PDP) help boost privacy in a SSOA?

  To answer this question, first a security architecture for the GENSOA was devised that allowed the arbitrary placement of PDPs along a certain axis. An evaluation of this proceedings is affirmative.

- What will an implementation look like?

  As already mentioned, both, the GENSOA and its security architecture (SEC) have already been tried and tested in real-world conditions. Access-eGov and SPIKE can be expressed as instances of the GENSOA while GENSOA Security Architecture (SEC) was implemented as a proof-of-concept within Access-eGov.

---

[14]http://www.spike-project.eu
[15]http://cordis.europa.eu/fp7/

In the course of research work over a timespan of nearly four years, additional interesting questions emerged and are also answered in this thesis:

- Are SSOAs already usable? Do they introduce value added?
  A comparative evaluation in Chapter 15 contrasts GENSOA-derived implementations with a less complex, client-server architecture based implementation.

- Can semantic- / knowledge-based technologies effectively be used in the Requirements Engineering phase of an architecture definition?
  Semantics indeed seem to be an interesting solution when it comes to build a shared vocabulary over development and requirements teams. Section 10.2 examines the suitability of this approach.

1.3. Chapter Structure

This thesis is structured into six parts, of which the current part, the Introduction, fulfills two main goals. Firstly, it describes the research methodology behind this effort. The Motivation chapter thereby constitutes the "Awareness of Problem" phase of the Design Research lifecycle by detailing which issues SSOAs try to solve and discussing whether these issues are worth the given attention.

Parts I and II illustrate the "Suggestion phase" in which a comprehensive and concise overview of the current state of the art of relevant research areas is given. Part I introduces the complex topic of Software Architectures and related concepts including the developments that finally lead to the inception of the Service Oriented Architecture (SOA) paradigm. Special attention is also paid to the very important requirements engineering phase as well as the extensive topic of security in software architectures. Knowledge and especially knowledge based technologies in all shapes relevant to SSOAs are described in Part II.

A "[r]eference process for the design and implementation of SSOAs" is introduced in Part III. Its chapter structure follows a software architecture lifecyle by first describing a specific Requirements Engineering process in Chapter 10 followed by a detailed description of the GENSOA architecture in Chapter 11. Introduction of a concise security architecture wraps up this part in Chapter 12. Part III is the counterpart to Design Research's "Design" phase.

Access-eGov and SPIKE, the two application cases, are described in Part IV and serve as a foundation for theoretically evaluating the proposed GENSOA. Still in line with the Design Research methodology, Part IV indicates the "Evaluation" phase where the previously elaborated design is checked for its suitability for the tasks at hand.

The last part, Part V, furthers this evaluation by extending the theoretical statements with a comparative evaluation also taking into account the implementation of Access-eGov, the preliminary implementation outline of SPIKE, and an alternative implementation that could be viable for the tasks at hand.

Part I.

Software Architectures

2. Introduction

A suggestion phase in a design research endeavor has a defined outcome. It should catalog available solutions, processes, technologies or best practices in order to be able to present a balanced view of the world of discourse at the point of research initiation. This common view, however, does not appear to be enough in the case of the SSOA where the outcome is a whole set of selected and matched technologies, connected by procedures. Describing a particular result only verbally is neither efficient, nor in any way comprehensive, thus leading many researchers to work in the field of system architectures and their description formalisms.

The first sections of this part are therefore devoted to a definition of software architectures and accompanying sections on their creation, formalization, and evaluation as well as the evolution of architectural styles. A generic process model for creating software architecture artifacts concludes these observations. Security in software architectures is elaborated on in the last section of this part.

2.1. System-, Software- and Information System Architecture

Today's inflationary use of the term "architecture" mandates its thorough definition in order to be successfully and correctly used. At the very heart of the whole topic the terms system-, software-, and information system architectures have to be discerned.

System Architecture

System architecture, concisely defined by Matevska-Meyer et al. as "structural decomposition of a system into subsystems and their connections" [MMHR04], is a term that has been in use in a software context since the early days of computing. Clements gives a good summary of the early evolution of the term by tracing it back to the late 1960s when Edsger Dijkstra first described a partitioning and structuring of software systems [Cle08]. The advent of new, inexpensive hardware and as a result, the growing size and dimension of information systems in the late 1980s and early 1990s lead to increased interest in software system design. Garlan et al. acknowledge the reuse of system organizations as one of the driving forces behind system architectures [GS93]. The authors still detect a total lack of system architecture theory but observe that system architectures are already widely used in practice.

In 2000, Hofmeister et al. still describe the ongoing lack of any standardized and practical means of architecture descriptions [HNS00]. Good software architecture for them is a key success factor for large software systems, especially taking into account the required complexity of those systems. Having a strong practitioner's record, Hofmeister et al. introduce guidelines and techniques for good architecture design, all of which are proven in real-world usage. The major benefits of software architectures are two-fold: architectures shall serve as a design plan (likened to a blueprint) and additionally shall help conquer the complexity involved in such systems. Adding views to the architecture description methods pool is also proposed in order to introduce a structured and above all comparable frame for looking at architectures. A conceptual, a module, an execution, and a code view are the main pillars of architecture description in this framework. These views are rather self-explanatory, initially looking at the system from a distance in the conceptual architecture view, and ending with detailed implementation considerations in the code view.

Software Architecture

For many researchers in the late 1980s, the semantics of the term "system" seemed to shift from describing a specific hardware and software combination towards a more integrated approach, also taking into account users, their tasks and roles, and their processes. Thus, what was formerly called system architecture is now more often called software architecture.

Perry and Wolf define the term software architecture through the use of the triple {Elements, Form, Rationale} to document possible constituents of a software system (Elements), constraints on those elements and their relationship (Form) and - on a rather untechnical level - the rationale behind the choice of used elements [PW92].

The authors also already propose the notion of architectural styles and, even more importantly, the concept of views, albeit somewhat limited in scope: Data, process and connection views are the only views mentioned by Perry and Wolf. These views largely overlap with the views contained in the Zachman architecture framework introduced in the next Section. Architectures in general should be the technical and managerial basis for the design and implementation of a system. Architectures also enable consistency and dependency analysis and act as the pillars on which a substantial portion of a system can be reused.

Siedersleben adds another view on software architectures to scientific discussion by introducing their Quasar[1] framework consisting of the following four labels: ideas and concepts, terminology, standard architectures and interfaces, and standard components [Sie05].

Clements et al. in [CKK02] on the other hand defines software architectures through their benefits for "large, complex, software-intensive systems". Benefits arise when software architectures have one or more of the following roles:

- *a vehicle for communication among stakeholders*

- *a manifestation of the earliest design decisions*

- *a reusable, transferable abstraction of a system.*

This thesis uses the term software architecture according to this definition given by Clements et al.

Information System Architecture

As early as 1987, Zachmann wrote one of the first research papers trying to formalize a so called information system architecture in contrast to a system architecture as described above [Zac87]. By deriving it from architectures in other contexts (e.g. building a house), the authors arrive at three types of architecture descriptions: data model, process model, and communication model. These descriptions are viewed from different perspectives, namely owner-view, designer-view and the technological view.

Roughly at the same time Krcmar defined an information system architecture as the structure of elements of a system, represented by functional, process-oriented, and temporal models [Krc90]. In addition to the former conceptualization of the term architecture, Krczmar also includes technical infrastructure, business objectives, and organizational structure into the architecture description. It is very interesting to note that he also surveys the contemporary goals of information system architectures in the early 1990s and identifies four main groups of goals: Horizontal- and vertical integration, comprehensibility and flexibility.

---

[1]Qualitätssoftwarearchitektur - quality software architecture

Conclusion

In general, lots of examples can be found that use the terms information system architecture [BS07] [BSW07], system architecture [CW00] [BME$^+$07] or software architecture [BCK03] [KWB03] interchangeably to describe basic properties like the structure and constituents of a data processing system. While a concise and generally accepted definition has not evolved so far, Bass et al. offer a definition for a system architecture that is both, general enough to fit current theoretical and practical usage while still being detailed enough to deliver an actual, comprehensive definition of the term [BCK03]:

> "The software architecture of a program or computing system is the structure or structures of the system, which comprise software components, the externally visible properties of those components, and the relationships between them. The term also refers to documentation of a system's software architecture. Documenting software architecture facilitates communication between stakeholders, documents early decisions about high-level design, and allows reuse of design components and patterns between projects."

2.1.1. Architectural Styles

Above definition puts its main focus on the detailed description of a software system that is going to be implemented. In order to be able to spot similarities between architectures and facilitate architecture reuse, the concept of an architectural style has evolved. Dewayne et al., for example, describe two levels on which an architectural style has its impact [PW92]:

- Descriptively
  meaning a "particular codification of design elements and their formal arrangements".

- Prescriptively
  meaning that the style limits the choice for both the elements and the relationships between them.

A first step into applied usage of architectural styles was taken by Shaw and Clements in [SC96] with the description of the components and connectors out of which systems are built as well as constraints on their composition. The authors also acknowledge the need for some sort of description standard for architectural styles and, using this standard, some organizational system for different styles.

Throughout this thesis, an architectural style is seen as an entity conforming to the definition of Shaw and Clements.

2.2. Reference Architectures

One of the main instruments used for answering some of the research questions posed in Chapter 1.2.4 is the creation of a reference architecture and process for SSOAs as presented in Part III. Thus, it is important to introduce basic concepts of reference architectures before proceeding with the actual design.

2.2.1. The Best of Best Practises?

In IT, many reference publications exists, ranging from reference architectures to reference systems or reference processes. A first, intuitive, "reference architecture" definition could describe an architecture design that is not written out in full, but leaves open many degrees of freedom for implementation efforts. If that architecture additionally is important for an application domain[2], the designed system is very likely a reference architecture.

Reed, of IBM (formerly Rational) fame and the Rational Unified Process (RUP) (cf. [Kru00]), denote the reference architecture as the *Best of best practises* [Ree02]. The following paragraphs will shed more light on this appraisal.

Reference architectures are not solely confined to the field of software architectures. Wyns et al. introduce a very interesting set of properties for reference architectures in the area of workstation design [WVBVB96]. In an online addendum to this publication ([WVBVB]), the authors go even further and devise a concise list of properties defining reference architectures:

- Unified terminology
  Bigger development teams entail increased complexity and increased error proneness. Quite often, these kinds of problems result from simple misunderstandings caused by diverging term definitions within the development team. A unified terminology is a big step in the direction of accumulating and re-sharing the combined knowledge.

---

[2]If it can generate enough interest in a scientific community, for example, or if landmark potential users build systems that are instances of the architecture.

- Simplicity of the design process
  A concise and well-represented software architecture considerably helps lowering the cost of implementation in projects as many of the often tedious and time-consuming activities surrounding the design process have already been carried out.

- Quality considerations
  If authors of reference architectures manage to get their architecture into widespread usage, the architectures will automatically be peer-reviewed, thus iteratively leading to improved design.

- Reusability
  If interfaces and even ready-to-run objects have been designed once already, possibilities of reuse arise in a setting which would otherwise have required a complete redesign of all components.

- Traceability
  In real-world applications it sometimes proves useful if the evolution process can be shown by comparing successive implementations to the underlying architecture.

One of the more prolific researchers also working in the field is Kruchten, who coauthored the Rational Unified Process (RUP) together with Reed [Kru00]. A reference architecture in Kruchten's terminology has the following distinct features:

- "A predefined architectural pattern or a set of patterns" belonging to a given business domain.

- A technical context guided by the architectural patterns.

- "Supporting artefacts to enable their use".

Later on, he was able to extend his work in [Kru95], where it is postulated that reference architectures should be designed in close relation to the 4+1 view model of software architecture defined there. This 4+1 view model is described in more detail in the following chapters.

In the light of these findings, a survey of a multitude of different publications on reference architectures has been undertaken during the work on this thesis. Reference architectures examined in this process can usually be grouped into only two distinct groups.

- Goal-oriented reference architectures
  Narrowly defined reference architectures that cannot be instantiated for anything other than their original target domain. Examples include PROSA, a "reference architecture for holonic manufacturing systems" [VBWV+98] or the reference architecture for the component factory of Basili et al. [BCC92].

- Academic reference architectures
  PERA, "[t]he Purdue Enterprise Reference Architecture and Methodology" [Wil98] or the "framework to define a generic enterprise reference architecture and methodology" [BN96] are representatives of this second group. Their defining factor is that they were able to generate interest in the research communities but failed to reach the real world system architects.

One notable exception to this categorization is the OASIS SOA Reference Model (SOA-RM), which will be introduced in the next section. It is a widely acclaimed reference architecture used both, in academia, and in practical projects.

2.2.2. The Oasis SOA Reference Model

The SOA-RM is one of the best-known examples of a comprehensive reference architecture. The following paragraphs summarize key concepts that are part of the specification [MLM+06].

Stakeholder

The first important property when modeling a system is the set of stakeholders involved. The SOA-RM distinguishes the following different types of stakeholders in a SOA context. All users actively partaking in the SOA, the *participants* are divided into service consumers and providers. *Service consumers* consume services that *service providers* serve. In between *consumers* and *providers* are *service mediators* which are a very diverse group, ranging from service registries to "filtering services" that for example provide cryptographic capabilities like end-to-end encryption. Another layer of indirection is added by the *agents*, which, acting on behalf of *consumers* and *providers*, make the services available while at the same time providing functionalities to electronically interact with services. Outside the SOA is one last group, the so-called *non-participating stakeholders*, which have a stake in the SOA while not directly interacting with the components[3].

---

[3]The example given in [MLM+06] is that of a state body charging taxes for certain services.

Resources

The group of authors continue their architecture design by modeling the modes of resource usage from different viewpoints. The underlying resource model is simple as it only consists of *resources* described by a *description* which in turn is denoted by a referebced *identity*[4].

Ownership of a resource comes with *responsibilities* and *rights*, both of which can be shared among stakeholders.

In another sub-model *needs* and *capabilities* are contrasted. *Needs* represent the wishes of a *participant* while the *capability* represents the providers' points of view.

Social structure and context

A large portion of the SOA-RM documentation is concerned with social structure, interaction and contexts which, while being important for certain research disciplines are not of importance to the considerations given in this thesis.

Realization of SOAs

Closest to the lower levels of an architecture description is the view on "Realizing Service Oriented Architectures" which gives detailed hints for necessary infrastructure components for service discovery and service execution. A *service description* in this case is the first artifact used to describe an actual service. It is made up of many different *annotations*, each of which originates at its own point of view. Examples for the included *annotations* are information on service reachability, functionality or on its interfaces. This view also elaborates on service execution and its contexts.

Service Visibility

Based on the *description* element previously introduced, *service publication* (called "attaining visibility"), and *discovery* (called "service awareness") is also described in full detail.

---

[4]Identity, at least for researchers active in the security field, is a dangerous term as it is usually used quite narrowly. In the SOA-RM, however, it summarizes the set of all characteristics an entity has.

Message Exchange Patterns (MEP)

Describing MEPs, the authors discern a "request / response" MEP and an "Event Notification" MEP, both of which act according to their name. Thus, the former is used for communication with the services while the latter conveys information on possible effects the service execution had on the environment, or on other events that have originated somewhere inside the system.

Composition of services

Another topic extensively reviewed is the composition of services including orchestration and choreography, a topic which is later described extensively (cf. Section 8.1.2 and 8.1.3).

Governance

Governance issues are also handled in the SOA-RM documentation.

Security and Trust

The last major part in the document describes security and trust issues. In the current version of the SOA-RM, it can be seen as the most complete part where the most important security and trust topics are described in every detail.

In summary, the SOA-RM leaves a mixed impression. Some aspects are very elaborately devised, like social aspects of the architecture. Other aspects, like the MEPs, are unnecessarily complicated. Technical aspects of SOAs generally are not described in such depth.

All in all, it can be considered as a good starting point for SOA projects. Projects based on the SOA-RM still need to make a huge number of organizational and technical decisions that are not guided through the SOA-RM, however.

2.2.3. The Generic Semantic Service-Oriented Architecture

In the previous sections, the complex topic of reference architectures has been introduced briefly. Its benefits are obvious and tangible even for small software projects. Since the main aim of this thesis is to improve the SOA concepts by using semantic technologies it is immediately clear how the resulting software project can benefit from the advantages of reference architectures:

- Unified terminology
  SSOAs compared to other architectural styles are relatively new and terminology is not stable, yet. Thus, prospective users will be able to use this unified terminology for unambiguously communicating about the SSOA.

- Simplicity of the design process and reusability
  While it usually is not possible to use a reference architecture directly, creating an instance of it to serve as a blueprint for the new system is considerably easier and less resource intensive than designing the system once again.

- Quality considerations and traceability
  If more projects share the same common ancestor, it is highly likely that best practices, know-how, and experiences gained find their way back into further revisions of the reference architecture, improving quality and traceability.

The SOA-RM on the other hand shows, that every reference architecture has to find a balance between topics relevant to practitioners, and topics mostly relevant to research communities. Comparing the room that is given to sociological discussions to the amount of technical content suggests that technical content could be underrepresented. Depending on the envisioned scope of application however, this diagnosis requires individual judgment.

Nonetheless the output of this thesis will be a reference architecture and process for a SSOA, named the GENSOA (cf. Part III). In order to be of more use to practitioners in the field, the GENSOA will omit many aspects present in the SOA-RM that are not directly concerened with software design and implementation.

2.3. Evaluation of Software Architectures

Having defined the terms system architecture and reference architecture, it is also important to review different methodologies for evaluating resulting architectures, especially considering the fact that architecture specifications are central to copious IT projects. Many projects, however, refrain from evaluating their work, with the possible effect of having to explain an expensive failure to management and customer. Clements et al. acknowledge this [CKK02] and add security and performance shortcomings and growing customer disaffection to the problems caused by unevaluated software architectures.

After all, the architecture design phase is the phase where setting the course of the system towards being well performing, secure and maintainable is most easily accomplished. Every single day into the implementation phase increases problems that even slight changes to the architecture entail. To make things worse, every architecture usually features some key design choices that cannot be undone without having to restart the implementation effort from the very beginning.

2.3.1. Context of Architecture Evaluation

Every architecture evaluation effort is constrained by a set of properties introduced in the following paragraphs.

Point of time

Architecture evaluation should be done as early as possible, ideally before any implementation work has been carried out. Abowd et al. name as a good starting point the phase right after requirements were elicited [ABC+97]. Other sources are less accurate, placing the initiation of evaluation efforts in an early development phase [BCK03].

It is generally agreed upon that major changes of the requirements or other important parameters of the system may need a re-evaluation of the whole architecture. For obvious reasons, changes on such a scale should be avoided at all costs. A thorough requirements engineering phase as explained later in Chapter 10 is a worthwhile effort to keep the probability of such events to a minimum.

Methods also exist that are geared towards late evaluation but the aim of such undertakings is usually not averting a bad software product but rather measuring whether changes to existing architectures yield the designated results or are about to fail.

Participants

According to Clements et al., there are two main groups of participants [CKK02]. Firstly, the evaluation team, mainly concerned with running the actual evaluation, and secondly, representatives of all of the stakeholders involved. In this context, the group of stakeholders is made up of developers, users, and decision makers at management level. Financial concerns usually make it very tempting to (re-)use members of the actual development team in the evaluation team. Since this is a genuine conflict of interests, this approach is to be disapproved whenever possible.

Result of the evaluation

The result of an architecture evaluation is not standardized. In general, however, it is agreed upon that architecture evaluations answer the question of suitability[5] of a given architecture for a given set of requirements, or that of better suitability of items in a set of different architectural choices [CKK02].

Classes of Evaluation methods

A very basic distinction of evaluation methods can be made between evaluation methods that are quantitative and those that are qualitative. Drawing a strict line between those two genres is hard, however, especially because there is a certain overlap between both classes[6]. Thus, in the remainder of this thesis, the classification also used by Bass et al. in [BCK03] is used, grouping the methods in questioning and measuring methods. Figure 2.1 gives an overview of the hierarchy of evaluation methods involved.

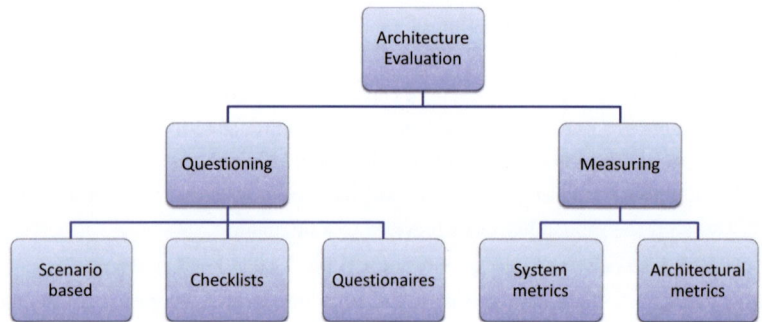

Figure 2.1.: Classification of Architecture Verification Methods, Extending [BCK03]

Measuring methods are quantitative and usually target either properties of a running system, or metrics that can be extracted from design documentation. While being a common usage for quantitative evaluation methods[7], extracting the target properties from a running system requires exactly that – a running system. In the

---

[5]Suitability, in this case, means that a resulting system implementing an architecture meets all relevant requirements and is at the same time realizable with existing resources. Examples of the resources in question include monetary and personal resources or prerequisite software like legacy systems.

[6]The later introduced CBAM for example is indeed questioning stakeholders for qualities, but always calculates quantitative measures in the last phase of its usage.

[7]The naming varies, some authors simply call such a method a metric for instance.

context of architecture validation, this approach therefore is questionable, even if it does not mean that the whole system has to be implemented to a usable state. It is quite possible to gather these metrics' values from a prototype since prototypes for systems with a main focus on their graphical user interface might be reasonably easy and fast to implement using a modern Integrated Development Environment (IDE) or prepackaged graphical toolkits or widget sets. For more complex systems, however, this approach is not advised.

Extracting quantitative values from the design documentation on the other hand is always possible, even if potentially very complex and time consuming when the documentation is in formats that cannot be automatically parsed.

Questioning methods follow a different approach and are concerned with unmeasurable[8] attributes of an architecture.

Evaluated quality criteria

A first challenge in evaluation is identifying suitable properties, for example a measure of performance or reliability, the degree of security in a system or the degree of compliance a system fulfills in relation to documented requirements[9].

Each of the exemplary methods introduced below has no predefined set of quality attributes but provides facilities for flexibly creating them, at least in the case of measuring evaluation methods. Quantitative methods on the other cannot be as flexible: since they involve calculations, the nature of the measured value is an integral part of the method itself.

Even after enough suitable attributes or appropriate quantitative methods are selected, the most important task is still to be carried out: assessing the exact degree of conformity in case of qualitative attributes or the exact measurement of a specific metric in the quantitative case. Close cooperation between the stakeholders and the evaluation team is of utmost importance in this phase [CKK02].

2.3.2. Evaluation Methods

In order to give an overview of the broad range of evaluation methods, both questioning and measuring methods have been examined and are exemplary introduced in the following.

---

[8]The definition of unmeasurable is extended to also include only temporarily unmeasurable attributes. Attributes, such as response times, which can only be measured once the system is already implemented, also fall into this category.

[9]Methods for evaluating the elicited requirements also exist, but are not in the focus of this thesis.

2.3.2.1. UML Metrics [LGZ⁺07]

Li et al. propose three characteristics that can be inferred from UML diagrams in a post-implementation setting:

- Information content
  is calculated by weighting all UML model elements with their supposed entropy and summing them up. The resulting characteristic measures how much information an UML model conveys.

- Visual effect
  is the sum of each element's physical area in the diagram. It characterizes how difficult an UML model is to understand, practically giving a metric of how confusing a diagram is.

- Connectivity degree
  measures the associations each model element has. Results in a value for the complexity of the architecture.

Measures for cohesion and coherence are computed from those three numbers using simple mathematics, yielding a qualitative way to judge interdependencies within the architecture and therefore its maintainability.

This method is interesting for two reasons. First, cohesion and coherence are central attributes of any architecture and any software or system design. A quantitative approximation is very valuable since quantified values can easily be compared without margin for subjective interpretations. In addition, its orientation towards UML, which is used in the majority of today's modeling tasks, furthers its relevance.

2.3.2.2. An Empirically-based Process for Software Architecture Evaluation [LTC03]

Using an in-house information system for experience sharing and organizational learning as a testbed, researchers at the Fraunhofer Center for Experimental Software Engineering evaluate two versions of the EMS in order to prove that redesign of the software was indeed a success. Dissatisfied with existing metrics, the researchers derived their own characteristics:

- Coupling-between-modules (CBM)

  A measure that does not take into account intra-module coupling and only focuses on inter-module coupling. CBM for any given module is the number of classes that are part of the coupling. Very important in this metric is the distinction between the CBM_{all} for all modules and the CBM_{nolib} which leaves out library classes in those computations.

- Coupling inside a module (CIM)

  Based on a number representing the relations between classes of a module (Coupling between classes (CBC)), the CIM is defined as the average of all classes' CBCs.

Both of these measures are used to indicate a quantitative notion of maintainability for an examined architecture.

CBM and CIM are closely related to cohesion and coherence as mentioned above and another good criterion for the interdependencies and associated maintainability[10].

Both, the UML metrics and this method eventually measure very similar properties and therefore should not be viewed as contenders but as complementary methods.

2.3.2.3. Architecture Tradeoff Analysis Method(ATAM)

One of the most effective architecture evaluation methods, the Architecture Tradeoff Analysis Method (ATAM) consists of activities in four broad groups:

- Presentation of the architecture

- Investigation and analysis

- Testing

- Reporting

It is carried out in four phases [PBG07]. After an initial preparation phase where the evaluation team is selected and organizational issues are clarified, the main evaluation activities commence:

---

[10]It is however doubtful if any ex-post metric on maintainability can be significant when it leaves out a measure for code documentation.

Presentation

In a first staccato of presentations, the method itself is introduced before spokespersons of the business side present the business drivers. Finally, a member of the architects' group (usually the chief software architect) presents the architecture that is the evaluation target.

Investigation and Analysis

The architectural approach plays a key role in the first activity in this group. The architect should explain the general approach in an objective way, without already adding evaluation hints. Usually included in this stage are high-level architecture views and information on the proposed architectural styles and patterns used. The central construct in this group is the "Utility Tree", which conveys a compressed representation of the most important quality attributes in the individual evaluation project, and additional, project-specific scenarios that can be prioritized before finally being analyzed.

Both, the architectural approach and the "Utility Tree" are matched against each other in order to assess the suitability of the selected approach with regard to selected criteria, usually including accordance to the elicited requirements.

Testing

Testing in the ATAM is scenario-driven. In order to crosscheck the scenarios contained in the "Utility Tree", this phase takes the scenario creation in front of a bigger audience which in turn could and should lead to modifications of the "Utility Tree". Three kinds of scenarios are important in this step:

- Use case scenarios are oriented towards the functionalities of the system.

- Growth scenarios are reasonable future projections of the software under evaluation. They serve as starting point for answering the question whether the system can cope with anticipated growth rates.

- Exploratory scenarios are the exaggeration of the growth scenarios and represent an unrealistic worst case.

Reporting

The last step in this process is the presentation of the evaluation results.

2.3.2.4. Active Reviews for Intermediate Designs (ARID)

This method follows an approach different to the ATAM because it does not require the existence of a complete architecture but can instead be used to rate partial designs. It is made up of nine steps in two phases:

Rehearsal (Phase 1)

Phase 1 is carried out only by the chief architect and the review leader. After setting up the team of reviewers, a presentation of the architecture is prepared and already rehearsed with the review leader as sole audience. Both participants then prepare sample scenarios that serve as a basis for phase 2. Rounding up this phase are organizational preparations for phase 2, including scheduling the review meeting and packaging the previously compiled scenarios and presentations.

Review (Phase 2)

This is the main phase of the ARID, starting with a presentation on the method itself, followed by the architecture presentation developed in phase 1. The plenum builds upon the sample scenarios in order to create system-specific, meaningful, and eventually prioritized scenarios.

Since the reviewers all are developers, they are now asked to use the architecture (or the part thereof) to implement the most important scenario in terms of pseudo-code. During this step, the architect is not allowed the slightest hint as long as the reviewers stay on track and only intervenes, should they become stuck or enter an erroneous path. Journaling of these cases is mandatory.

This step is repeated multiple times before final results are gathered. Issues that turned up during the previous phase and also the opinion the reviewers voiced on the architecture are also considered.

2.3.2.5. Cost Benefit Analysis Method (CBAM)

In sharp contrast to the objective of the ATAM or the ARID, which are both evaluating mainly technical criteria, the Cost Benefit Analysis Method (CBAM) is concerned with the economic implications of different architecture types [ABC+97]. It builds on ATAM scenarios and the overall description of the future system. Therefore, the CBAM is no technology that can be used on its own but requires extensive preparative steps which are typically covered by an iteration of the ATAM.

Building on the prioritized set of ATAM-scenarios, the CBAM collects different alternatives to the current architecture design for each scenarios and calculates costs and benefits for each alternative. Both values are related through a measure called desirability of the architectural alternative.

As a last step, the evaluated alternatives are ranked according to their desirability index.

While this approach might present itself as straight-forward, many problems exist on a detail level. Especially the calculation of the benefits has much uncertainty attached, while the calculation of the costs can partially be solved by standard software engineering instruments [KAK01].

2.4. The Generic Semantic Service-Oriented Architecture and Evaluation

After having described some diverging evaluation methods to show the broad range they occupy, the most important question in the context of this thesis is whether the GENSOA will have to be evaluated or not. This question, however, is not specific to the GENSOA but pertains to any reference architecture analysis.

In general, evaluating reference architectures is possible and has been done before. Gallagher used a modified ATAM to evaluate a government reference architecture in a two day workshop [Gal00]. While the participants were content with the results of the evaluation, they still unearthed a number of problems within the reference architecture. To which extent the architects should take these findings into consideration requires good judgment on the architects' part. Attending to every single user comment may well violate one of the main principle of a reference architecture: being generic about use cases. A reference architecture cannot, and must not, be as complete and comprehensive as a final system architecture.

Thus, the GENSOA itself will not be evaluated, but every user basing an own software system on it is well advised to use suitable evaluation methods on his derived architecture. In the case of this thesis, the Access-eGov system has been evaluated (cf. Section 15.1.3).

3. Evolution of Software Architectural Styles

In this chapter, the evolution of architectural styles leading up to the SSOA is elaborated by showing the different predecessors of SSOAs. System architectures initially were monolithic because of several constraints inherent in the then prevalent computer systems. Complexity back in these days was largely due to the used algorithms as they had to be geared towards restrictive system resources[1].

Introduction of multi-user systems increased the level of system complexity. Issues created by sharing of resources had to be solved at implementation time in code, and at design time in a suitable software architecture.

Today's architectures feature some of the most complex software systems designed so far. SSOAs certainly are no exception, but their complexity comes with convincing benefits as is shown later in this thesis.

3.1. Sources of Classification Criteria for Architectural Styles

Classifying architectural styles in the early days of software architecture frequently was topic of original research. In the following paragraphs, two selected classification approaches will be presented to serve as basis for our own scheme introduced later.

Renowned for their seminal work on software architectures, Garlan and Shaw introduced an initial classification of contemporary architectural styles [SG96]. The groups they used were:

- Call-and-return systems
  Garlan and Shaw interestingly grouped both, procedural ("main program and subroutines") and object oriented systems in the same class. Today, this sim-

---

[1]Current software systems often follow a different path. Complexity these days stems from dependencies and complex runtime environments that encapsulate the used algorithms.

plification is no longer justified, considering the way procedural and object oriented programming have diverged over time.

- Dataflow systems
  Among the dataflow systems, the authors place "pipes and filters" showing a common criteria for this class: arbitrary dataflow between different components.

- Independent components
  Independent components were used as a class for systems based on communicating processes[2].

- Virtual machines
  Garlan and Shaw used this term for interpreters and rule-based systems. Today, virtualization has even more meanings and therefore the item would require a distinction into at least three different flavors of virtualization: Virtual machines as enabled by processor virtualization[3], virtual machines like the Java sandbox, and finally Knowledge-Based Technologies (KBT)s, the term used as container for, among a wealth of other technologies, rule based systems today.

- Data-centered systems
  This class is unfeasible today. Databases have come to be the foundations almost every software product builds upon, and are a product in their own right today, not any longer an architectural style.

Shaw et al. further these concepts introduced in [SG96] by devising a formal set of criteria for architectural classification and exemplarily applying the resulting schema to two different architectural styles [SC97]. Components and connectors are the primary classification properties which do not, however, suffice to unambiguously distinguish architectural styles. To overcome this problem, the authors add control disciplines and data organizations, and as a dynamic element, the interaction of control and data as additional discriminators.

Another source of classification criteria is the ISO-9126 document [ISO01]. It is divided into four sub-parts, of which the applicable part is concerned with quality metrics of software systems such as functionality or reliability.

---

[2]The Remote Procedure Call (RPC) paradigm was already widely used at the time of publication.
[3]Some see this as basis for cloud computing, in itself an architectural style.

The last important source for classification criteria is Roy Fielding's thesis in which he examines architectural styles from his very own point of view, the view of one of the principal authors of the World Wide Web (WWW) [Fie00].

3.2. Quality Criteria for Architectural Styles

Drawing from the previously investigated sources, describing the architectural styles is done along a number of dimensions that are presented in this section.

Distribution of architectural entities

The possibility to distribute entities of the architecture across organizational and/or technical boundaries is vital for modern software systems. In earlier systems, the only mode of distribution was that of using separate physical devices. Increasing usage of virtualization, however, demands an easy and stable distribution scheme. Deployment units steadily decrease in order to minimize unwanted side-effects and interconnections between different services or hardware devices. A successful architectural style has to be able to support fine-grained services, opening up the opportunity to distribute service execution both in terms of localization and of capacity in arbitrary ways. Garlan and Shaw used the property topology to describe similar facts about the system [SC97].

Complexity

Two distinct views on complexity of architectures define this discussion. Architectures should be able to represent arbitrarily complex systems while at the same time being not overly complex themselves. The more complex the system, the more error prone and less maintainable it is after all.

Grady Booch devotes a whole chapter of his seminal book on object-oriented analysis and design to complexity in software systems [BME+07].

Extensibility

Extensibility, among other sources postulated in [ISO01], is a key requirement in certain types of software systems. Systems like SOAs or SSOAs are mainly concerned with extensibility since they are no self-contained system offering functionality extending that of a plain execution environment. The chapters on requirements engineering of the GENSOA and of the implementation projects are proof for this claim (cf. Part III). There are many degrees of extensibility of which the most important distinction in this thesis is, whether they are dynamically extensible[4] or just statically, involving recompiling or at least substantial reconfigurations.

Integration facilities

Integration is commonly divided into at least two distinct methods [Bus03], data integration and functionality integration. Integrating different data sources is one of the major types of integration tasks in many software systems that have to interface to legacy systems. Even if no legacy systems exist, integration of third party data[5] often is a key requirement.

Integrating functionality cannot always be precisely discerned from data integration. If, for example, the integrated functionality results in data that is made available to the integrating system, the borders between both tasks become blurred.

What is often described as a third facet of integration, for example in [Bus03], is event integration. Again no accurate distinction exists. Event integration can also be viewed as the basis on which functionality and data integration operate, at least as long as dynamic systems are concerned.

Reliability, Availability, Security

Reliability issues arise on many levels, with very common reliability problems on the hardware level. All of these problems, however, have a corresponding mitigation strategy, ranging from the inexpensive use of RAID enabled storage devices to limit the impact of failures in disc drives to complex high availability solutions encompassing two identical copies of a machine connected through automated failover mechanisms. Thus, it is important to carefully restrict the discussion to reliability issues inherent in software.

Availability is the ultimate prerequisite for each software system. Unavailable systems obviously cannot be accessed in any way, thus rendering all other properties of the system meaningless. A large amount of different technologies implemented in both, hardware and software, is available to any system integrator that has to add so-called "high-availability"[6] provisions to his system. Thus, the possibilities to make use of such availability enhancing technologies have become a key property of any software architecture.

---

[4]In addition to the obvious dynamic extension mechanism of using services, also the plugin mechanism is very widely used to offer extensible interfaces to applications.

[5]Business to Business (B2B) Commerce is one of the main drivers of such integration efforts.

[6]This term's abbreviation *HA* has become the industry term for all these technolgies.

Finally, ISO-9216 [ISO01] places the security of a system in the functionality group, a classification that does not do justice to the importance of the subject and also does not take into account the interconnections these three concepts have. They, however, are subject of their own research efforts. Laprie et al., for example, describe their role in the bigger picture of - a rather technical - dependability [LRL04] while Bharat et al. on the other end of the spectrum fit these terms into a organizational QoS terminology.

Performance

Performance of a system is among key criteria used by Fielding in his classification of WWW-related architectural styles [Fie00]. As with reliability aspects, performance is no distinct property of the architecture alone, but a function of the performance of all components. To discuss the architecture's performance it is therefore vital to consequently separate the architectural elements from the rest of the execution environment.

Interoperability

For many application scenarios, it is vital that the architecture can easily be configured to interoperate either with a different software system or with another instance of itself.

Maintainability

"Constant change", the often heard metaphor for quickly changing markets and environments is the main driver behind extended expectations towards maintainability. If requirements on a system change on a scale that creates the need for substantial modifications to it, going beyond (re-)configuration abilities of the software and into code modifications, it is of utmost importance that the underlying software is well-documented, and based on proven standards and methodologies. It is also part of the ISO-9126 standard [ISO01].

Portability

Portability indicates how easy it is to operate a software system in other environments as those it was planned and designed for. Especially in the case of architectures, the portability aspect means more than portability of the code[7]. The ability of two components of the same architecture communicating to each other if they are run on different target platforms is very important as well[8].

3.3. Current Examples of Architectural Styles

All of the following styles except peer-to-peer and REST styles are evaluated against the previously introduced set of criteria. They have been selected for evaluation because they are, to a varying degree, ancestors of the SSOA. Peer-to-peer and REST are two currently promising approaches that are interconnected with the SOA world for various other reasons to be explained in due course.

3.3.1. Client / Server

Client / Server computing is one of the oldest architectural styles [CS93]. Its simplicity led to huge popularity especially in the CPU and memory-strained early days of networked computing.

The basic idea behind it is that the data storage and processing is done by a server component, while the user interface and possibly certain aspects of the data processing are executed on a client component. Server and client usually are two different hardware devices, with a server that usually has more resources than clients. One server concurrently serves a number of clients which is only limited by its hardware configuration and resource consumption of the server code. Figure 3.1 illustrates this communication relation.

Criterion	Assessment
Distribution	Client and server always communicate directly, clients need to know the location of the server beforehand or at least have to have some means to locate it (e.g. directories, name services). As long as these allocations do not have to be dynamically discovered at runtime, flexibly distributing different servers throughout networks is possible.

---

[7]The ability to recompile source code for different target execution environments without modifying it substantially.

[8]This property describes the communication on a purely technical level, i.e. matching character sets and communication protocols as opposed to interoperability introduced before.

Complexity	This style is very straight forward and has a very low degree of complexity. Even if augmented by load balancing and redundancy facilities, a Client / Server system stays easily manageable and clearly structured.
Extensibility	Adding new servers and clients is unproblematic. The only provisioning to be done is to make the new server known in whichever components are used for server location (cf. Distribution).
Integration facilities	Integration can happen both on the client (by connecting to and using more than one server) and the server (by using more than one datasource or recursively calling other servers).
Reliability	No provisions for reliability are made inside the architecture itself as a Client / Server system's maximum reliability is always bound by the least reliable of its components. While it is possible to build fully redundant servers or clients, this way of reliability enhancing is always transparent to the architecture.
Availability	No provisions for availability are made inside the architecture but standard methods apply. One of them is increasing availability through redundancy. This, however, is a daunting task in a Client / Server system as there is no standard way of sharing data across multiple instances of servers in a consistent way. Each server also constitutes a single point of failure if no measures to boost reliability are taken.
Performance	Depending on the individual performance of the participants, a Client / Server solution can be very well-performing, mostly due to its simple design, low complexity, and short data paths. Performance requirements above a certain limit, however, require the use of load-balanced server components which can be easily implemented with the exception of the data redundancy problem mentioned before. Architectures extended this way are, however, N-tier approaches.

Security	Communication between clients and servers is straightforward and can be secured with communication protocols that fulfill the security requirements of the designed system. Many stock protocols and protocol extensions already exist, greatly simplifying security-related software development in a Client/Server case. Additionally, direct interconnections between clients (meaning no dynamic reconfiguration of the systems) allow filtering of (possibly) malicious clients on the network layer, already.
Interoperability	Many Client / Server systems use specially crafted communication protocols, most often proprietary or undocumented. Therefore, apart from REST services described in detail in Section 3.3.7, only a small fraction of Client / Server applications rely on standardized protocols like HTTP or XMPP[9]. Even if they do, these protocols are often only used as transports and carry proprietary data formats.
Maintainability	No provisions for maintainability are made inside the architecture itself.
Portability	The protocol is the most important factor for portability in Client / Server environments. Binary protocols are inherently hard to port since many issues with representation of the data on the wire may arise (signedness issues are among the more frequently seen problems). Text-based protocols on the other hand usually pose no problem[10] when run on different platforms.

Table 3.1.: Characteristics of Client / Server Architectures

---

[9]The extensible messaging and presence protocol, http://xmpp.org/.

[10]The used character sets play an important role as some character sets are incompatible to others or the availability and quality of implementations differs between host and Operating System (OS) architectures.

3.3.2. N-Tier

N-tier approaches to architectural design are a flexibilization of the Client / Server paradigm. Instead of a mandatory direct relation between client and server, N-tier-based systems allow for additional layers between client and server. One of their usages is to partition the workload across multiple server components. Load-balancing can be one of those layers as well and therefore be modeled by means of the architecture itself.

Figure 3.1 shows a selection of possible layers in an N-Tier system. The leftmost vertical column shows the traditional Client / Server mode, split up into an independent presentation layer and the actual application layer taking care of business logic and data access in the second column. Further to the right, more layers are added, dividing the task into more partitions. The three rightmost columns show how load balancing is integrated into the N-tier approach.

Criterion	Assessment
Distribution	Flexible partitioning supports distributing the functionalities of the software system over different network nodes.
Complexity	Adding layers increases interconnections between layers. The result is an exponential increase in complexity, but overall complexity still is low.
Extensibility	cf. Client / Server
Integration facilities	cf. Client / Server
Reliability	Basically the same as in the Client / Server case. Adding more layers, however, adds more modes of failure to the whole system.
Availability	cf. Client / Server
Performance	cf. Client / Server
Security	cf. Client / Server
Interoperability	cf. Client / Server
Maintainability	cf. Client / Server
Portability	cf. Client / Server

Table 3.2.: Characteristics of N-Tier Architectures

41

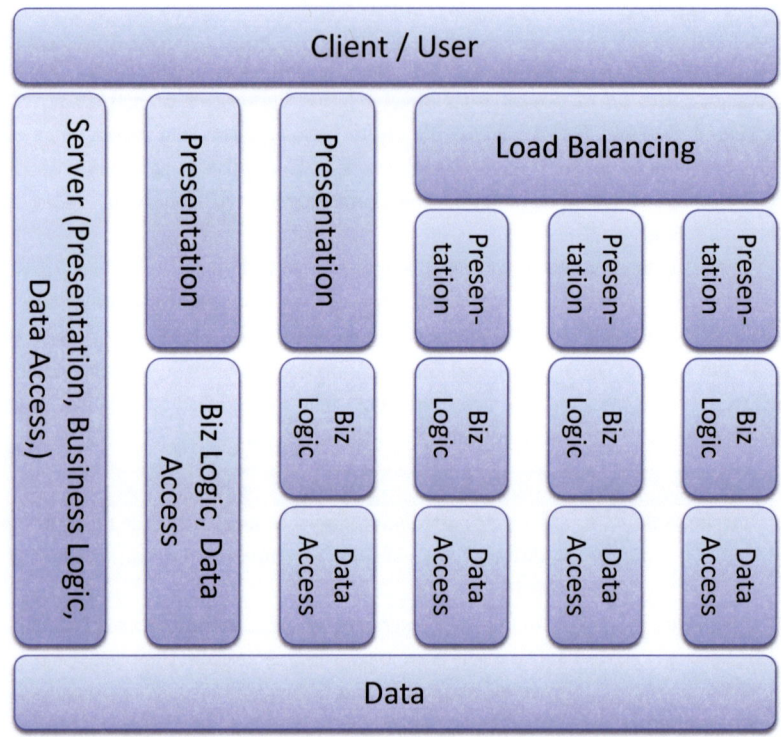

Figure 3.1.: Schematic Structure of Client / Server and N-Tier Architectural Styles

3.3.3. Pipes and Filters

This architectural style[11] has already been in use long before it was formalised by Meunier in [Meu95]. The basic idea behind it is to have a multitude of small utilities called filters and a mechanism to connect outputs and inputs of those filters. The best-known implementation is the Unix operating system. Many filters (e.g. cat, grep, sed, awk) can be connected through pipes, resulting in a system that quite closely resembles the functionalities of the SOA as it allows dynamic reconfiguration and addition of new filters (services),if the used tools are intelligent enough.

---

[11]Calling a pipes and filters system an architectural style might seem an oversimplification at first. But considering the fact that the unix community has a long tradition of building even most complex software applications from a set of independent tools, pipes and filters are indeed an architectural style.

Criterion	Assessment
Distribution	Depends on the pipe mechanism. Unix pipes as the most common implementation cannot easily be used in a distributed fashion. Replacing the interconnection mechanism by a network aware version however, allows for certain degrees of distribution.
Complexity	Each of the filters is very simple, combinations on the other hand not only gain functionality but also a certain level of complexity.
Extensibility	As long as the implementation is able to talk to the pipe, just adding new filters extends the whole architecture.
Integration facilities	New filters could also allow integration of external data sources or external functionalities.
Reliability	No provisions for reliability are made inside the architecture itself.
Availability	cf. N-Tier.
Performance	The slowest filter is going to be the bottleneck that limits overall performance, provided that the pipe mechanism itself is adequately performing.
Security	Transporting security information between invocations of filters is not standardized. Standardized inter-filter protocol do not exist, either, making every implementation of a pipe and filter system quite unique. Thus, security problems have to be solved repeatedly.
Interoperability	cf. Client / Server.
Maintainability	cf. Client / Server.
Portability	The filters underlie the same portability considerations as every other software artifact. Text-based filters additionally suffer from character set issues as explained for the Client / Server case. The pipe mechanism itself is not important, the host of such an architecture only has to support a specific implementation.

Table 3.3.: Characteristics of Pipes and Filters Architectures

3.3.4. Distributed Objects

Every common programming language nowadays has acquired some form of support for distributed objects. Java, for example, extensively uses a concept called Remote Method Invocation (RMI) to make components aware of their counterparts at different locations in networked environments. Microsoft devised their own scheme, calling it Component Object Model (COM), COM+ and D(istributed)COM successively. An industry standard body created a distributed object technology called CORBA, the Common Object Request Broker Architecture, with the added benefit of not only not being platform-independent but additionally being language independent. Raj explains three of these most widespread technologies in more detail [Raj98].

Common aim of all these technologies is to use the Object-Oriented Programming (OOP) paradigm in a distributed environment. Discerning between local and remote objects is no longer mandatory as ideally both cases use the same call semantics [OBDA08].

Table 3.4 explains the classification of this architectural style.

Criterion	Assessment
Distribution	Native part of the technology.
Complexity	Every access usually involves stubs and proxies and the usage of a resource locator. All of these components can be auto-generated but increase complexity of the resulting system.
Extensibility	One of the main drivers behind OOP was its good extensibility.
Integration facilities	A wide range of different integration schemes exists, some of which are more useful than others. In some cases, external data or functionalities are integrated through the use of wrappers. The preferred solution for data integration is, however, if the data or functionality that is to be integrated is available through a set of remote objects that are compatible with those used by the integrator.
Reliability	No provisions for reliability are made inside the architecture itself.

Availability	No provisions for availability are made inside the architecture itself.
Performance	The considerable overhead of wrapping/proxying and locating remote objects has to be considered. Caching strategies can alleviate these performance penalties.
Security	Not all of the inter-object protocols support encrypted transports, leaving it up to the application to encrypt transfered data in certain cases.
Interoperability	Within technology families, interoperability is very good. Interoperability with other components follows the same considerations as in the Client / Server case.
Maintainability	Encapsulation of different components is quite good, resulting in a good maintainability of the whole system. Components can be replaced or modified at will as long as only the interfaces are stable.
Portability	Portability depends on used technology families. Not every computing platform has a usable DCOM implementation, making it impossible to port a DCOM based application to a different platform even if the original programming language itself is available on the target. This is shown in the case of UNIX with its support for C# but not for C#'s DCOM.

Table 3.4.: Characteristics of Distributed Objects

3.3.5. Service-Oriented-Architecture (SOA)

Many people and organizations claim to be the inventor of SOAs but apparently the SOA was not invented but has evolved over time. The history of the terminology has already been laid out in Chapter 1.

The very foundations of SOA as we know it today are web services. The term web service has been in use in different contexts for some time but commonly describes "a software system designed to support interoperable machine-to-machine interaction over a network" [BHM+04], usually achieved through the usage of Simple Object Access Protocol (SOAP) (currently specified in version 1.2 [GHM+03]) and eXtensible Markup Language (XML)-encoded data. SOAP resembles other object access protocols in that it allows the user to call methods in remote objects, optionally passing in arguments and receiving a return value. Exception handling is also standardized in SOAP.

Without the help of analysts and viewed from a researchers' perspective, SOAs are a logical advancement of all the architectural styles introduced so far in this chapter, glued together by web services and SOAP. They draw the following influences from the corresponding styles:

- Client / Server
  SOAs reuse the general model of communication between networked entities acting in different roles. Microscopically, the communication between a SOAP-client and one single service can be seen as a Client / Server relationship.

- N-Tier
  Breaking up the rigorous relationship between the client and the server by introducing intermediary layers is mimicked by SOA through the introduction of web services which all have their very own, self-contained functionality and can be called one after the other, cascading data between the respective calls.

- Pipes and Filters
  Pipes and filters is quite similar to SOA as an imaginary, tuned up, example of a pipe and filter implementation shows: Each filter is offering its service through a SOAP-capable interface and all the pipes connecting the filters are also implementors of SOAP and intelligently pass on the data.

- Distributed objects
  SOAP already was designed in the spirit of distributed objects as, it is a protocol that allows representing remote services as objects and performing methods on these objects.

SOAs nowadays are defined to have a number of distinctive properties as summarized by Erl in [Erl05]. The first major property is loose coupling. Loosely coupled objects seek to ensure that objects only have minimal mutual dependencies. Objects communicate only through methods pre-defined in a service contract and in general are autonomous and reusable. All of these properties were already present in the previous styles and do not automatically make the SOA an improvement. Two other important pieces of functionality therefore exhibit the real novelty of the SOA: *Composition* and *Discovery*.

Composition is the ability to string together a set of web services in order to arrive at a new, meaningful, composite service while *discovery* makes available methods to search through databases of web service definitions and retrieve the ones fitting a requested functionality.

Unlike earlier styles, a SSOA needs a platform that is capable of carrying out the composition and discovery dynamically.

Table 3.5 describes SOAs according to the common criteria catalog.

Criterion	Assessment
Distribution	Communication between distributed nodes through standardized SOAP makes distribution a native property of the SOA.
Complexity	Proportional to the number of involved services. If done in a dedicated way, the number of services easily reaches a few hundred[12].
Extensibility	Inherently supported by composition and discovery.
Integration facilities	Standardized interfaces as well as composition and discovery allow for integration of every component with a working SOAP stack. Even for objects not capable of SOAP a solution exists in the form of wrappers.
Reliability	No provisions for reliability are made inside the architecture itself.
Availability	No provisions for availability are made inside the architecture itself.
Performance	Overhead caused by the added complexity[13]can cause significant performance hits.
Security	Many standardization efforts are underway. Basic security services like confidentiality and integrity of the transferred data are already supported by versions of these standards.
Interoperability	Every SOAP-capable entity can be integrated without modification. Otherwise, wrapper technologies are used.
Maintainability	The high degree of loose coupling lightens the burden of maintainability considerably.

---

[12]One SAP manager told an astonished crowd at a keynote about their flagship SOA-based "SAP business by design" product, that it had incorporated more than 1.000 web services.

[13]The more dynamic a system is, the less statical binding between components is possible, obviously. Thus, communication relations incur considerable overhead.

Portability	The very high degree of encapsulation of particular web services reduces portability problems to those of standard software systems, i.e. the need to get an executable binary for a specific platform. Other issues, such as byte order or characterset conversion problems are dealt with in the SOAP stack which is not part of the designed system but a runtime library.

Table 3.5.: Characteristics of the SOA Approach

3.3.6. Semantic Service Oriented Architecture (SSOA)

After SOAs have been introduced in Chapter 1, their added value is not clearly visible, at least for many of its touted characteristics, as Table 3.6 shows. It compares SOA's characteristics by Thomas Erl to their possible implementations in traditional software development technologies.

SOA characteristics	Non-SOA implementation
Loose coupling	Interfaces, data encapsulation / hiding. These are classic object-oriented concepts, enforced in all object-oriented languages and also nowadays emulated in procedural languages[14].
Service contract	Interfaces[15] are ideally suited to offer service contracts.
Autonomy	Autonomy of components can also be controlled by designing appropriate objects and modules in the conceptual phase of software development.
Abstraction	Interfaces additionally offer a varying degree of abstraction.
Reusability	Components can be modeled to allow their easy reuse.
Composability	No direct counterpart in traditional software technologies.

---

[14]Depending on the application area. Embedded systems design or operating system kernel developers will not want to use high-level software techniques like these, but use better performing approaches even at the risk of loosing maintainability in their codebase.
[15]Two examples are the header files in C++ and the Interface concept in Java.

Statelessness	This is a characteristic that is not shaping the term SOA but nonetheless is present in [Erl05]. Many developers will look at it as a nuisance rather than a feature.
Discoverability	No direct counterpart in traditional software technologies.

Table 3.6.: SOA vs. Traditional Software Engineering Approaches

This analysis shows that all but discovery and composition have proven support in conventional software engineering.

Discovery in SOAs is usually done through the use of so called registries that adhere to the Universal Description, Discovery and Integration (UDDI) standard [BCE+02]. UDDI exhibits the typical information retrieval problem as the fields describing service usage in the registries are filled with free-form text. Free-form text is a very subjective approach to describe services, leading to obvious problems with the quality of the retrieval results. Automatic discovery is an unrealistic idea as the returned services certainly have to be checked by human experts to assess if their description fits what they actually can perform.

Composition of services is usually done manually for two distinct reasons[16]. The first is a validation of the capabilities the discovered services offer, the second is to alleviate the problem of finding a meaningful order of execution of discovered serviced.

Trying to solve these issues requires standardized knowledge on web services inside the repositories. KBTs as explained in Part II deliver technologies and methodologies for exactly that task. With these tools at hand, the SOA can finally be transformed to the SSOA, which is subject of an exhaustive description in later chapters.

To close this subsection, however, Table 3.7 describes the SSOA-approach by means of the usually examined properties.

Criterion	Assessment
Distribution	Communication between distributed nodes through standardized SOAP makes distribution a native property of the SSOA, as well.

---

[16] Automated composition is researched, for example in [BCDG+03], those research results did not find their way into practical SOAs yet, though.

Complexity	In addition to the complexity considerations given for SOAs, the usage of KBTs further increases the overall system complexity.
Extensibility	cf. SOA.
Integration facilities	Web service integration in a customary sense is not different to SOAs. Integration of the KBT-based system components, however, is challenging.
Reliability	cf. SOA.
Availability	cf. SOA.
Performance	Even more overhead is caused through KBTs. Their knowledge-intensive computations affect performance considerably.
Security	cf. SOA.
Interoperability	A generic interoperability feature for KBTs is unavailable at present. Even if currently researched, this task needs too much Artificial Intelligence (AI) support for being feasible at this time.
Maintainability	cf. SOA.
Portability	cf. SOA.

Table 3.7.: Characteristics of the SSOA Approach

3.3.7. Representational State Transfer (REST)

REST-style architectures [FT02] follow another approach by looking at a web site/application as a virtual state machine formed by its pages. Whenever a link is followed or a form or other data is submitted, a state transition occurs and the new state is "represented" (the R in REST) to the user. Thereby the web is broken down into resources representing an information provider which is addressed through an URI. Access to the resources is achieved through a small set of operations using a Client / Server protocol that is stateless, cacheable, and layered.

While Fielding and Taylor describe their architectural style as open and generic enough to be used without the WWW, RESTful architectures practically only play a role in WWW contexts, where they increasingly gain momentum on SOAP by offering a very simple and solid interface as opposed to the complexity added by SOAP and its underlying XML foundations.

This architectural style is rooted in the Client / Server environment. Table 3.8 further describes the previously used key criteria for Representational State Transfer (REST) styles.

Criterion	Assessment
Distribution	cf. Client / Server.
Complexity	cf. Client / Server.
Extensibility	cf. Client / Server.
Integration facilities	In contrast to the Client / Server style, REST-based architectures offer a minimum amount of structuring (Create, Retrieve, Update, Delete (CRUD)) for the communication relation between client and server. Thus, certain semantics are available.
Reliability	cf. Client / Server.
Availability	cf. Client / Server.
Performance	cf. Client / Server.
Security	cf. Client / Server.
Interoperability	cf. Client / Server.
Maintainability	cf. Client / Server.
Portability	cf. Client / Server.

Table 3.8.: Characteristics of REST Architectures

3.3.8. Peer-to-Peer Architectures (P2P)

As opposed to all other variations previously introduced, P2P architectures rely on central components as little as possible. Conventionally, data in P2P networks is transfered between two arbitrary clients. Some network node or protocol feature has to exist that helps clients locate other clients. Once these peers have been connected, the data transfer is handled directly.

Peer to peer protocols are perceived as protocols geared towards receiving of content. In reality, however, the opposite is true. In order to support effective retrieval of content, it has to be stored effectively. Lots of research has been undertaken in this field (e.g. [SMK+01] and [RD01]). Despite all its usefulness, the Peer-to-Peer technology still has negative connotations attached[17].

---

[17]Napster, the first widespread file sharing system, helped coin the term P2P and was mainly used for trading copyrighted audio files.

Table 3.9 summarizes the properties of such systems.

Criterion	Assessment
Distribution	Native part of the system.
Complexity	Data transfer between peers is straightforward. The algorithms to locate certain bits of information can quickly get out of hand when the number of peers reaches a critical mass. Several approaches to levitate these problems exist, however. As the latest generation of Peer-to-Peer based file download facilities prove, those protocols nowadays scale well.
Extensibility	Extending the network is a native feature of the protocol.
Integration facilities	No direct integration facilities exist but wrapper technologies could induce additional nodes to the network that do not natively support a specific P2P protocol.
Reliability	The whole system is very reliable if a critical mass of users is reached. From this point on, content can be distributed redundantly among the nodes. Below a certain number of nodes reliability is problematic, however. If one node goes offline, it quite possibly could take with it the only copy of a portion of content existing in the whole system.
Availability	Availability is among the key features described for Peer-to-Peer (P2P) architectures
Performance	Depending on the effectiveness of data distribution on nodes, retrieval of data can be very well performing. The actual data transfer always is dependent on the hardware and link specifications of both connected peers. A problem could be that there is no potential for easy optimization as the platform is not centrally operated.
Security	Trust between nodes is heavily researched but no final solution seems to emerge [AD01]. Also, encryption of content is problematic as, again due to the lack of a central authority, PKI is not easily implementable, while symmetric cryptography cannot cope with the amount of nodes in huge P2P networks.

Interoperability	Only nodes implementing the same protocol can communicate with each other and with external requesters.
Maintainability	No central point of control in turn means no central point of administration either, making maintenance of the system a challenging task.
Portability	The protocols exist for many platforms already and, apart from that, much of the original research work is available and can be used to deduce algorithms that need to be implemented in order to join a P2P network.

Table 3.9.: Characteristics of P2P Networks

Figure 3.2 shows the relations between the presented architectural styles.

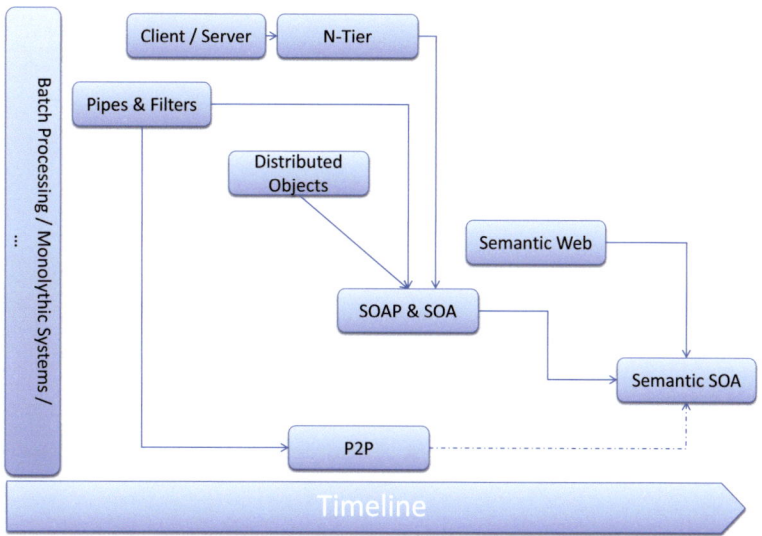

Figure 3.2.: Interconnections Between Presented Architectural Styles

As is frequently the case, no single solution is enough to form an innovative and stable system that fulfills the user requirements. Part III will draw on many of the introduced styles in order to build a progressive follow-up to the SOA that has the ability to overcome most of the weaker points of SOA concepts.

4. System Architecture Design

After having reviewed basic quality parameters of software architectures and thoroughly explained the evolution of software architectural styles, it is now time to discuss the actual design methodology of software architectures.

4.1. System Architectures in the Development Lifecycle

Many process models exist in today's software engineering communities, and many of them are similar or overlapping. Thus, in order to place the architecture development inside the general software development process, it is not necessary to go into detail regarding all those process models. For the rest of this thesis, it is enough to briefly look at an example process model, only to identify coarse steps and locate the architecture design within them.

One of the most widely used models today still is the spiral model, devised by Boehm in 1988 [Boe98]. Its main activities are (simplified):

1. System Requirements

2. Design

3. Prototype

4. Feedback cycle (After evaluation of the prototype, go back to step 1) and update the requirements with the results of the evaluation)

System architecture design often takes place in Step 2), the design phase, and is concerned with translating the user requirements into implementable units or modules. Both steps will be explained in more detail in the next sections.

Prior to that however, two different modes of architecture design have to be discerned:

Retrofitting Software Architectures

A lifecycle model for retrofitting architecture design is primarily interesting for software development efforts within a single organization. Software systems in many organizations have been upgraded to support new protocols and technologies, oftentimes neglecting the bigger (organization wide) picture. To get back on a clear and oriented software development track, the following three distinct and consecutive activities, described by White et al., appear to be a good starting point [WLO97]:

- Architecture extraction
  Architectures of already existing systems are extracted. Depending on the quality of already available (design) documentation this step could possible involve reverse engineering or other exploratory methods. White et al. claim that architecture extraction is beneficial to the source architectures as well, as it improves maintainability by enhancing their - often weak - documentation.

- Architecture generalization
  Elaborating the similarities between the sourced architectures allows the designer to abstract from individual architectures, thus resulting in a generalization.

- Architecture reuse
  Subsequent implementation efforts can largely benefit from the collection of generic architectures as only a fraction of the source architectures have to be modified for every new instantiation.

On a different technical level, Katzman et al. describes a similar approach for working with already existing software systems [KC99].

Integrated Design of Software Architectures

As opposed to the suboptimal case of retrofitting software architectures, a design environment that is able to initially start with at least a preliminary architecture is a better way to design software systems.

4.2. Requirements Engineering Phase

The days of developer-centric software systems are long gone. Nowadays, the most important participant in a software development project is the user. Requirements engineering, the art of surveying the users' exact wishes and desired functionalities has been a research hot topic for nearly three decades. The following paragraphs introduce this area of research by firstly giving a definition of the matter before subsequently explaining one approach to successful requirements engineering.

4.2.1. Defining Requirements Engineering and its Environment

According to the IEEE, the most basic term, the "requirement" is defined as follows [JM90]:

1. a condition or capability needed by a user to solve a problem or achieve an objective.

2. a condition or capability that must be met or possessed by a system or system component to satisfy a contract, standard, specification, or other formally imposed document.

3. a documented representation of a condition or capability as in (1) or (2).

Reknown for the important role the IEEE plays in the research community, their definitions usually are viewed as a de-facto standard by many researchers.

This very definition, however, is too shallow to be really useful in real-world projects. On the contrary, having no other kind of constraint on the `condition` and `capability` than (1) and (2) paves the way for gold-plating[1] of systems which has to be avoided at all costs. It raises general system costs not only by making systems more complex and therefore more error prone, less manageable and also less intuitive from a user interface point of view, but also more costly to develop. Systems with a limited user group are in no imminent danger of gold-plating, the probability rises with the size of the relevant user group: A system like the Microsoft Office Suite, built for millions of users worldwide, is bound to have many distinct features that are very important to one user group and at the same time being totally ignored by other users. This is obvious: a technical writer for a car manufacturer, possibly working in a team, is requiring a largely different set of features than a student writing his first seminar work.

Feature-ladden software suffers from severe usability problems as the users are swamped with unknown menu entries or pictograms. Usability in turn is directly

---

[1]An even less formal term for gold-plating is featureitis, both meaning the introduction of features that are not needed in systems if those systems should only adhere to user requirements specification and not fulfill additional requirements.

connected to user satisfaction, a key goal of (commercial-) software development. Microsoft for example acknowledges this fact through using a self-adapting menu system able to hide unused menu items while prominently placing frequently used items right in the middle of the menu strip.

Not implementing unneeded features at all is better in terms of developer productivity and user satisfaction than hiding them away, however.

Some constraints obviously are missing in this first definition and are added by Zave which, in a compressed and self-contained short paragraph, gives the most suitable definition of requirements engineering [Zav97]:

> "Requirements engineering is the branch of software engineering concerned with the real-world goals for, functions of, and constraints on software systems. It is also concerned with the relationship of these factors to precise specifications of software behavior, and to their evolution over time and across software families."

4.2.2. Process Model

Many sub-disciplines of information system design have generated their own, often highly specialised process models for requirements engineering. This work in contrast builds on the generic and widely acclaimed process description introduced in [ABDM01] which is extended to fit into the reality of SSOAs. Four distinct phases make up the core of the requirements process in this process model: elicitation and analysis of the user requirements, a formal specification of the elicited topics, and validation, all of which will be introduced in the following paragraphs.

4.2.2.1. Elicitation

Elicitation of user requirements[2] is a complex process that can resort to quite a number of distinctive methods. Table 4.1 lists commonly used methods and the perceived share each of the three entities requirements engineer (RE), development team (DT) and users (UP) have in their realization.

Method	Description	RE	DT	UP
Introspection	The RE analyses the system in question and extracts requirements.	++	–	–

---

[2] Also called "gathering of user requirements" which oversimplifies things as the process is much more complex than that, involving different user groups and skilled requirements engineers.

Method	Description	RE	DT	UP
Structured Interview	The RE interviews users according to a predefined sequence.	++	–	++
Unstructured Interview	The RE has a freeform conversation with the UP.	++	–	++
Questionnaire	UPs fill out a questionnaire in order for the RE to reproducibly obtain information.	++	++	o
Scenario	RE and UP design detailed use cases of the architecture in design.	+	–	++
Round-Tables	Users gather for an informal discussion lead (and directed) by the RE.	++	++/–	++
Workshops	Similar to round tables, workshops also feature discussions mostly among UPs with a supporting role of the RE. Workshops however have an (at least partial) agenda.	+	++/–	++
Focus Group	Differs from a round-table only in the participants. While round-tables generally are open, focus groups are attended by specifically selected participants who all meet certain constraints.	o	++	++
Rapid Application Development	DT uses RAD tools to quickly design prototypes which evolve over time through UP interaction.	-	++	++
Protocol Analysis	A key person in the UP writes down all specific steps of a process and lets the RE extract the requirements thereof.	++	–	++

Method	Description	RE	DT	UP
Laddering	RE interviews a user by starting with questions about a fact on a very high level of abstraction, decreasing the level with every new question. The user has to assess how important those "child facts" are. The end result is a tree-like representation of the initial fact and all the relations the user has, giving a detailed image of the users' knowledge and assessment of the specific fact's context.	o	−	++
Card Sorting	Users are given cards with requirements written on them and are tasked with sorting them into distinct groups. They also have to give the rationale behind the division criteria chosen.	+	−	++

Table 4.1.: User Requirements Elicitation Methods and the Degree of Involvement of Peer Groups

4.2.2.2. Analysis

After finishing the elicitation process, the result usually is a large document of more or less freely (as in non-formally) described user requirements. This list in its current form has no value to the software design process, however. All requirements need to be grouped and weighted before further phases based on them can commence.

Classification

Usually, classification is done along one of the following axes (or even a combination of them):

- Functional vs. non-functional requirements
  Functional requirements are directly mapped to the input, output, and effect of the designed system while non-functional requirements measure quality criteria like bandwidth or response time.

- Origin of requirements
  Different parts of the system generate different requirements. Examples for this schema include the user interface, the system backend, or a system API.

- Legal requirements
  Those requirements come in two different forms, one concerned with generally significant law restrictions, the other directly connected to the designed system through contract issues.

- Product or process
  Does the requirement target the product (i.e. the system) or rather the process of using it?

- Priority
  Not all user requirements necessarily are equally important. Observations that the teams tasked with requirements engineering make during the elicitation process are a good starting point for a priorization of requirements.

- Stability
  Requirements change over time. An assessment of their stability might be necessary to judge whether the adoption of a requirements engineering management processes and accompanying software tools is necessary.

Conceptual modeling

Complex systems account for complex requirements documents, but adequate visualization and modeling technologies can alleviate their complexity. While being an important tool in the process, modeling on a conceptual scale is out of scope of this thesis.

Architecture Design

This item is included in [ABDM01] but the requirements process model used in this publication is different. It explicitly does not design any architecture components before the whole specification document is finished.

Conflict Resolution

While being important in the case of peer groups having different priorities or a different general idea of a system, a description of conflict resolution strategies is not a topic discussed in this thesis.

4.2.2.3. The IEEE Software Requirements Specification

Many different approaches to documenting the actual software requirements exist, ranging from informal or loosely formalized, text-only descriptions to complete requirements specification languages and accompanying tools. Since most of the collected requirements are kept in unstructured textual representations, valid requirements documents are not confined to one and only one style of formal document. Part III explains why SSOAs require very flexible and apt ways of documenting the requirements.

In this light, the IEEE saw a need for a formal basis for all the requirements documents in as early as the 1980s and successively developed a complete and complex framework for such documentation.

The template for specification of the requirements of a software project, the so-called "Software Requirements Specification" (SRS) [IEE98] is presented by the IEEE in IEEE-830-1998. Its main contents are grouped into two blocks. Firstly, the overall description, organised as follows:

- Product perspective
  Describes the relation the system in question has to other systems, to remote and local hardware, and to its users.

- Product functions
  A section that explains the required functionality of the product.

- User characteristics
  A short summary of the expected users' characteristics.

- Assumptions and dependencies
  The place for all factors directly or indirectly influencing the SRS.

- Apportioning of requirements
  Priorisation of requirements in requirements having to immediately be implemented and requirements that can be delayed to later versions.

The second part of the SRS, the so-called "Specific Requirements", advances into the details of the analyzed system:

- External interfaces
  Description of all inputs and outputs of the system.

- Functional requirements
  This most important part describes the functionality that is planned for the system.

- Performance requirements
  Quantitative analysis of expected performance requirements and usage figures.

- Logical database requirements
  Section on the data that the system should be able to handle.

- Design constraints
  A collection of design constraints to which the design has to adhere to.

- Software system attributes
  A collection of attributes that have to be assured in the design and in the final system.

4.2.2.4. Assessing the Quality of a SRS and its Validation

An SRS (or any other form of a user requirements document) is the central dictionary for the users' view on a new system. Therefore, quality control measures have to be put in place as to not allow a flawed user requirements document to jeopardize the whole project's user acceptance and therefore implicitly, the success of the whole project.

In this light, assessing the quality of the SRS becomes quite important. Simple, quality attribute-oriented methods as described in [DOJ$^+$93] are often used. A set of attributes is defined by the authors that range from the completeness and correctness of the collected requirements to their reusability. The expressiveness of these criteria is low, however.

Automatic approaches like the Natural Language Software Requirements Specification (NLSRS) quality model [FFGL00] evaluate linguistic qualities of natural language SRSs by computing the linguistic quality of individual sentences and those sentences in context of the whole specification. It is questionable if such complex approaches are neccessary at all, given the mandatory availability of key personell and the expected moderate size of the resulting document.

In general, requirements specified using formal languages are easier to validate since a finite set of expected content elements is already predefined. A validator can check a given specification according to these rules and it is guaranteed to arrive at a conclusion.

The most promising approaches are the ones that tie together the design and validation processes as is shown for an UML-based requirements formalism in Sukumaran et al. [SSV06]. It specifies a visual notation and uses a triad of formal analysis, automatic scenario generation based on model-checking, and rapid prototyping approaches to validate the resulting set of requirements.

Some, in another effort, uses Use Cases to describe a system and related scenarios to verify them [Som05]. In addition, this model also features a prototypical graphical tool. Fenkam et al. follow a similar approach [FGJ02].

4.3. Architecture Design Phase

Unlike for the requirements engineering phase, there is no step-by-step process model for designing the actual architecture. The reason thereof is, that architecture design is not a specific process but highly individual to both, the project and the architect.

Even well-respected authorities in the field of system architectures like Eberhardt Rechtin cannot tangibly define the role and attached tasks of a system architect. In [MR00] for example, Rechtin et al. speak of the architecture design as being "both an art and a science". They go on to describe the foundations of system architecting and include, among more tangible properties like a "purpose orientation", a number of very informal terms such as "ultraquality, certification, and insight".

Reflecting on this work, Koopman elaborates six core competencies of a system architect in [Koo00]:

- Knowledge in system lifecycle activities and in candidate technologies.

- Experience in different architectural styles.

- Ability to handle complexity.

- Ability to present the findings of key facts about system architectures.

- Ability to cope with systems that have not evolved according to a plan but rather just "happened".

- "Good taste" to create reasonable architectures.

Other publications do not add much scientific content to this discussion. Considering the complexity, the breadth of tasks, and individuality of the projects, this is not really surprising. Thus, in this thesis the system architect role will simply be defined to be that of an experienced person that

1. uses all suitable tools and methodologies (cf. Part I)

2. to pick technologies (explained throughout this work) and architectural styles (cf. Chapter 3)

3. in order to describe (cf. Section 4.4) systems that reflect and fulfill the system requirements (cf. Section 4.2).

4.4. Describing Architectures

Describing a designed architecture can be done using different approaches. Studying the real-world usage of different methodologies seems to imply, however, that most of the time architecture descriptions are needed, they are realized using diagrams based on Unified Modeling Language (UML) in an often arbitrary mix.

The following sections introduce formalisms before describing one of the few standardized architecture description frameworks in detail.

4.4.1. Architecture description languages (ADLs)

In this work, so far two different formats of architecture descriptions have been shown. Architectural styles in Section 3.3 for example have been described in a text-based manner. The SOA-RM in Section 2.2 used a hybrid of text-based description coupled with diagrams, most of which are UML-based.

While there are some well-known modeling viewpoints and associated diagram styles for describing software architecture, none of them is formally defined. IEEE/ISO Standard 1471 (IEEE1471) is prototypical in this respect. It only describes the actual content of the resulting documents, but not to which detail level they are to be described. Formalisms are not even mentioned. Information technology is full of examples showing that not formalizing integral parts of any entity yields problems with unambiguity, with transformation of the results and also with critical reviews thereof. Exactly due to these reasons, software architecture research long has been actively looking for a formal way to describe all artifacts.

Thus, a multitude of different formal languages geared towards architectural descriptions evolved. In sharp contrast, quality attributes for Architecture Description Language (ADL)s are not nearly as evolved even if it is very important to have methods at hand to compare ADLs and pick the best suitable candidate. Worst of all, the transfer of ADL from the research domain into practical usage has not happened on a broad scale.

Medvidovic et al. survey a huge number of different ADLs [MT00]. Their spectrum ranges from general purpose system description languages to languages describing the semantics of architectural interconnections. Some ADLs are based on models and accompanying tools while others are pure formalization. The authors go on to show a classification scheme that consists of two pillars, the *components* and their *connectors*, and an additional aspect called *architectural configurations* which denote the combination of components and connectors.

Currently it appears to be the case that ADLs as introduced in [MT00] are used only in a small minority of projects[3], with the vast majority of projects relying on UML for their modeling and description needs.

One thing has to be considered when talking about ADLs and [MT00]. At the time of publication of [MT00], UML did not have the significance it has today but was in an early adopters phase. Kande et al. [KCSS02] is one representant of the increasingly important research direction of trying to bridge the gap between formal ADLs on one hand and the UML on the other.

In the remainder of this work, ADLs other[4] than UML are not considered. There is no general need for the complexity of a formal proof of software systems. Systems which require such proofs are ill-advised to build upon a highly dynamic system like the SSOA in any case. Dynamic reconfiguration of services presents a challenge for validation efforts that has not even been met for the more restricted OOP paradigm [SR90].

4.4.2. IEEE/ANSI 1471-2000

One of the most concise architectural description frameworks in existence today is the one proposed by the IEEE and ANSI organizations, commonly known as IEEE 1471 and described in much detail in [RW05]. It is based on four key concepts:

- Stakeholder
  Usually a group of persons, a single person, or a (legal) entity that has an interest in solving a particular problem. Examples include the users, the decision makers or the architects.

---

[3]Projects actively using formal ADLs can usually be found where formal verification of the designed architecture and according implementation are required. The need for formal verification, however, is not a SSOA or SOA specific requirement but originates at different, non-technical levels withing projects.

[4]No universally accepted position exists on whether UML is indeed an ADL or not. From a formal point of view, it certainly is not, but it could be fit into the schema of [MT00] as far as the description task is concerned.

- Viewpoint
  Viewpoints collect patterns and templates for a specific purpose.

- View
  Applying the viewpoint to the system in question results in the view.

- Perspective
  The main difference between a viewpoint and a perspective is that the perspective can encompass more than one view and that it is concerned with only a single quality property.

[IEE00] identifies five key requirements for conforming architecture descriptions:

1. Conforming architecture descriptions have to identify stakeholders and particular concerns they have with regard to the system.

2. Those concerns shall be represented by appropriate viewpoints as described above.

3. For every viewpoint have a view documenting that particular property or requirement.

4. Consistency-check the whole document and denote any derivations.

5. Document reasons behind key architecture decisions throughout the whole document.

Identifying a set of views and viewpoints is an individual and complex task [RW06]. An experienced architect will have no problems selecting the right constituents, but a novice architect needs some guidelines. [PW92], already mentioned earlier in this document and not connected to [IEE00], defined the three views of data, processing, and connections. While back then groundbreaking, software systems long since have gotten more and more complex, effectively creating the need for more than these three views.

A *Module View Type*, explaining the decomposition of a system into distinct implementation units, is one of the views that is proposed in [CGB+02]. The relations and interactions of components are described in a *Components and Connectors view type*, while the *Allocation View Type* details software engineering related aspects of the modeled system.

[Kru95] identified four views long before IEEE 1471-2000 was devised and already named the main notations for each of them. A *logical architecture* is an object-oriented description of the system in a specific notation based on Booch[5]. A *process architecture* divides the system into a hierarchy of processes and independent tasks, visualized in another suitable Booch notation. A software-engineering type of view is the *development architecture*, which decomposes the systems into subsystems or modules. Again modeled a variant of the Booch Notation, the authors propose to stack these views in order to arrive at layers having "narrow and well-defined interfaces" between them.

Extending [Kru95], Rozanski et al. propose six viewpoints and consequently six views [RW05]. A *functional view*, describing functionalities of the system, is at the centre of the architecture description. All data-related tasks are subsumed in an *information view*. Concurrency, especially important in the kind of multi-user systems this thesis is concerned with, has its dedicated view as well. All developmental issues are summarized in the *development view*, the *deployment view* is devised accordingly. The operations phase, the last and hopefully longest lasting phase of a typical system lifecycle, is taken care of in the *operational view*.

As a last example, Hofmeister et al. again use four views to model a system in UML [HNS99]. The *conceptual view* comprises of components with so-called ports acting as sole interface to the components. Connectors have roles describing their bindings to ports. A further decomposition of the subsystems into modules is the task of the *module architecture view*. The path from modules to an executable artifact is modeled in the *execution architecture view* and the *code architecture view* lists a preliminary file system tree for the components.

4.4.3. Describing a generic Semantic Service-Oriented Architecture

In order to describe the GENSOA, the name given to the generic SSOA designed in this thesis, all of the previously introduced methods were candidate technologies. The final decision, to use IEEE 1471, was made based on the following considerations:

- Predefined structure
  IEEE 1471 details an outline of an architecture documentation that, when

---

[5] At the time of writing this paper, UML was not available. The Booch notation, however, later was one of the foundations of UML.

followed carefully, covers all important issues with relation to architecture design.

- Integration of UML
  UML diagrams can easily be integrated, allowing for standardized, widely used, and effective modeling of different facets of the system.

- Effectivity
  Even though the structure of the whole documentation is predefined, the resulting outline is still terse but complete. All of the included items have a relation to the actual architecture and implementation effort.

- Developer familiarity
  Every modern developer is familiar with UML. Many of the prototype developers additionally have had experience in IEEE 1471-based software projects in the past.

5. Security Considerations in Software Architectures

Only 20 years have passed since Bill Cheswick's amusing look at a security incident [Che90] in which he gives a detailed account of the computer security environment in the early nineties of the previous century. Today, almost every aspect has changed. Numerous new threats emerge each day, a flourishing global black market of computer crime tools exists, and black hatting turned into a million dollar business. Thus, having a clear picture of security in each newly designed system is unavoidable and, if performed wholeheartedly, also improves the quality of the resulting software system.

5.1. Standard Security Objectives

Each software project requires its own set of adapted security functions, defined in the requirements documentation. While these functions can be highly individual in each project, they share the same building blocks, usually called "standard security objectives". Eckert is a good starting point that defines the following common[1] security objectives [Eck06]:

5.1.1. Authenticity

Subjects and objects need to be authenticated countless times throughout their lifecycle during which the following three scenarios have to be discerned:

- Subject authentication
  The subject authenticates to the object in a way that is verifiable and accepted by the object. In general, this means that the object provides a set of constraints on properties that the subject must fulfill.

---

[1] The presented security objectives are also considered by e.g. Verschuren et al. in [VGV93] and in a web-based context in Dridi et al. [DFP03].

User authentication, meaning that a user presents credentials in order to get "logged in" to his user profile, is one of the main use cases for this mode.

- Object authentication
  While identical from a technical point of view, the situation reverses if the object needs to authenticate to the subject. The roles are simply reversed.

  In this scenario, users have the possibility to assess whether the object is indeed the one they want to interact with and no impersonator. This is especially important when users have to provide personal data to the object like their login credentials.

- Mutual authentication
  A logical consequence of the two previous scenarios is that authentication can – and in many cases should – be mutual. The subject first authenticates the object in order to assess that it is not posting its private data to an attacker and only if this check is valid does it continue to the next step, the subject authentication. There the subject transmits values for properties that the object wants to have checked in order to authenticate the subject.

For SSOAs, special requirements for authentication exist; the authentication process has to be as flexible as possible in order to facilitate the extensibility of SOA-based architectures.

Depending on the nature of requested properties (also called attributes in the authentication context) there are many different facets of object authentication. If the attribute is for example describing the creator of an object, the assured quality is "origin", and possible mechanisms to verify the creator of a document are by no means confined to digital entities, ranging from wax seals to asymmetrically signed Message Authentication Code (MAC)s.

Subjects often need to authenticate themselves against access control modules usually using mechanisms in one of the following three groups:

- ownership-based
  The most wide-spread ownership-based authentication token is an identity card which is in use in almost any company of considerable size. Those identity cards, however, do not allow access to computer systems in their most basic forms. Extending this concept are cryptographic certificates[2] stored on suitable identity cards.

---

[2]Albeit being around for more than two decades, cryptography-based certificates never gained widespread usage so far. Even in the considerably sized German market, it took until 2009 when

- knowledge-based
  Today, knowledge-based methods are still the most frequently used authentication methods, mainly because of their most notable representative: the login / password combination.

- biometric-based
  Many verifiable properties of the human body can also be used as authentication means, for example fingerprints or retina patterns.

5.1.2. Integrity

Integrity, often specifically called data integrity, is at least as important as authenticity. If integrity constraints are violated it is always through one of two different mechanisms: Either data is altered[3] or data inconsistencies are introduced. The difference between both mechanisms is that in the latter case the data was altered by the system itself as opposed to the first case, where an actor external to the system is responsible for any alterations.

Many solutions exist to ascertain integrity of data. Of practical relevance in the SSOA case are the following two categories:

- Prevention of unauthorized modifications (active)
  When any access to data is controlled by an access control component, the data is save from unauthorized modifications and therefore unauthorized loss of integrity. Intruders with enough access control permissions can endanger the integrity of any system without any possibility to manage such behavior. Formally verifying the access control component is the only effective way of assuring integrity of data controlled or processed by an application. This, however, incurs much overhead and complexity and is therefore seldomly carried out. Additionally, many situations mostly in highly dynamic systems exist which produce unverifiable constellations [SR90].

- Detection of data modifications (passive)
  MACs are one cryptographical example which are used to ascertain that a

---

with ELSTER online (the German tax data transfer application) one first, wide-spread application offered the method of authenticating and at the same time protecting the confidentiality with a standardized cryptographic certificate.

[3]Whether this data is accidentally or maliciously altered is irrelevant for the definition of integrity.

specific portion of data has not been tampered with. Auditing also falls in this category as logging access to data also can uncover modifications[4].

5.1.3. Confidentiality

Confidentiality is a quite complex security goal. It mainly means that the information in the system is under the control of a certain entity that prohibits unauthorized information flows and therefore inhibits unauthorized subjects from gaining knowledge that is not directed towards them. This explicitly includes all communications links which are vectors for unauthorized information flows. Closely related to confidentiality is again access control, this time as a service allowing the controlled disclosure of data.

Every software architecture needs to have facilities for the confidential storage, processing, and for secret transfer of data. Otherwise, authentication and authorization is impossible.

Protecting the confidentiality of data features an additional difficulty because detecting data disclosure is not always possible. Auditing can only support confidentiality to a certain degree. Data that is conveyed to a passive attacker via eavesdropping, for example, is not necessarily detectable.

5.1.4. Non-repudiation

Many legal events require a complete chain of evidence that in the case of Alice sending a message to Bob, neither Alice nor Bob can deny that the message transfers happened [KMZ02]. Evidence is required to assess the truth of these claims, both for the sender and for the receiver. In this context, it is very important that non-repudiation is implemented in a fair way, meaning that either both communication partners get and produce the evidence or none does.

In the context of SOA and SSOA, non-repudiation is especially important. Dynamic inclusion of services can have negative consequences once one of the included services is malignant. Even without malevolent attackers, some usage scenarios for non-repudiation exist. One, for example, is the billing between service providers and service consumers in the SSOA.

---

[4]Logging itself is a very complex topic. If not done correctly, the logs itself can be tampered with and therefore rendered unusable. Thus, cryptographic methods will have to be deployed for log systems as well.

5.1.5. Availability

Availability is commonly seen as the relation of real system uptime to expected system uptime and as such another crucial objective of the system. Availability of the whole system is always a function of the availability measures for all its constituting parts.

Availability in general is seen as a safety mechanism, rather than being related to security in its classical meaning [FP00].

5.1.6. Anonymity and Untraceabilty

All so-far introduced objectives exist to protect the system from attackers, thus protecting it from a subset of its users. Provisions for the opposite objective of protecting the user from the system also have to be taken into account. Anonymity of entities and untraceability of communications between entities is a prerequisite for successful privacy preserving methodologies.

5.2. Threats and Vulnerabilities

Each SSOA-based software system, like any system connected to today's Internet, is in the line of fire of a whole spectrum of different cyber criminals. The following chapters will review the threats a SSOA faces.

5.2.1. Classification of Threats

According to Bishop, a threat is a "potential violation of security" [Bis03], which links this definition back to the previously introduced security objectives: Any possible violation of them can be classified as a threat. According to Pfleeger, threats need to have a corresponding vulnerability in order to be actively exploited [PP07]. The authors introduce the categorization of vulnerabilities into three broad groups: hardware, software, and data-related vulnerabilities. Describing assets of computer systems that are in need of protection, another category is added in [SB07], the "communication facilities and networks".

Classifying threats is highly dependent on the used schemes and, as always in cases where objective criteria are missing, highly subjective. Formal criteria and a large number of subcategories can boost objectivity and uniqueness of the categorization but comes at the cost of added complexity. For the remainder of this document it is therefore assumed that the four categories are sufficient, especially since they are only used as a loose ordering schema.

Table 5.1 presents a generic overview of vulnerabilities in the different assets of an Internet-based system.

Attacked entity	Complexity of the attack	Assessment
Networking infrastructure[5]	Increasingly easier due to availability of flourishing black markets for botnets or shares of botnet usage time.	Very problematic. These sorts of attacks are potentially unavoidable. While many of the most sophisticated attacks can eventually be tracked down and hopefully mitigated, it is the brute force attacks, often employing tens of thousands of hosts, that are hardest to protect of. In a worst case scenario, when all available bandwidth is exhausted, the situation results in a Denial of Service (DoS) no matter which additional security measures have been taken.
Implementation	Only possible if bugs exist. Once they are discovered and exploited, applying these exploits is trivial. Discovering the bugs and writing initial exploit code is often only possible for highly capable personal, however.	While protection mechanisms exists, not every software development team is aware of them and actively using them. Hence attacks through software components still top computer anomalies lists and often are the basis on which botnets are created.
Human personnel	The so-called social engineering requires specially trained and talented personnel[6].	Hard to protect from, but tools and technologies exist to mitigate the effects that these attacks possibly have.

[5]Hardware assets providing the infrastructure.
[6]Many social engineering approaches include impersonation of colleagues, for example.

Links (DoS, Loss of Integrity, seldomly: Loss of Authenticity)	A typical attack on a link is eavesdropping which, with good availability of required tools, is easy.	Not problematic if existing protection schemes are employed.

Table 5.1.: Common Threats Shared Between all Considered Architectural Styles

5.2.2. Consequences of Threats and Vulnerabilities

Consequences associated with vulnerabilities and thus with threats are equally important. RFC 2828 [Shi00] is a widely accepted list of such consequences of which a summary is shown in Table 5.2.

Threat Consequence	Description	Triggers
Unauthorized Disclosure	Access to data without proper authorization.	Exposure, interception, inference, intrusion
Deception	Failure to protect the authenticity and integrity of the data.	Masquerade, falsification, repudiation
Disruption	The equivalent of DoS and Distributed Denial of Service (DDoS).	Incapacitation, corruption, obstruction
Usurpation	Unauthorized control of parts or the whole system.	Misappropriation, misuse

Table 5.2.: Threats According to [Shi00]

5.3. Standard Security Services

Now that security objectives and associated threats have been defined, it is important to assess which methodologies are available in order to support implementing these objectives and protecting the system against these threats accordingly.

5.3.1. Atomic Functionalities

Core[7] security objectives in an architectural context can be split into atomic functionalities, resulting in a list of the following services[8]:

- Authentication
  A prerequisite for subsequent functionalities, authentication is used to achieve the objective "authenticity".

- Authorization
  Checks whether a subject is allowed to access an object in a specific way and is therefore often realized by access control mechanisms.

- Encryption
  Encodes a given portion of data using a specific cypher.

- Decryption
  Reverses the encoding action.

- Hash
  Computes a MAC using a given algorithm.

- Verify Hash
  Verifies if a given data object's MAC is correct.

- Sign
  Cryptographically sign a portion of data.

- Verify Signature
  Checks if the signature on a certain portion of data is correct.

- Log
  As a basis for audit trails, events generated at different sources have to be preserved in a secure, unmodifiable store.

---

[7]Organizational functionalities such as Public Key Infrastructure (PKI) functions like key managment are not explicitely described.

[8]This list originates at [VGV93]. The labels have been updated to reflect both, the changing terminology in the field overall, and the different terminology in this document. Also, the descriptions have been updated.

5.3.2. Implementations

Implementations of these atomic security functionalities are commonly called security services. Verschuren et al. already introduced a security architecture and accompanying security services [VGV93]. This architecture, however, was targeted at the network and carrier level as opposed to the abstract, software-based security architectures that this document is concerned with.

Table 5.3 maps discoverd atomic functionalities to existing, real-world implementation efforts.

Atomic functionalities	Existing implementation efforts
Authentication	X.509 Certificates, Login / Password, Challenge / Response, Watermarking, Multifactor authorization
Authorization	Policy languages (XACML), Access Control Lists, Rules
Encode & Decode	Symmetric and asymmetric cryptography
Hash & Verification	MD5, SHA-*
Signature & Verification	PKI
Auditing	Logging, Remote Logging

Table 5.3.: Atomic Functionalities Mapped to Implementations

Verschuren et al. also introduce an initial set of security services which can be described using previously mentioned atomic functions [VGV93]. Table 5.4 shows an attempt at this mapping.

Security Service	Implemented by
Authenticity	Authentication
Integrity	Authentication, Authorization, Auditing
Confidentiality	Encryption, Decryption, Authorization
Non-repudiation	Auditing
Availability	Authorization, Authentication, Auditing

Table 5.4.: Atomic Functions and Their Implementors

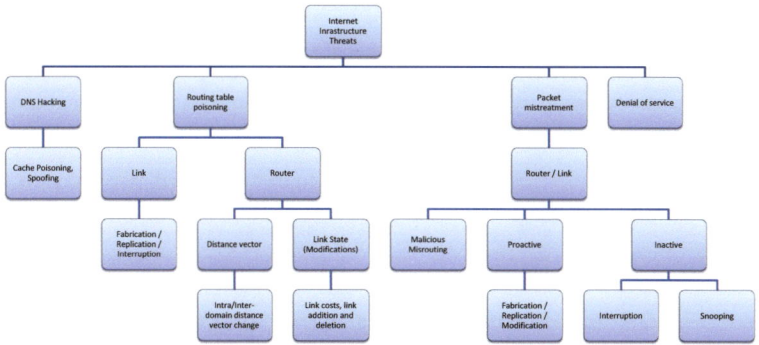

Figure 5.1.: Internet Infrastructure Threats (Based on [CM02])

5.4. Security in Different Architectural Styles

In order to position the SSOA paradigm with regard to security requirements, security in some of the milestones of the introduced architectural styles is assessed before finishing this section by looking at security requirements for a SSOA. The evolution of the line of software architectural styles encompassing those milestones that led to the SSOA paradigm has been shown in Section 3.3 while their respective security issues are introduced in the following paragraphs using the classification of threats devised in Section 5.2.1.

5.4.1. Client / Server

Infrastructure

One of the biggest Client / Server implementations in existence today is the Internet. Chakrabarti et al. assess the direct threats to the Internet's structure [CM02]. The Internet itself is definitely the worst case[9] infrastructure scenario for a Client / Server system design and therefore ideally suited to study possible threats against these kinds of systems. Figure 5.1 illustrates the numerous security related threats and issues today's Internet faces.

---

[9]In the sense of a massive system that has grown in its own way, without external guidance.

Hardware

Considerations on hardware vulnerabilities are very similar in all considered styles: Protecting the hardware from being tampered with is the key to a successful threat prevention strategy. Without secure locations for servers and other hardware components are exposed to physical attacks[10].

Software

Another critical component is the software of the Internet-based system. Every interface or component with contact to unchecked (so-called tainted) data is potentially suffering from problems with input validation. Depending on where the actual failure in the software is located, the results may be corruption, incapacitation, and obstruction of services and associated data.

Unauthorized disclosure of information is possibly caused by faulty portions of code in the software system if they enable an attacker to bypass the access control mechanisms. Many high-profile scenarios prove that this is happening quite frequently.

Well-known issues with operating system reliability show that systems do not only suffer from problems with input validation but can also have problems due to faulty code paths that do not get in contact with input data. While these usually cannot be directly exploited, the case of a notorious bug in a previous version of the Microsoft Windows operating system that shut it down after 48 days of uptime is an example of a self inflicted DoS attack.

Data

Attacks on the data are not exclusive to the Client / Server paradigm. After all, data has to be defended from any unauthorized usage or tampering in any possible way. Standard methodologies of doing so exist[11].

---

[10]Most computer systems are only poorly protected against attackers that have direct access to system consoles, mainly because each system has to have a mean of interaction with it which is out-of-band to the network in order to be able to recover from network problems or other serious problems that possibly require (re-)configuration of key system features.

[11]Existing methods range from very low-level usage of MACs to ascertain integrity and possibly authenticity of data to highly complex systems using query rewriting or other technologies to mitigate the possibility of inference attacks on the data sets.

5.4.2. N-Tier

N-Tier approaches are the logical consequence of Client / Server systems. Therefore the previous assessment also holds true for this type of architecture. Additionally, the N-Tier approach has one defining characteristic: It multiplies the problems of Client / Server architectures for each of the included tiers.

Infrastructure

N-times more layers result in up to $\frac{n*(n-1)}{2}$ interconnections between the tiers, each of them their own part of the infrastructure. Consequently, N-Tier infrastructures multiply the possible points of attacks to exploit the previously introduced infrastructure threats.

Hardware

Since the N layers usually are executing on separate systems, hardware vulnerabilities are multiplied as well.

Software

Every layer is responsible for its own input validation schema. Obviously this setup increases the complexity but the effects can fractionally be mitigated by reusing input validation components or libraries.

Every layer of such a system also can be a new source of malicious data after having been brought under control by an attacker. Well-separated layers, on the other hand, have the potential to secure the whole system if, and only if, the components are only loosely coupled: Intrusion in one component does not alter the state of any other component in this case.

Data

The assessment put forward for the Client / Server case holds for N-Tier systems as well.

5.4.3. Service Oriented Architecture

The most complex in the list of already reviewed architectural styles is the SOA. From a security point of view, however, it is not as different to a Client / Server system as could be expected at a first glance.

Infrastructure

SOAs not only rely on an Internet infrastructure[12] with its previously described problems, they additionally advance this infrastructure with additional repositories (UDDI), adding extra connections. Each of these new links is another point of attack and increases the SOAs susceptibility to infastructure-related threats.

Hardware

SOAs bring true diversity to the architecture at the cost of added complexity. Hardware security in this case is way out of scope of this document as it requires the physical safety and security of network components and computers at many[13] different premises.

Software

SOAs partially behave like N-Tiers in that every service[14] needs its own input validation code. Unlike N-tiers, however, all communication is standardized. Thus, no extra effort has to be made to implement input validation as existing libraries, together with Web Service Description Language (WSDL) information, can check and validate input, finally leading to acceptance or rejection.

Data

Due to the vast amount of data stored for each service, attack vectors increase accordingly.

5.4.4. Semantic Service-Oriented Architecture

Compared to SOAs an SSOA does not build upon different base technologies but extends the concepts through the addition of semantic data.

---

[12]The basic protocols, at the lowest level of the SOA, are the Domain Name System (DNS) and Hypertext Transfer Protocol (HTTP)/HTTP Secure (HTTPS).

[13]Depending on the scope of the SOA. SOAs that are used as Enterprise Application Integration (EAI) facilities inside one enterprise are only placed on a small number of different hosts at different premises. SOAs with a goal of integrating different companies rely on nodes situated inside many different organisations.

[14]A simplified but not 100% correct translation would be to compare services to either a Client or a Server according to the role they play in a specific interaction.

Infrastructure and Hardware

Infrastructure and hardware is not different from the SOA case, thus the considerations made there are valid for the SSOA.

Software

A SSOA is the most complex system considered in this thesis. Its use of semantic data introduces additional problems because the whole system has no strict boundaries anymore. Included services can originate at many different locations, yet have to be trusted to a certain degree by the platform. Correct handling of any sort of data, no matter whether valid or maliciously injected into the system, is of utmost importance.

Data

Not only handling the data formats is precarious, however. KBTs with their links between data portionsallow the compromisation of a whole SSOA if an attacker successfully introduces altered versions of data (for example service descriptions) into the data repositories.

5.4.5. Security Requirements for a Semantic Service-Oriented Architecture

Summarizing the last paragraphs, Table 5.5 maps native SSOA-related security threats and threats inherited from predecessor architectural styles to security services.

Security Threat	Mitigating Security Service
Data threats, Software threats	Authenticity
Data threats, Software threats	Integrity
Infrastructure threats	Confidentiality
Infrastructure threats	Non-repudiation
Infrastructure threats, Data threats (partially), hardware threats	Availability

Table 5.5.: Resulting Threats to the SSOA in Contrast to Standard Security Services.

The most important finding of this chapter is that the SSOA can be supported by the set of well-known standard security services introduced earlier and does not require non-standard mechanisms in order to be secure.

5.5. Existing Tools and Technologies for Standard Security Services

Standard security services have been around for a considerable amount of time. Thus, lots of implementations for all of their functionalities exist mostly in the form of programming artifacts (source code, libraries, components), but also in the form of processes or methodologies[15]. In a SSOA context, security services and accompanying functionalities have found a home within the WS-Security framework and the XACML standard, both of which are going to be introduced in the following sections.

5.5.1. WS-Security

WS-Security, currently in version 1.1 [NKMHB06a], is a specification on equipping web services[16] with tools and functionalities necessary to support the following security-related tasks:

- Transporting security tokens[17]

- Integrity

- Confidentiality

WS-Security, however, does not offer solutions for any of the addressed problems by itself. Instead, it acts as a common umbrella for standards and technologies that implement solutions for these problems. Integrity is ascertained with the help of XML Signature [RSY+09]. It is the continuation of well-known digital signature technologies[18] into the web services world. Confidentiality of the data in the SOAP messages is guaranteed by encryption[19] [ERI+02].

---

[15]Authenticity, authorization, integrity, confidentiality are usually solved in code, availability and non-repudiation often are methodologies, sometimes accompanied by components or other software artifacts.

[16]WS-Security only considers SOAP-based web services.

[17]The term *security token* references any textual or binary artifact that can be used to verify an identity or the result of a security related decision (e.g. access control decision).

[18]So far, digital signatures were mostly seen in PKI contexts.

[19]Note: All the web service security functionalities, including encryption, are optional; they are not specified in any prerequisites for any web service protocol.

The glue between XML Signature, encryption technologies, and further external functionality is provided by the WS-Security framework. One of its success factors is the stacking of security information: The `<wsse:Security>` element can appear more than once, allowing senders to attach different security entities for different recipients. Recipients are able to pick only the element addressed to them. Such behavior is extremely useful in highly dynamic situations like in the SOA or SSOA context, where initial requests may be transformed by a whole chain of services before finally reaching a recipient.

Each `<wsse:Security>` element is a subclass of *Security Token*. A basic instance of such a token is the `wsse:UsernameToken` which, however, is only of limited use in the SSOA case because usernames are not defined on an organization-wide level. Much more important is the ability to attach tokens created by external entities like a XACML instance or a Kerberos system. The `<wsse:BinarySecurityToken>` and an unspecified generic "XML Token" type allow exactly that.

A selection of the most important tokens is briefly explained in the following enumeration:

- UsernameToken
  Contains an username and the corresponding password which may be hashed. More sophisticated concepts like a nonce which is cached on the server and prohibits replay attacks, are specified in [NKMHB06b].

- X.509 Certificate Tokens
  [NKMHB06c] describes how the X.509[20] universe is linked to web service security via the usage of X.509 security token types.

- SAML Tokens
  Based on the Security Assertion Markup Language (SAML)[21] effort, this profile (cf. [MKN+06]) not only describes how a SAML token, containing authentication or authorization information is transported in a `<wsse:Security>` element, but additionally introduces a method to use XML Signature to securely bind the actual assertions to the SOAP messages.

- Kerberos Token
  Extended[22] Kerberos is the Microsoft way of authentication, authorization,

---

[20]Many PKIs in use today build upon the X.509 ITU.T recommendation [ITU08] as underlying standardization effort.

[21]An XML-based language to transfer authentication and authorization messages.

[22]Microsoft is often credited with the motto "Embrace and Extend" and indeed, many of their products show exactly this behavior. Kerberos, where Redmond used a MIT implementation

and especially Single Sign On (SSO). While the Microsoft implementation is not totally open, it has to be admitted that interworking with Active Directory is possible without much effort. Thus, Kerberos tokens should be taken into account in any Authorization and Authentication Infrastructure (AAI), especially in inter-organizational settings, where Active Directory (or compatible) directories have already been deployed. Moralis et al. in [MPG$^+$07] add another reason in favor of Kerberos: performance figures are considerably better for Kerberos - at least in their individual test scenarios.

The profile itself is specified in [LKN$^+$06].

5.5.2. eXtensible Access Control Markup Language (XACML)

The eXtensible Access Control Markup Language (XACML) as introduced in [M$^+$05] is a modern, XML based language for expressing access control policies and decisions. In addition to the language, it also features a reference architecture for a XACML-based access control system.

5.5.2.1. Basic language components

The global goal of every XACML-based interaction is to arrive at an *Authorization Decision*, which usually either allows or disallows the *Access Request* of a *Subject* to a *Resource* for a specific *Action*. In certain cases the *Access Request* result might not be determinable[23] or the *Access Request* might not be applicable at all in the current environment.

To achieve this goal, XACML defines three top-level elements, *Rules*, *Policies*, and *PolicySets*:

- Rule
  A discrete expression that can be evaluated without context of other rules or other top level elements and yields a boolean value. A direct usage of rules is not envisioned in the standard, access is rather foreseen through policies and policy sets, respectively.

- Policy
  A container for *Rule* elements which has an additional property to denote rule combining strategies.

---

and extended it to fit their own version of a directory service called "Active Directory" is no exception.

[23]For example if attributes needed to evaluate the Access Request are not available due to privacy reasons.

- PolicySet
  A container for *Policy* and *PolicySet* elements recursively, annotated with a policy combining algorithm.

Rules and policies, as already mentioned, can be combined in the XACML framework. While the Rule combining takes place inside the policies and is therefore important for evaluation purposes, the fact that policies also can be combined opens up an interesting possibility: XACML is not restricted to evaluating policies that are directed at a resource but can use the combining algorithms to additionally include policies originating at a subject into the evaluation. Therefore, it is now possible that not only the provider of the resource enforces the presence or value of certain attributes of the subject, but also vice versa.

An example: a subject is asking for a SSL-encrypted connection when having to transfer a credit card number, accepting the possibility of the transaction to ultimately fail in case the provider cannot fulfill the constraints of this request. The service provider wants a payment for service usage but does not offer SSL. Rule combining algorithms now can be used to arrive at the (correct) access decision of Fail, even though no direct rule for the given situation existed previously.

XACML also offers a formal way to describe situations relating to the four-eyes-principle by introducing the opportunity to have more than one subject in an access request.

Due to the possibility of evaluating access requests with attributes from both the subject and the resource, Attribute-Based Access Control (ABAC), a fairly recent extension of classic access control approaches, is natively supported by XACML. ABAC after all describes just that: Access control through combination and evaluation of subject and object rules and attached policies [PDMP05]. A suggested initial set of subject attributes is based on LDAP standard attributes like a distinguished name.

5.5.2.2. XACML Architecture

In addition to the language elements, XACML also proposes an architecture that is capable of handling access requests according to its own standards document. Figure 5.2 illustrates these components and their interdependencies which are listed in the order they are called in the following list:

- Policy Administration Point (PAP)
  Policies have to be retrieved by other components. Instead of hardcoding

them or retrieving them from a database, XACML introduces the Policy Administration Point (PAP) from which policies can be retrieved. One mode of retrieval is retrieval by query, meaning that for each XACML query, a request to the PAP is made. Another mode of operations is loading all policies in advance at initialisation time. Both modes have their distinct advantages and disadvantages, and every implementation has to pick the individually best suited approach.

- Access Requester
  The subject seeking access to a resource.

- Policy Enforcement Point (PEP)
  The Policy Enforcement Point (PEP) usually is just an abstraction, representing an entity enforcing the final access decision. It does not have to be a stand-alone component and is integrated into a service or another XACML component. There are virtually no limitations on accessing this service, SOAP and other web service protocols are only examples of available connectors.

  As of late, some new examples of PEPs include PEPs built into fileservers, used for example in data leak prevention tools such as Nextlab's "File Server Entitlement Management"[24].

- Context Handler (CH)
  Coordinating facility that directs interactions between the other components.

- Policy Decision Point (PDP)
  Responsible for identifying suitable policies according to an individual request. After retrieving the policy, the PDP instructs the context handler to relay its attribute requests to the Policy Information Point (PIP) and subsequently uses these attributes to arrive at an access decision. A response context object is used to transport the result of the decision back to the context handler.

- Policy Information Point (PIP)
  Retrieves the attributes that the PDP requested. There are three types of queried attributes: subject, resource, and environment attributes, each with their own well-defined use.

- Resource
  The actual resource that is protected by a specific XACML instance.

---

[24]http://www.nextlabs.com/html/?q=file-server-entitlement-management

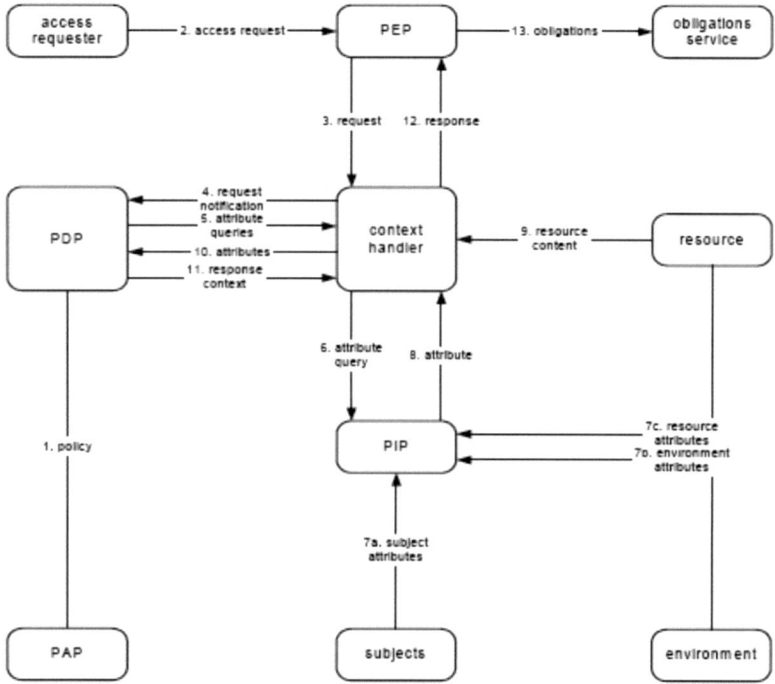

Figure 5.2.: XACML Components ([M+05]

- Environment
  Container object for information pertaining to the environment of this XACML instance.

- Obligations service
  Obligations in XACML terms are used to trigger events on successful or unsuccessful authorization attempts. One possible use for obligations is the logging of failed access attempts.

5.5.2.3. The XACML process

The following enumeration lists the steps taken by a XACML-based system in order to arrive at an access control decision.

1) Policy enumeration request
   On bootstrapping the system, the PDP issues a request to the PAP in order to get all available policies[25].

2) Access request
   An access requester issues an access request to the PEP. Usually the PEP is an integral part of the access requester as far as standard XACML is concerned, making the PEP a rather virtual construct.

3) Access request is forwarded to the context handler.

4) Request notification

5) 6) Attribute query
   PDP uses the context handler to relay a query for attributes to the PIP.

7) PIP attribute gathering
   The PIP gathers subject (a), environment (b), and resource (c) attributes. The storage location of these attributes is not formally specified and is implementation dependent. In many cases it is a Relational Database Management System (RDBMS) backed repository.

8) Attribute query response

9) Resource content
   The actual requested content is sent to the context handler.

10) Attributes
    Attributes are sent to the PDP.

11) Response Context
    The CH receives an XML code portion contains the result of the access control evaluation from the PDP.

12) Response
    The response from the previous step is enriched and relayed back to the PEP.

---

[25] As previously mentioned, there also exists the possibility to get the policies on a per-query base which is not performing well since the policies are XML objects of considerable size. It, however, does not convey the whole set of policies at once which could be important to the service provider, depending on further components of the security subsystem in place.

13) Obligations

The PDP induces execution of this request's specific obligations, which is at least the access to the resource content.

5.5.3. WS-XACML

WS-XACML, the Web Service Profile of XACML [And06], acts as the glue between XACML and the previously introduced WS-Security framework by making available four new entities:

- XACML Authorization Token
  A new instance of WS-Security's Security Tokens conveying XACML authorization decisions.

- XACML Assertion
  WS-Policy as the emerging policy standard [BBC$^+$06] does not natively support XACML Assertions but supports an extension mechanism through which the XACML Assertions are added.

- XACML P3P Policies
  Linking Platform for Privacy Preferences (P3P), XACML, and the Web Services world, this entity adds support for a XACMLPrivacyAssertion element.

- XACML Attributes in SOAP Message Headers
  Integrating XACML Attributes into SOAP headers is done through the use of a SAML assertion.

5.6. Relevance to the Semantic Service-Oriented Architecture

This chapter presented a detailed look at security in software architectures in general before elaborating on security in different architectural styles. Looking at security considerations for previously introduced architectural styles provided a very important result: Throughout the evolution of the described line of architectural styles, standard security services deduced in Section 5.1 were (and are) able to fulfill all tasks directed at protecting the system.

SOAs and SSOAs are no difference and are well handled by those common security services. In fact, the only real difference between those styles is the growing complexity with regard to security topics. Security objectives and associated atomic functionalities can be reused from Client / Server architectures to the SSOA without modifications.

For the SSOA specifically this means that it can draw on a wealth of already implemented security mechanisms that come in various forms, ranging from strictly nontechnical best-practice process models to complete frameworks and low-level libraries.

Especially WS-Security with all its subcomponents and standards as well as the XACML language and architecture prove very useful as they were designed to service XML-based systems natively.

Chapter 12 is completely devoted to presenting a security architecture for an SSOA, building on WS-Security and XACML while recursively employing itself to find and execute additional security-related services.

Part II.

Knowledge and Knowledge-based Technologies

Every day, hundreds of millions of people use the most famous hypertext system, the WWW. Starting from a very simple model that was not based on any adjacent research in the hypertext area, physicist Sir Tim Berners-Lee invented a Client / Server system for easy publishing of information and links between different portions of the information. Quite early in its lifecycle it became evident, however, that information retrieval in the WWW was problematic. This fact, together with the general aim of improving his creation, probably contributed to his vision of the Semantic Web as introduced later in this thesis. Tim Berners-Lee did not invent all facettes of the Semantic Web on his own. He rather built upon already proven research and technologies, which interestingly enough are ancient compared to "young" technologies like web services or even the WWW. After all, systems for working with knowledge as opposed to working with data were among the first drivers of computing research right after the second world war.

This part as a whole is dedicated to introducing and elaborating KBTs and their areas of usage, especially in a SSOA context.

6. Foundations

In this chapter, the underlying foundation of KBTs, the ontology, is introduced and explained before briefly listing currently widespread uses of knowledge.

6.1. Ontologies

Ontologies[1] have become the research hot-topic of information scientists, cognitive scientists, and business information science researchers alike, especially since Tim Berners-Lee proclaimed the semantic web in the late 20th century. Outside of the computing world, primarily in philosophy, the term has been used for a long time. Arguably the first mentioning of the latin term "ontologia" dates back to 1607 [ØAS05] when Jacob Lorhard in his "Ogdoas Scholastica" used it to describe metaphysics.

Ontologies in the modern, IT-centric point of view, as they are relevant to the semantic web, are defined (e.g. [Gua98]) as being a

- Vocabulary

- With attached assumptions on the intended meaning of the terms in the vocabulary.

These assumptions often appear in the form of a first-order logic representation of relations and facts concerning the concepts (terms of the vocabulary) and instances of these concepts.

Tom Gruber's definition of the term is frequently cited in the semantic web services community [TLH07]: "An ontology is an explicit and formal specification of a conceptualization". Both definitions are complementary, with the first one describing the contents and the second definition postulating formal qualities of ontologies.

---

[1]Some researchers introduce a strict separation of the terms ontology in a philosophical sense and formal ontology in a technical sense. The remainder of this thesis is concerned with formal ontologies and therefore this distinction is not made.

6.1.1. Application Areas

In order to be able to better assess the usefulness of ontologies in general, looking into current usage scenarios of ontologies is a good starting point. McGuiness states that ontologies have "come of age" [McC05]. She backs this claim by listing a wealth of possible applications for ontologies. Grimm et al. basically share this view and also give a number of application cases for ontologies [GHA09]. Summarizing both publications yields the following groups of ontology usage:

- Information Integration
  Interoperability between different data stores is a tough task for practitioners. It can be guided by ontologies when they are used as a mediator between different data representations.

- Information Retrieval
  Ontologies can considerably improve information retrieval results through intelligent narrowing or broadening of query result sets. Also completing partial user information is interesting in this environment.

- Knowledge Management
  Expert systems need no longer be solely based on rules but can be improved through the use of inference on ontological bodies.

- Data Verification
  Instead of having to codify constraints on data in rules, ontologies allow for a streamlined description of these constraints. A quick glance at the object-orientation paradigm suggests that many, if not all, constraints required for input validation can be inferred from the data type the data is packaged in.

6.1.2. Types of Ontologies

Often ontologies are only categorized into two distinct groups. Upper ontologies, that contain all available information on the discourse world and domain ontologies, which are specific to only a subset of this information.

Grimm et al. summarize prior work in the field, formulating an enhanced distinction. Figure 6.1 explains the connections between the introduced four categories [GHA09]:

- Upper Ontologies
  Upper or top-level ontologies are defined as stated above, containing all available knowledge of the whole world of discourse.

- Domain Ontologies
  Only contain domain specific knowledge.

- Task Ontologies
  In direct relation to the domain ontologies, the task ontologies hold the knowledge needed when processing a certain task. Ideally, task ontologies should be independent from domain specific knowledge, and domain ontologies should not contain task-specific knowledge [GHA09].

- Application Ontologies
  These kinds of ontologies limit task and domain ontologies to information only valid within a single application context.

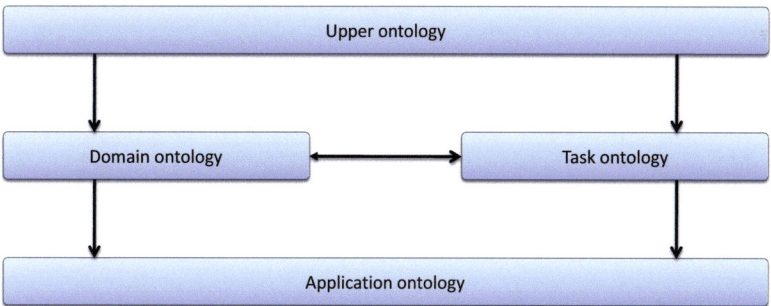

Figure 6.1.: Classification of Ontology Types Based on [GHA09]

6.2. Established Usage of Knowledge

Semantic Web technologies are only a very recent applications of formalised knowledge. Previously, knowledge has already been in use for a surprisingly long time. The following examples want to give the reader a rough idea of the various tasks knowledge is involved with today before exploring the semantic web world in detail.

6.2.1. Knowledge Management

A major task that companies are facing in today's highly knowledge-dependent work environments is the overall management of a company's knowledge. Knowledge is deeply integrated into processes, and is even sometimes formalized within organizations but most of the time only implicitly available.

Figure 6.2 gives a brief account of the development of information processing, enumerating six milestones in which the area of information processing progressed. It is an interesting observation that only the last step, beginning in the late 1990s, introduced knowledge as a dimension worth discussing. Previous knowledge processing was implicitly contained in data processing.

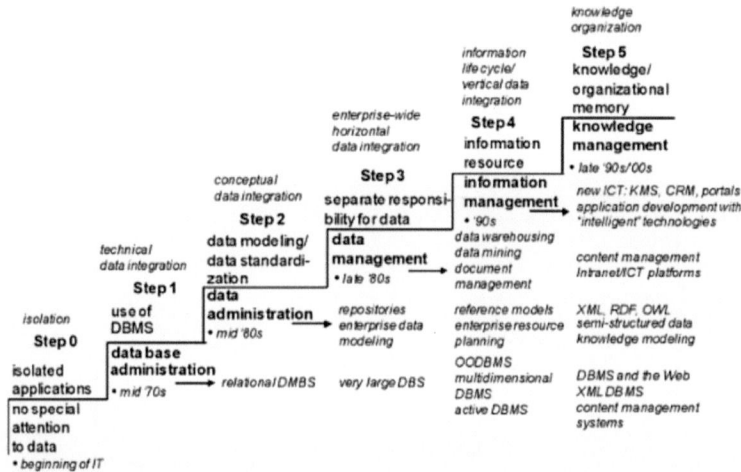

Figure 6.2.: Information Processing over the Course of Time ([MH09])

Nowadays, Knowledge Management and Organizational Memory are well-respected disciplines of business information scientists, who have discovered and designed a vast array of instruments. [Ear01] propose a division of knowledge management as a discipline into three distinctive "schools", which also can be reused to classify knowledge management tools.

A first school is described as being technological. Its instruments range from truly technocratic IT-supported knowledge bases[2] and map-based "Knowledge Directories" up to the holistic process-based approach.

The economic or commercial school views knowledge as a core asset that not only is an ingredient in manufacturing, management, and other processes, but is

---

[2]According to the author, this is the oldest approach to knowledge management. Since it builds on codification of the knowledge, however, it is the most important approach in the light of this thesis, which is mainly concerned with knowledge preservation in machine readable form.

a product all in itself. Knowledge is seen as an intellectual property that can be marketed and profitably used as own product without the need for further design and manufacturing processes. The most prominent representatives of this school are enterprises like IBM that annually earn billions of dollars with their patent portfolio and resulting license fees alone.

Behavioral aspects define the last school. Their main aim is to improve knowledge sharing and exchange in many organizational, spatial, and strategic ways.

Tools support exists for every phase of each of these schools.

6.2.2. Expert Systems

On a more tangible scale, expert systems were a key research topic since the mid 1960s[3] and reached considerable proficiency.

A typical textbook on expert systems (e.g. [Nik97]) would name the following components as constituents for its architecture:

- Knowledge base
  Facts the system knows about are stored inside a knowledge base in a suitable knowledge representation format. Often extremely simple, rule-based approaches (e.g. If-Then rules) are used, because their simplicity boosts performance while at the same time not requiring new development methodologies.

- Inference engine
  An Inference Engine is the entity in the architecture that generates new knowledge from existing concepts and rules.

- Explanation module
  This component provides the knowledge worker with feedback and could be nicknamed a "knowledge debugger". It visualizes the steps that had been taken in order to come to a conclusion to solve the current problem.

- User interface
  The user interface is the point of contact for all users of the system.

- Knowledge acquirement facility
  An input module for knowledge, this component is very specific to the individ-

---

[3]Terminology was not advanced back then. The term expert system was only one in a large set of terms describing systems closely related to what later became known as expert systems. [Sim65] for example described "question answering" systems.

ual expert system. Knowledge cannot just be imported, it needs to be heavily pre-, and post-processed.

All these systems follow a similar approach. Starting from a given state of the world, they search their knowledge base for suitable knowledge (usually rules). Those rules are executed on the initial set of facts and the results are sent to the user via the user interface.

Expert systems are in use in many fields with frequently described fields of application including banking (lending) and general troubleshooting in call-center environments.

6.2.3. Case-Based Reasoning - CBR Systems

Case-based reasoning (CBR) systems are based on expert systems with a number of additions and differences [AP94]. The main characteristic of CBR systems is that they draw on historical instances of knowledge usage. Thus, their basic strategy is to find a very similar set of properties as the one describing the current problem and infering an extended solution from this input. CBR systems learn from previous solutions by updating the underlying case base (knowledge base) with the results of the current problem solving action.

Case-based reasoning always takes place in at least two steps. The first step searches the case repository to find cases that have a relationship to the problem under review. This process is not trivial because the case bases can be large and complex and searching them can be very resource consuming. The type of knowledge representation is additionally important because not all approaches are equally well suited for being searched on.

Once the relevant cases have been located, the solutions have to be updated to reflect the specifics of the currently reviewed problem as a new case.

After the solution has been compiled it has to be implemented, dependent on the area in which the CBR system is operating in. If the solution can be automatically tested, the feedback loop does not require any human interactions. Usually, the user is not directly connected to a CBR system, however, but has an operator in between (again, a call-center type of interaction is an example). The feedback usually is given by the user and input manually into the system.

7. Semantic Web

The WWW was by no means the first system offering linked documents, so called hypertexts. Tim Berners-Lee wrote his implementation of a hypertext system, clearly detached from the hypertext / information retrieval scientific community[1] of that time. Perhaps one of its biggest success factors was its simplicity. Every user could provide content according to their own definition and rules. The whole information space of the early web was held together by initial versions of an easily usable markup language called HTML. Exponentially growing, the WWW quickly showed associated problems, however: Millions of documents with unstructured descriptions leading to a severe information retrieval problem as was already recognized as early as 1994 [Lic94]. Many researchers contributed possible solution approaches, among them Brin and Page [BP98] who later became the creators of the Google search engine and founders of the related company.

7.1. Semantic Web Layer Cake

Tim Berners Lee himself also acknowledged this problem and identified the need for added semantics on WWW documents in 1998 [BL98]. It was still a rough idea that quickly was refined and culminated in a seminal Scientific American publication [BLHL01] that brough the idea to a larger audience. A so-called semantic web layer cake, a now famous diagram of the constituents of the semantic web is a good starting point to explore its theoretical background. The semantic web consists of the building blocks laid out in the following sections.

7.1.1. URI / IRI

The Uniform Resource Locator (URI) is a standardized way of addressing resources as specified in RFC 3986 [BLFM05]. In the tradition of the WWW and associated protocols, an URI is very simple and open, its generic form only consists of two

---

[1]Tim Berners Lee wrote the first incarnation of a WWW server and client at the Swiss CERN, a particle physics laboratory.

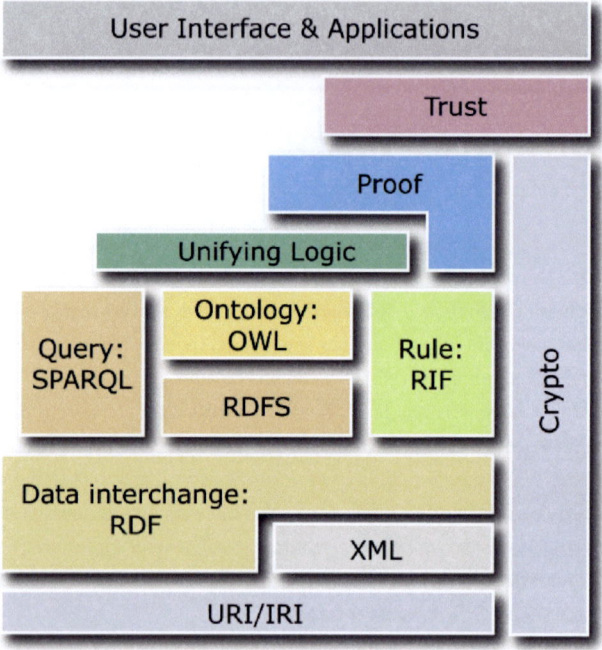

Figure 7.1.: The Semantic Web According to the W3C [Sem07]

elements:

$$scheme:scheme\text{-}specific\text{-}part$$

Uniform Resource Locators (URLs) are one of two[2] subtypes of URIs, describing how to locate a specific resource. Many well-known schemes exist, for example the HTTP (http://) scheme extensively used in the WWW.

Internationalized Resource Identifier (IRI)s are defined in [DS05] as the internationalized version of URIs, separately introduced to avoid compatibility issues. IRIs support UTF-8 and are therefore suited for nearly any known languages and character set.

---

[2]The other subtype, the Uniform Resource Name, is not relevant for this work and therefore omitted.

7.1.2. RDF / XML

Resources pointed to by URIs and IRIs are encoded on two stacked layers. XML is the data representation of choice for semantic web. Since data in XML does not have a semantic meaning[3], Berners-Lee picked the Resource Description Framework (RDF) [KCM04] as format of interchange for the Semantic Web data.

RDF is based on directed graphs, representing a subject (entity that is to be described), a predicate (labeled type of the relation) and the object (value of the relation). This relationship is usually that of a *statement* that describes the *subject* with the value *object*.

RDF was designed with the following goals in mind:

- simple data model

- formal semantics

- provable inference

- extensible vocabulary (extension mechanism based on URI)

- XML-based syntax

- possibility to use XML-Schema based data stores

The RDF specification [KCM04] adds one last goal, which is "allowing anyone to make statements about any resource". This goal, however, is not interesting for the GENSOA as it is merely an organizational and even more so political issue, not a technical one.

This layer constitutes the combined low-level encodings of data in the Semantic Web.

7.1.3. RDF Schema (RDF-S)

While RDF is already suited to describe properties of objects, there is no direct way to describe these properties themselves. Thus, RDF-S was introduced with the goal of providing means to instantiate type systems in RDF [BG04].

The underlying generic type system of RDF-S revolves around *classes* from which all other elements are derived. Pre-defined classes are chosen to cover and extend the expressiveness of RDF. Thus, *rdfs:Resource* extends *rdf:Statement* and *rdf:Property* to define the well-known basic RDF elements.

---

[3]Semantic meaning is only introduced by an XML application which usually is specified through an XML-Schema or a DTD.

7.1.4. Ontologies - Web Ontology Language (OWL)

One way of codifying ontologies in the semantic web is the Web Ontology Language (OWL). [MVH+04] introduces OWL as a comprehensive language to "represent machine readable content". As with many knowledge formalisms, OWL as well has different flavors. Those flavors are distinguished by their respective degree of expressiveness and the scalability of reasoning approaches [SGA07]:

- OWL-Lite
  A very restrictive subset of OWL, geared towards easy and straight-forward tool-support. Basically, OWL-Lite only provides constructs for subclassing and property restrictions [DCvH+02], making it suitable for simple classification ontologies.

- OWL-DL
  OWL-DL relaxes many of the restrictions put in place by OWL-Lite and is strongly tied to descriptive logics. All remaining restrictions together make sure that OWL-DL constructs use the maximum possible subset of OWL-Full while still staying decidable [DCvH+02].

- OWL-Full
  Finally, OWL-Full does not only subsume all OWL-DL and OWL-Lite constructs, but acts as a full mapping[4] to RDF(S) as introduced above.

Mappings also exist to transform OWL into RDF [DCvH+02].

7.1.5. Rule Interchange Format (RIF)

RIF is one of the most prominent proofs of the evolution of the Semantic Web. Earlier versions of the layer cake did not include rules at all while later versions included a generic box for "Rules". Only in very recent instances of the layer cake (the one shown in Fig. 7.1 and onwards), RIF is explicitly included. RIF itself is not finally specified as it is under heavy development. At the time of writing, the RIF WG website[5] did not feature final documents and also did not list any implementations of RIF and RIF-capable reasoners and rule engines.

The strategic approach is quite viable, though: the Semantic Web community wants to provide support for representing knowledge through either OWL or rules or possibly a combination of both. The belief that both OWL, and rules have their

---

[4] All OWL-Full classes are indeed also rdfs:class
[5] http://www.w3.org/2005/rules/wiki/RIF_Working_Group

advantages as well as disadvantages depending on the specific area of usage seems to have penetrated the semantic web community[6].

7.1.6. Query: SPARQL

Independent of the deployed knowledge representation scheme, SPARQL [PHS$^+$08] is projected to be the future query language of the Semantic Web. Integrated with RDF, SPARQL queries have the well-known constituents subject, predicate and object with the only exception that each of these three constituents may be represented by a variable.

SPARQL queries can be performed against a growing number of RDF Triple Stores[7].

In conjunction with future implementations of SPARQL interfaces for Rule Interchange Format (RIF) repositories, it is easy to see that this layer has the potential to be a layer for querying knowledge contained in the layers below it.

7.1.7. Unifying Logic and Proof, Trust, Crypto

Starting at the layer of unifying logic, the Semantic Web description leaves the paths of exact science and starts to describe future visions. The idea behind this unifying logic is, that every usage of reasoning can be translated into unified logic representations in order to be able to compare the reasoning sequence and therefore arrive at a proof of the reasoning that all involved parties can agree upon.

Instantiating trust in large systems is challenging. Often trust is achieved through reputation systems[MMH02], either in the form of user-centric platforms or of automated evaluation.

The last of the constituent layers is cryptography, which is mainly used for authenticating XML-based messages and can draw on a wealth of already existing technologies many of which are part of the WS-Security family (cf. Section 5.5.1).

---

[6]http://www.w3.org/2005/rules/wiki/RIF_FAQ#How_fast_are_RIF_processors_compared_to_RDFS_inference_and_OWL_inference.3F

[7]Naming any form of database that can hold RDF triples a Triple Store might be inaccurate as it does not take into account the inner workings, nor the suitability of the underlying database. Nonetheless, this nomenclature is universally used in the Semantic Web context.

7.2. Current Status

Semantic web topics undoubtedly are challenging, interesting, and exciting. Semantic web research is, however, mostly confined to the lower levels of the layer cake. Unifying logic and especially proof are still niche topics, researched only - if at all - theoretically.

How the semantic web will fair in the future remains to be seen. Currently, however, there are almost no real-world applications implementing the idea. Companies claiming to support latest semantic web technologies in reality seldomly support more than Dublin Core[8].

SSOAs on the other hand, are independent from the semantic web and, the most important distinction, do not rely on trust, proof or unifying logic to the extent the semantic web does. SSOAs therefore, as the following chapter will explain, have a much larger implementation base than semantic web technologies.

---

[8]A family of predefined metadata properties available at `http://dublincore.org/`.

8. Semantic Web Services

Semantic web services try to put the intended logical layers and software agents of the semantic web into practical use today. Logic and inference can work much better in a confined setting like a semantic web services framework. The idea of the current WWW transitioning all its content into the Semantic Web in contrast is unrealistic at present. The following paragraphs describe key properties and concepts in the semantic web services environment.

8.1. Supported Functionality

Semantic web services are the amalgam of web services technology as used in classical SOAs (cf. Section 3.3.5) and the concepts of the Semantic Web introduced in Part II. A semantic description of web services shall support software systems with the following tasks [AFO+09]:

- Discovery

- Composition

- Orchestration and choreography

- Reasoning

All of these functionalities are explained in detail in the following sections.

8.1.1. Discovery

Maximized automation in the discovery of web services is impossible with conventional technologies. An inherent information retrieval problem[1] leaves no option

---

[1] Textbooks on information retrieval like the well-known Baeza-Yates et al. book on "Modern Information Retrieval" [BYRN99] describe the information retrieval problem(s) in great detail. Of all the many facettes, the most problematic one in the context of this thesis is text understanding through software. If texts cannot be understood by agents, there is no possibility to infer the functionality of web services from their textual descriptions.

other than manual intervention when it comes to filtering web services according to their functionality rather than their description. In contrast, semantically annotating web services allows components to match the offered functionality of the system together with common web service data like associated costs (both in terms of monetary resources, and computing/networking resources) in order to find not only the best service fitting this, rather weak set of criteria but instead finding the service fitting those criteria while at the same time being able to perform the task in question.

Web Service Discovery is the art of "identifying relevant services" [SGA07]. Before strategies for effective and correct discovery can be designed, it is important to have a clear definition of the relevance of a web service in relation to a user's specific goal.

Relevance of a service is usually binary, unlike relevance metrics in general information retrieval. Either the service can carry out the task it is asked to, then the service is relevant. or it cannot, in which case the service is irrelevant. Nuances do not exist. The actual comparison contrasts something that users want to be done with what services are able to do. Formally, this can be described as comparing the services' capabilities with the goals of the users. The users, however, do not directly interact in the discovery process but are represented by agents.

Studer et al. [SGA07], based on [Pre04], define the concept of correct or complete semantic annotations: correct annotations have all elements of the model of the service appear in the abstract service. Annotations are complete when any element of the abstract service has to appear in its model.

Consistent with [SGA07], the two essential properties of semantic service discovery in this thesis are defined to be:

- Annotations (static view)
  Describes the services' capabilities and the users' requested goals in a formal way.

- Process Model (dynamic view)
  Describes the sequence in which the services have to be executed in order to achieve the users' goals.

Semantic matching is the defining subtask of discovery. The most important approaches to matching are listed in the following [SGA07]:

- Matching through inference
  Knowledge about capabilities and goals is represented in the form of descriptive

logic statements. A degree of matching is computed as the degree of overlap between both.

- WSDL-S descriptions
  Tied to UDDI and WSDL-S, this approach employs so-called "concept similarity measures" to compute a semantic distance between capability and goal.

- OWL-S service profiles
  OWL-S inherent, this strategy uses the OWL-S service profile, and the individual input and output parameters to compute the match.

- WSMO discovery
  The most promising approaches in WSMO currently compare pre- and postconditions in order to find out if the examined service offers any transition between both states.

- Rule-based discovery
  SWSF[2] proposes a matching based on executing queries against a rule database that stores the descriptions of the web services.

8.1.2. Composition

In addition to the notion of Composition used in the SOA world[3] ([PG03]), KBTs support automation of this task, at least to a limited extent.

While different ways of composition exist, this thesis is only concerned with the goal-oriented composition. Goal orientation according to Studer et al. [SGA07] gives the user the possibility to voice his goal in terms of:

- Input data

- Restrictions to this data

- Outputs that are expected from the service provider

Furthermore, the authors explain that composition relies on atomic goals, roles, and composition goals. Atomic goals abstract from particular web services while roles abstract from messages that are needed to address the services. Composition services finally are agglomerations of atomic goals with accompanying interconnections and constraints.

---

[2]http://www.w3.org/Submission/SWSF/
[3]To understand the further explanations, it is sufficient to think of generic SOA composition as a way to integrate different web services, both on a technical, and a semantic level.

Assuming these preliminaries, the actual act of Composition can be summarized as a two-step process. First, the composition goal is constructed from the user's goals and inputs (either (semi-)automatically or manually). The composition goal is "resolved" to an executable chain of web services.

[SGA07] gives a detailed and thorough state of the art assessment of this topic.

8.1.3. Orchestration and Choreography

The terms *Orchestration* and *Choreography* describe two viewpoints of the same situation ([BDO06] [Pel03]), namely the interaction of different web services in order to realize a common goal.

Choreography is concerned with interactions of the services, either among each other or between services and (possibly automated) clients.

Orchestration looks at the way services interact from outside the system, by detailing the order, constraints, and additional properties involved when web services collaborate to solve a given problem.

8.1.4. Reasoning

Reasoning, at least in the semantic web services field, is a fuzzy term. The broad range of definitions for this term can be seen by comparing the usage of reasoning in two exemplary publications. McIllraith et al. do not formally define reasoning but implicitly call any evaluation of semantic content reasoning, including the special case where actual additional knowledge is generated about the discourse world [MSZ01].

Stollberg reviews reasoning tasks especially in the semantic web services environment in [Sto05] and identifies two key areas of application. Service choreographies, where reasoning is used to check for the existence of at least one valid choreography of a given set of web services by determining whether a valid chain of interactions between services exists that complies with the following statements:

- Usage of homogenous ontologies throughout the services.

- Information compatibility between service invocations meaning that the exchanged content payload is compatible.

- Communication compatibility, meaning that the communication protocol over the whole chain has at least one defined initial state and is guaranteed to arrive at a termination state without needing additional input.

Reasoning also is used in order to validate orchestrations of web services by assuring that each interaction with and between web services can be accomplished successfully.

8.2. Process Modeling

Not all users' goals can be resolved by SSOA systems for the simple reason that only parts of the discourse world are known to the system. Likewise it does not know about all available services. Thus, at least some sort of hinting at the expected composition has to be possible and is indeed supported by most of the semantic web services frameworks.

Usually workflow-related technologies are used to support this goal. Graphical Business Process Management (BPM) tools in this context are very important for users of the system as they allow designing a specific process model in a Graphical User Interface (GUI), usually without having to be a knowledge expert[4]. Business Process Modeling Notation (BPMN) emerges as one of the most widely used graphical workflow description facilities [ABFG+08]. Resulting graphs need to be translated to executable workflows [ABFG+08] in which discipline Business Process Execution Language (BPEL) is the current market leader.

Figure 8.1 and Listing 8.1 show the general process model for obtaining a building permission which was part of the Access-eGov pilot (cf. Chapter 13) in BPMN and its accompanying BPEL representation [ABFG+08]. Comparing the figure and the listing shows, that both technologies can – and should – be used simultaneously, since BPMN is graphical and thus easy to grasp, making it ideally suited for human workflow creation editing while BPEL is machine processable.

So far, however, neither BPMN nor BPEL are directly supported by SSOA technologies. Thus, each of the efforts has to implement its own schema of integrating workflow technologies. In the subsequent description of semantic web services frameworks, the corresponding process model is explained in more detail.

---

[4]The modeler still has to be a domain expert, though.

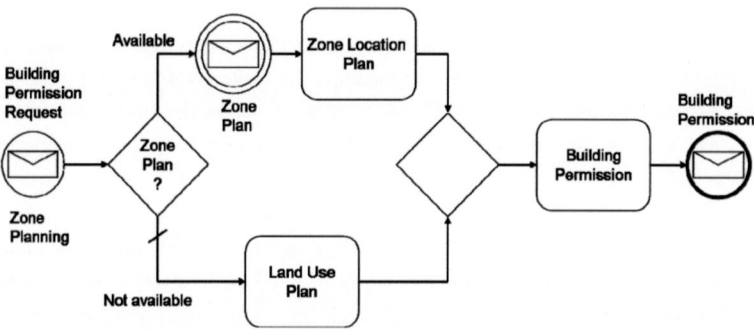

Figure 8.1.: Example BPMN Process from the Slovak Access-eGov Pilot (taken from internal developers' documentation)

```
1  <process name="BuildHouse" xmlns="http://docs.oasis-open.org/wsbpel/2.0/process/executable">
2  <sequence name="BuildHouseWorkflow">
3    <receive variable="processData" createInstance="yes"/>
4    <switch name="ZonePlanningAvailable">
5      <case condition="bpws:getVariableProperty(processData, ZonePlanAvailable)=true">
6        <sequence>
7          <receive name="ReceiveZonePlan" variable="processData"/>
8          <invoke name="ZoneLocationPlan" inputVariable="processData"
9            outputVariable="processData"/>
10        </sequence>
11      </case>
12      <otherwise>
13        <invoke name="LandUsePlan" inputVariable="processData" outputVariable="processData"/>
14      </otherwise>
15    </switch>
16    <invoke name="Buildingpermission"
17      inputVariable="processData" outputVariable="processData"/>
18    <reply variable="processData"/>
19  </sequence>
20 </process>
```

Listing 8.1: The process in Fig. 8.1 expressed in BPEL (taken from internal developers' documentation)

117

9. Semantic Web Service Frameworks

Following the goals outlined in Chapter 8, different frameworks for semantic web service environments have emerged. As is the case with all new research fields, the associated terminology is not yet stable. Different projects introduce new terms for a semantic web service environment almost daily. In this thesis, the term "semantic web service" (SWS) is used in order to denote systems that feature web services with semantic enhancements.

Most SWS frameworks have one thing in common: they are split into two basic building blocks; the ontology for modeling and persisting the knowledge (cf. Section 6.1) and a process model (cf. Section 8.2) to help with chaining and composition of web services. In the following survey of different SWS technologies, both parts will be described for each technology accordingly.

The three selected SWS frameworks, namely OWL-S, WSMO, and WSDL-S have not been randomly picked but were selected for different reasons:

- OWL-S
  OWL-S is based on OWL and therefore can rely on a widely used knowledge formalism.

- WSMO
  WSMO has a strong practitioner's following, especially from within European research communities.

- WSDL-S
  WSDL-S builds on the industry standard WSDL which is the most important description standard for non-semantic web services at the time of writing.

9.1. OWL-S

Building on the Web Ontology Language as introduced in Section 7.1.4, the OWL-S framework currently is described in a W3C member submission [MBH+04]. It is widely used in academia, probably because of its relation to OWL.

9.1.1. Ontology

OWL-S claims to be an upper ontology for services whose information needs are grouped into three distinct categories.

Firstly, the "What?" of the web service's qualities is described in a so-called *ServiceProfile*. Although not formally specified[1], three main elements of knowledge constitute an instance of a ServiceProfile:

- Provider information
  Information on the service provider is given in this part of the description. Highly nontechnical, information such as contact details or sales representatives is kept for administrative tasks.

- Functional description
  A formal description of the preconditions the service has, the input and output that the service requests and delivers, and the effect[2] the service execution has[3]. An often made mistake in this context is to equate the output to the effect. These two information bits do not necessarily have any relationship. Output is always tangible, while the caused effects might not be visible directly but may be as abstract as an altered legal status of an entity, for example.

- Service features
  In addition to two predefined and self-explanatory attributes named category and quality of service, OWL-S also allows the addition of arbitrary additional attributes.

A *ServiceModel* contains the actual semantic content. It describes in detail the expected semantics of the involved input and the possible outcomes of the service execution.

---

[1] There is a class "Service" in the OWL-S specifications which can be subclassed. However, this is not mandatory nor endorsed.

[2] Also sometimes called postcondition(s).

[3] The set of these values is often called Input, Output, Preconditions, and Effects (IOPE), especially in European semantic web efforts.

A *ServiceGrounding* contains the exact details on how a specific service can be connected. This technical data contains information on the protocol, address (URI), and port as well as mappings between the used semantic concepts and the service's input.

9.1.2. Process Model

OWL-S follows a process model that modifies the popular notion of a process as a sequence of events by also including the interactions within one service as a process. Thus, OWL-S has a dangerously different understanding of the widespread distinction between atomic processes and composite processes. Atomic processes here are a solitary entity which, in every invocation, is only called once and only returns one result.

OWL-S's composite processes, on the other hand, are not necessarily composed of atomic subprocesses or of subprocesses at all. They are rather called a number of times by the same caller while keeping internal state, effectively leading to a situation where each call advances the execution of the process by one step. To complicate matters even more, another chapter of the specification describes composite services as the well-known chain of either recursively or sequentially defined atomic or composite services.

The two main purposes of processes here are to firstly generate new information from existing (input-) information and outside/world knowledge and to leave visible traces in the discourse world when looking at postconditions and effects.

Grounding

OWL-S provides a formal specification of the relationship between WSDL and OWL-S content by introducing WSDL extensions. They are quite lightweight, only adding one property for semantically describing the data types and, optionally, serialization hints.

WsdlInput|OutputMessage and wsdlInput|Output specify mappings from semantic (ontological) data[4] to data "on the wire", meaning the data types encoded in WSDL.

---

[4]The more semantic context in the description, the less the notion of a data type in the convential terminolgy is justified, since semantic types are much more powerful, possibly encompassing types as complex as the object carrying the effects that a marriage has on the legal status of a person.

Formalism

Since OWL-S is formalised in OWL, the syntax as specified in [PSHH04] holds and was already briefly evaluated in Section 7.1.4.

9.1.2.1. Evaluation of OWL-S

Table 9.1 gives an indication of the usefulness of OWL-S as specified in its current form.

Strenghts	Weaknesses
• Complete specification of all SWS-related functionality • Strong community through good links to OWL • Widespread usage in OWL related projects	• No seperation between provider and consumer view • Open questions pertaining the process modeling • Parts of the terminology conflict with most other SWS-related efforts
• Taking part in the OWL community which is closer to semantic web efforts	• It is not clear yet whether OWL-S is enough to provide every facette of business process modeling support that is needed for SSOAs
Opportunities	**Threats**

Table 9.1.: SWOT Analysis of the OWL-S SWS Framework

9.2. WSMO

WSMO is a conceptual model for management of semantic web services [dBBD+05]. Unlike OWL-S with its obvious research background, WSMO has a practical grounding in a number of EU-funded research and development projects[5], which helped shape the design and appearance of WSMO towards a practical solution to the SWS problems.

9.2.1. Ontologies

As an universally integrated component within the WSMO framework, ontologies constitute the formal semantics on which the other components build upon. Concepts, their relations, functions and axioms, instances of the concepts with their corresponding relations, and non-functional properties are the core concepts that are actively used to describe certain facts of the discourse world. Used mediators and links to other ontologies can be seen as meta-data to each individual WSMO ontology.

Goals

Goals have already been introduced to denote the objectives a user of a system has in mind when accessing the system. WSMO's Goal element is inline with that definition as it conveys non-functional properties, used mediators and ontologies, and - most importantly - capabilities and interfaces. Capabilities in this context are the actual functional properties which a service has to fulfill, declared by IOPEs. Interfaces describe orchestration and choreography of represented services.

Web Services

Web services are described in exactly the same way as goals. In WSMO, web service description and goal are counterparts that are semantically matched against each other in order to automatically discover and compose processes from all the available web services.

Mediators

Mediators[6] are constructs that exist to help overcome semantic, conceptual or structural mismatches. WSMO in its current form knows four distinct types of mediators:

- OOMediator
  Mediates between two ontologies by resolving all representation mismatches.

---

[5]e.g. COIN, SemanticGov, SemBiz, SUPER, DIP, SEKT, ASG, to name but a few of the most prolific projects
[6]Mediators are explicitly mentioned in the specification as being one of the design goals of WSMO.

- GGMediator
  Connects goals by creating subTypeOf hierarchies.

- WGMediator
  Either links goals and web services through the goal's choreography or a web service to a goal via its orchestration.

- WWMediator
  Connects web services in order to setup cooperation. WWMediators concern the low-level, technical details of service choreography.

9.2.2. Process Model

The process model for WSMO is centered around orchestration (cf. Section 8.1.3). An Abstract State Machine (ASM) as the underlying formal model has the following defining features [RSF$^+$06]:

- State-basedness

- Representation of the state through an algebra

- Guarded transition rules to indicate state change

Using these components, the orchestration (and the related process model) can be described by adding a new non-functional property called *mode* to a WSMO ontology that declares which elements of the ontology have an associated state that can be changed, and by which entities. Transition rules can be formulated as arbitrary logical constructs.

WSMO differentiates itself from its competitors mainly through the priority it assigns to mediation, ultimately resulting in every orchestration process requiring the use of a mediator.

9.2.3. Grounding

WSMO has long suffered from incomplete grounding specifications but the situation has turned to the better lately. [KMRM07] shows different approaches of grounding data and choreographies.

Data grounding

WSMO-based systems keep all their information in the form of instances of concepts in ontologies as containers. Conventional web services cannot cope with this rich information, while even semantic-aware web services may have a knowledge formalism different from WSMO/WSML[7]. Thus, data has to be transformed to an interchange format and later transfered back into the realm of the ontology. These two complementary processes are called lowering and lifting, respectively. For WSMO objects, grounding rules to XML have already been described.

Choreography grounding

A very similar situation exists for choreographies. Conventional[8] web services will not be able to talk directly to semantically enabled clients and related web services. Again, lifting and lowering transformations come to the aid of the developers by mapping the ontology world to a data transfer syntax like XML and vice versa.

The latest approach in this field is the Semantic Annotations in WSDL and XML Schema (SAWSDL) effort described in [KVBF07]. It builds on the standard technologies WSDL and XML Schema, completed by XSLT for lifting and lowering.

9.2.4. Formalisation

WSMO is formalised in WSML, the Web Service Modeling Language [dB08], available in five different flavors that are either following their own text-based format or are XML-based:

- WSML-Core
  Based on the intersection of descriptive logic and Horn logic.

- WSML-DL
  Comparable to OWL-DL, drops the limitations of horn logic.

- WSML-FLIGHT
  Extends WSML-DL with rudimentary logic programming facilities and rules.

- WSML-Rule
  Adds full support for logic programming.

---

[7]ooMediators could be used but only if the mismatch is located at the ontology level, not on a formal level.
[8]Web services only speaking SOAP and described by WSDL.

- WSML-FULL
  Unification of the previous variants under "a common first order umbrella with non-monotonic extensions".

9.2.5. Evaluation

WSMO has a very active development community, not only boosted by the various EU-funded Framework Programmes in which the members of the WSMO consortium are involved in, but also due to the growing uptake in other, EU-unrelated projects. The clear and concise design undoubtedly contributes to its success.

While implementations of most of its components already exist, not all are suited for real-world applications, yet. The original implementation of the WSML languages called WSMO4J[9] was complete but very complex leading to all sorts of problems as described later in Section 15.1.1.2 when used in real-world settings. WSMO-Lite [VKVF08] and MicroWSMO [KVG08] both are successful approaches trying to improve the connection between industry developments and academia's semantic web service improvements by providing reasonably fast and straight-forward implementations of the WSMO object model.

Table 9.2 contains a SWOT analysis of the current WSMO environment.

---

[9]http://wsmo4j.sourceforge.net

Strengths	Weaknesses
• Complete specification of all SWS-related functionality • Clean design, loose coupling through extensive usage of mediation • Tight integration of Dublin Core constructs as metadata for all WSMO objects	• Parts of the specifications are unfinished or a moving target
• Ambitious and large development consortium • Large userbase in EU-funded projects • WSMO as central platform, other formalisms linked in via mediation	• Very complex process model. ASMs cannot easily be understood by SWS end users
Opportunities	Threats

Table 9.2.: SWOT Analysis of the WSMO SWS Framework

9.3. WSDL-S

9.3.1. Overview

In contrast to the WSMO framework which was designed from ground up, WSDL-S (Web Service semantics, [AFM+05]) as the name already implies builds on the well-known WSDL descriptions of web services by enriching them through the following constructs:

- modelReference
  Maps WSDL input and output elements to the semantic model in a 1:1 relation.

- schemaMapping
  Also aims at mapping WSDL inputs to outputs but based on a n:m approach, also allowing for the mapping of complex types or transformations.

- Precondition
  Comparable to IOPE preconditions.

- Effect
  Comparable to IOPE effects.

- Category
  Maps the web service to a category in a given taxonomy. Mainly used for discovery based on that categorization and is only of limited value for semantic matching.

9.3.2. Process Model

Not part of WSDL-S. The usual approach is to use OWL-S's process model.

9.3.3. Grounding

A distinction between data and orchestration grounding has to be considered. Data grounding in WSDL-S is possible via conventional XML translations (like eXtensible Stylesheet Language Transformations (XSLT)). Orchestration grounding exists via a mixture of IOPEs and Artificial Intelligence planning technologies [KRMF06].

9.3.4. Formalization

There is no standardized formalization in this context as WSDL-S is not geared towards a specific knowledge-representation methodology, but only provides links to external knowledge specifications.

9.3.5. Evaluation

Table 9.3 contains a SWOT analysis of the current WSDL-S environment.

Strengths	Weaknesses
• Most simple of the introduced appraoches • Only requires WSDL, no other dependencies exist • Also has a large following	• No provisions for orchestration and choreography within WSDL-S
• Independence of semantic formalisms makes WSDL-S very flexible	• Many questions remain open (choreography, composition) and are not going to be answered currently as they are deemed outside of scope by the WSDL-S community.
Opportunities	**Threats**

Table 9.3.: SWOT Analysis of the WSDL-S SWS Framework

9.4. Relevance to the GENSOA

All of the described SWS frameworks have their merits as well as shortcomings. While the GENSOA is not dependent on a specific SWS framework, it has been designed with Web Service Modeling Ontology (WSMO) in mind for the following reasons:

- It has a complete specification of all required functionality which was designed from scratch, thus eliminating the need for tweaks to allow for backwards compatibility.

- Its design is very clean. The important role that mediators play furthers the quality of the design as it opens up the possibility to cleanly link in any other formalism as long as mediators are implemented for it.

- The GENSOA evolved in the environment of EU-funded research and WSMO currently is the most successful SWS framework in these research communities.

Part III.

Reference Process for the Design and Implementation of Semantic SOAs

The topic of reference models and reference modeling is a research hot topic. Especially German business systems groups extensively research "Referenzmodellierung" (German for reference modeling) [VB03, FL06]. Groups outside of Germany do not follow this strict academic approach to reference modeling but rather prefer a pragmatic proceeding.

While usually little or no effort towards formalizing the perception they have of reference modeling is made by these groups, [MLM+06] arrive at one of the most coherent definitions by calling a reference model a framework that illustrates relationships between the constituting entities of a discourse world, in effect yielding a common vocabulary and common understanding of the world of discourse.

In line with [MLM+06], this thesis also sees the reference model as the most basic, most abstract form of description of a system. The first level of instantiation is the reference architecture, in more detail explained in Part I, which still is too abstract to be implemented. Thus, another level of instantiation is needed to arrive at a physical architecture which in turn can be built and deployed. Examples of this can be seen in Section 13.3 and Section 14.3, where actual deployments of SSOAs are described.

This part of the thesis is dedicated to describing a reference process for building a SSOA. The resulting system, called the GENSOA, is constructed along a typical software development lifecycle by first introducing a methodology to adapt requirements engineering approaches to SSOA realities, followed by the design of a system and a security architecture.

10. Requirements Engineering

Chapter 4.2 introduced the four basic phases of requirements engineering, namely elicitation, analysis, documentation, and verification. While the original sequence of phases remains unchanged, some of them have to be modified in order to make them better suited for the GENSOA approach.

The main questions to be answered in this case are whether to include KBTs at all and if yes, whether to include the semantic concepts in the requirements engineering phase already or later in the product development cycle. The following sections will explain the rationale for a decision on adopting KBTs or not and also consider the extent and the point of inclusion of those technologies.

10.1. Assessing the General Need for Knowledge Based Technologies

Introducing KBTs inflicts far-reaching consequences on decision maker(s) which usually are double edged. Complexity of any software system increases, as do costs.

An example: Coupling between data and data processing in the KBT case can be as low as in well designed software systems not relying on KBTs. Directly dependent on the coupling property is the maintainability of the examined part of the system. In decoupled systems maintainability of the platform is good. Maintainability of the knowledge, however, cannot be assessed generally. Depending on the used knowledge formalization system, even the initial knowledge elicitation techniques can overburden an uninitiated software development team, let alone their users. Many other possible problems can be anticipated but usually pertain organizational issues which cannot be handled in a software development process. Instead, this has to be taken care of by management.

Before any effort with regard to adopting KBTs is made, two questions have to be answered. The first of them is whether to include KBTs at all in the current project. Figure 10.1 presents a decision diagram assisting designers in their decision. The root branch of this diagram asks whether KBTs are a functional requirement defined

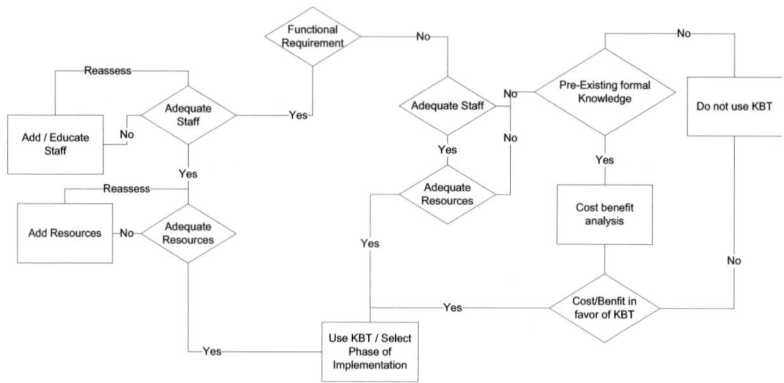

Figure 10.1.: Decision Tree for Selecting the Best Approach to Introducing Knowledge-Based Technologies

prior to starting the requirements process or not. If they are, no other possibility but to add them and educate the staff in their correct usage exists in any case.

If, however, the decision whether to use KBTs is initially open, the designer has a number of measures to judge in order to arrive at a conclusion. A first important question is whether the staff of the project is adequate both in size and in familiarity with KBTs. If the answer is positive, the same questions have to be asked for the resources booked on the project.

Once either staff or resources do not comply with the required skills and/or are not available at the required sizes, yet another criteria has to be used to support this decision. Availability[1] of formalised knowledge could influence the assessment in favour of KBTs: If the processes that make up the application system in design and the corresponding and required knowledge are already modeled in any knowledge formalism, a cost / benefit analysis has to be undertaken. In the likely event that the benefits indeed outmatch the costs, taking care of staff and resource issues as described above should pave the way for introducing semantic technologies. If the cost / benefit analysis decides otherwise or if no knowledge has been formalized in advance, introducing KBTs usually is not worth the effort.

In the remainder of this thesis, it is assumed that such an assessment has already been carried out and that the result was favoring SSOAs and therefore KBTs over any other approach.

---

[1]It is increasingly common to have knowledge management infrastructures (cf. Figure 6.2) in place.

10.2. Semantics in the Different Phases of Requirements Engineering

In this section, possible approaches for inclusion of KBTs in the requirements engineering process are discussed. Apparently, every phase of this process opens up a possibility, however KBT inclusion at a specific stage does not always proof effective in relation to the specific project and environmental surroundings.

10.2.1. General Considerations

Pinpointing a single ideal moment of inclusion of KBTs in a development cycle is impossible. Between the very beginning of the requirements engineering process and the beginning of the implementation phase, a lot of opportunities to include KBTs arise. Before describing them in greater detail, general properties of delayed or even sped up inclusion have to be analyzed. Deferred KBT usage incurs a number of disadvantages:

- User contact with semantics is delayed
  KBTs are complex. User groups that are brought in touch with them after requirements elicitation and analysis may feel alienated by technologies that are quite new to them. While this is of course true for every innovative technology, it is especially true in the KBT case as even experienced developers and researchers who had no previous contact with them have mixed feelings about the technology[2].

- Benefits of semantics cannot be used in initial phases
  As described later in this chapter, KBTs cannot only be used as additional markup to web services, but the underlying taxonomies and ontologies can already be used as shared vocabulary and conceptualization during development of the requirements. The later the usage of KBTs commences, the later these benefits can be realised.

- Semantics is moved to the backend
  Instead of having a prominent place in the architecture diagram, semantic additions are moved to backend services when not introduced until during

---

[2]The Access-eGov project brought this to light. Consulting partners of some of the user partners initially were very hostile against the whole SSOA concept and it took from months to years to convince them to at least half-heartedly support the cause. Lessons learned from Access-eGov are described in more detail in Chapter 15.

or after the specification process. Thus, the innovative aspects of KBTs are underrepresented.

Rarely any decision has only advantages or only disadvantages. This is especially true for decisions involving the application of innovative and novel technologies. In contrast to previously mentioned disadvantages, deferring implementation of KBTs can also have the following positive consequences:

- Straight-forward requirements
  Users are not alienated by new concepts and can utter their views just like they would in non-KBT based software development projects.

- Knowledge experts are not initially needed
  Full knowledge of semantic technologies is not needed in the design phase in this case, allowing to defer the employment of knowledge specialists as means to save costs.

- Validation of suitability of the SSOA concept
  If at the stage of finalizing the user requirements specification document still no real need for semantic additions arose and all required functionalities can be fulfilled without KBTs, the whole decision to use a SSOA should be reconsidered, possibly by an independent team.

10.2.2. Elicitation

Different models for requirements elicitation have already been mentioned in Section 4.2.2.1. All of them were of a rather generic nature, and not geared towards usage in a SSOA setting. In order to derive criteria for an elicitation method's aptitude towards SSOAs, the matter has to be further reflected on.

10.2.2.1. Definition

Section 4.2.2.1 assumed a rather colloquial definition of the term requirements elicitation but in a formal context, certain properties define requirements elicitation and its context. The following overview of the usage in common research highlights this observation. Requirements elicitation is

1. communicative
   Requirements elicitation is, with the exception of the introspection method [GL93], a very communicative approach. All methods are highly dependent

on communication between different groups. Thus, the better the information flows between stakeholders, the higher the degree of completeness of elicited requirements.

2. not formally defined

While certain formal languages for user requirements specification exist, they are always used at a later stage when the gathered requirements have been analyzed. Elicitation itself has no support in the form of formalisms and is natural language-based.

3. error prone

It follows from (2) that the process of elicitation is highly subjective and therefore its quality is intertwined with the person carrying out the task. Margin for errors is ensured.

4. not objectively evaluable

Again it follows from (2) that no means to objectively evaluate the elicited requirements exist.

5. targeted

Elicitation is always extremely targeted at the one specific purpose of the software system currently being designed. No generic or even partially generalizable subject of elicitation exist.

Combining above mentioned properties, a - still colloquial - definition of the term requirements elicitation is the following:

Requirements elicitation allocates methods for:

- (REL1) extracting

- (REL2) all possible requirements

- (REL3) connected to a specific software system.

10.2.2.2. Elicitation Methods and Knowledge-Based Technologies

Of all the methods introduced in Section 4.2.2.1, not all are (positively or negatively) affected by the addition of KBTs:

- Introspection
  This method does not really fit well within the others since it is solely carried

out by a requirements engineer. Accordingly, the impact semantic technologies have on it is at the requirements engineers' discretion. Like most of the methods, introspection can benefit from a controlled vocabulary and therefore from ontology usage.

- Structured interview
  The situation is similar with structured interviews. Using a controlled vocabulary, the engineer is able to prepare the interview results in a manner optimally suited for further elaboration in a team. One possible approach is to first derive an initial taxonomy or ontology from introspection and wrap the structured interviews around that ontology / taxonomy.

- Unstructured interview
  Unstructured interviews have a different focus as they are exploratory when compared to their structured counterparts. A too strict corset of terms can quickly become a problem as personnel not familiar with an initial selection of terms might be unable to voice their views using an unfamiliar terminology.

- Scenario
  Scenarios can benefit from KBTs because the interactions can be labeled with terms in the common vocabulary. Unlike unstructured interviews, there is no danger of being too tangled up in the controlled vocabulary since the exact aim is to extract interactions between the system and its users.

- Round table
  Round tables do not benefit from semantic technologies other than the controlled vocabulary. The requirements engineer is the main actor in a round table and the actual focus of this method is a discussion.

  Note however, that the case of creating ontologies can very well benefit from round tables [KUW06].

- Workshop
  With no clear distinction between workshops and round tables, the situation is fairly similar. Albeit workshops usually are focused on a certain topic, they also are moderated and can only benefit from the controlled vocabulary. Again, the ontology creation can benefit from a round of workshops because users are brought together with knowledge engineers to further the discussion about conceptualisation of the application's world of discourse.

- Focus group
  Yet another variant of round tables and workshops with the main focus being put on users, the above mentioned assessment of round tables and workshops holds true for focus groups as well.

- Rapid Application Development (RAD)
  In the case of RAD, two possible situations have to be discerned. One situation involves applications which are already planned to have a large degree of KBT integration. RAD is very well suited to support the situation by giving users the chance of having a first glance on the modes of usage of knowledge. RAD-based prototypes may very well be the first ever points of contacts with semantic technologies for users and can therefore influence the uptake of the technologies within the respective user group.

  If KBT usage is restricted to the backend of the system, it is highly likely that the users will not even notice the presence of a semantical framework, making the additional provision of RAD-prototypes not worth the effort if solely used for demonstrating KBT functionality.

- Protocol analysis
  Due to the small number of participants, this method usually progresses quickly and has a postprocessing stage in which only the requirements engineering team is involved. Thus, this method is ideally suited to define parts of the controlled vocabulary.

- Laddering
  Having a strong knowledge engineering background where it is used to elicit users' goals and associated concepts [WSSR06], laddering is usually a very successful approach for ontology generation.

- Card sorting
  Card sorting is also extensively used in knowledge engineering, making it the second well-fitted candidate for initial generation of ontologies.

10.2.3. Analysis

The next possible opportunity for including KBTs is the analysis phase, which was explained in detail in Section 4.2.2.2. One part of the analysis, the classification of the requirements, is a very good application for semantic technologies. A taxonomy or even an ontology can initially be used as a controlled vocabulary which in turn yields comprehensible and, above all, repeatable classification schemes for user requirements.

Two possible constellations for the usage of KBTs in this classification exist. One is employing a specific requirements engineering ontology. Terms like priority or scope of the requirements or more complex concepts like the distinction between functional and non-functional requirements can be modeled in this ontology and later reused. A probable setting involves a company with expertise in integration and software engineering in general. They might have an in-house software-engineering ontology at their disposal which should contain requirements engineering terms as well. The leading peculiarity of this approach is that the remaining phases (including remaining tasks in requirements engineering itself) do not necessarily benefit from including KBTs. After all, the used ontology is not connected to the system about to be designed but instead generic. No processes and concepts, in short no knowledge about the modeled system is ever included in the knowledge representation.

Another approach is using taxonomies and / or ontologies specifically geared towards the system being designed. If they are already developed at this stage, the clear formal picture of the discourse world encoded in them can be of immense help, not in classifying the requirements but in mutually validating requirements and semantic model. If, for example, certain concepts surfacing in the requirements engineering discussions are not expressible in the current vocabulary, those concepts usually are either superfluous or denote an incomplete ontology.

When a semantic model is already finished at this stage, it has another advantage: shared vocabulary eases communication among project team members.

Modeling in a semantically-enabled context can, in any case, be harder than using traditional elicitation approaches. Mostly however, this happens in cases where KBTs are openly visible to the respective user group. A prime example thereof is building large service databases, like in e-Government or B2B settings. Here, interactions and processes within the modeling task can grow quite complex and leave users and domain experts in dire need of KBTs.

If this is not the case, however, no difference between traditional conceptual modeling and the version of it used in a semantically-enabled setting can be distinguished.

10.2.4. Specification

In IEEE terms, the definition and specification of user requirements are two distinct tasks. A Software Requirements Specification (SRS) as introduced earlier is a specification and as such sufficiently technical to hold the complex semantic specification.

As far as the non-technical requirements definition is concerned, it is a matter of the requirements engineers' consideration if and to what extent semantic concepts are introduced therein.

If the semantic model is already available, the best approach is to publish it in a separate document and reference it from a SRS. This way, the SRS can make use of the set of concepts defined in the semantic model, making it more readable even for persons external to the project teams. The only prerequisite is that the semantic model has an appropriate quality and is sufficiently complete.

10.2.5. Quality Assessment and Validation

In this phase, KBTs cause a considerable amount of additional effort because they need to be evaluated separately. If semantic technologies were introduced after the elicitation phase, the previously mentioned validation can now take place by cross-checking whether all concepts in the SRS are represented in the semantic model and all semantic concepts are contained in the SRS. Mismatches do have to be resolved before the design phase can be commenced.

10.3. Different opportunities for Knowledge-Based Technologies inclusion

After inspecting how the different phases of requirements engineering can profit from inclusion of KBTs, this section will advocate two distinct scenarios:

Scenario	Assessment
Analysis	The only benefit in this scenario is, that KBTs give a clear formal picture[3] that can aid in cross checking the requirements during the classification process. This alone does not warrant the additional complexity of KBTs, however, as other methodologies exist that also support this goal.

---

[3]The additionaly mentioned usage of software engineering ontologies is interesting and probably very effective but out of the scope of a document on SSOAs as this technology can be considered for all kinds of software development efforts.

Specification	Whether a semantic model in any form exists or not has no influence on the SRS which could still be of low quality and unreadable even if backed by a perfect semantic model. A bad semantic model on the other hand does not necessarily entail an equaliy bad SRS. Another drawback of introducing the semantic model in this process is, that it cannot be of any help regarding the cross checking of requirements and concepts because the danger exists, that it follows the already elicited concepts much too closely.
Quality & Validation	The emerging semantic model is probably only a replica of the already elicited requirements and again does not warrant the additional effort.

Table 10.1.: Rejected KBT Inclusion Scenarios

Table 10.1, by eliminating unsuitable KBT inclusion approaches, lead to these two scenarios. A finding that is backed by Guarino, who comes to an equal conclusion by dividing the scenarios into the groups "ontologies at design time" (later called process 0 in this thesis) and "ontologies at runtime" (Backend only in this thesis' terminology) [Gua98]. His approach is, however, quite limited. Usage of software-engineering ontologies as proposed above is completely omitted as is the possibility of making the development of the ontologies part of the overall software development process.

10.3.1. As process 0

Prior to any other tasks, in this scenario the first undertaking is the creation of the semantic model. While earlier research assumed[4] ontologies coming from external sources, the research focus shifted towards designing individual ontologies for every project. Lee et al. describes an approach that was modified in this work because it seemed to be too complex: not only semantic concepts were included, but also new modeling notations and specific tools [LG05].

While the reasons behind this approach are clear, it can be suspected that the uptake of such totally new concepts is limited in practitioners' groups. Semantic

---

[4]The community was waiting for the advent of all-embracing "world" ontology [YM98].

concepts and KBTs currently are novel enough on their own. Forcing even more newly introduced concepts into the design process inescapably will result in a refusal to use them.

Therefore the approach in this thesis fosters professional uptake by partially making the semantic modeling process independent from the usual design process, allowing maximum flexibility in projects. One knowledge engineer is enough to start the semantic tasks by conducting initial interviews with stakeholders and formalizing the results into any knowledge formalism[5]. A resulting output of this formalization in turn has to be used and continuously updated by all project members.

10.3.2. Backend only

If not as process 0, the only other step in the process that is adequate for including KBTs is the implementation phase of the backend. In this scenario, the approach is totally different. Users are not burdened with KBTs at all, only the development team sees the modeled knowledge. While this approach might not make sense at first glance, a number of reasons speak for it.

- Close proximity to SOAs

  A project in question is highly distributed or modularized, and introducing the SOA paradigm as underlying design pattern is deemed inevitable. Then the next logical step, introducing semantic technologies (cf. introductory considerations in Chapter 1), should also be taken. An immediate benefit is an easy and well thought-out model for combining the contained scenarios which, unlike traditional SOAs, is an automated task.

- Gaining experience with KBTs

  A semantic backend can be a first step on a path towards a complete SSOA with limited risks. If only the backend uses these technologies, the whole development team can steer the degree of involvement of semantic technologies and thus reducing the chance of failure of the architecture.

- Future investment

  Investing in semantification of the backend also provides a future-proof system: Once more and more (electronic) webservices are available[6], not only

---

[5]It is not necessary but advisable to already decide on a knowledge formalism this early. If formalization is done in one of the better-known formalisms like OWL or WSML, however, mappings to other formalisms exist.

[6]SOA enthusiasts predicted that to happen since the SOA hype started in 2004. In 2009, the web service landscape still looks meek, however.

specialized research projects but the overall IT sector will want to harvest the benefits as explained in Chapter 1. The resulting architecture is well prepared for that case.

10.4. Requirements / Ontology Feedback - a Hybrid Approach

After having surveyed the role of semantics in all the different phases of the requirements process, three types of KBT usage have emerged according to their application area: Semantic technologies can either be used to support the requirements processes or the system in question or both. For reasons explained in the following paragraphs the latter possibility is to be prefered in almost all cases.

10.4.1. Modes of Operation

If KBTs are used to accompany the requirements engineering process itself, their main usage pattern is that of a controlled vocabulary. Nuseibeh et al. have an interesting line of thought by viewing an ontology as a set of objective truths about a problem domain [NE00]. Ontologies in this context are in contrast to epistemology and phenomenology. The underlying phenomena that are observable in the world are viewed quite differently by different peer groups which is a problem in many sorts of collaboration efforts, requirements engineering being no exception. Additionally, every peer group claims to have the only answers and explanations to each of those phenomena.

Ontologies in this case can act as a connector or mediator between different peer groups, if – and only if – the peer groups agree to adhere to the ontologies.

Extending the usage of semantic technologies to the whole system means directly describing the SSOA as is done throughout this thesis.

The biggest potential is realized by a hybrid approach. Requirements should be formalized in an ontology-guided way and a well-described feedback cycle should be used to validate both, the requirements against the ontology and the ontology against the requirements. This way, a common vocabulary can be used throughout most of the project lifetime, starting quite early in the requirements phase and carrying on into the operations phase of the system. In addition, crosschecking opportunities between involved peer groups guarantee added benefit for projects following this approach.

Ontologies seldomly are available in companies or generally in the stakeholders' sphere of influence today. Hopefully, this is a transitional phenomena because as the Semantic Web idea catches on, ontologies once will be as widespread as today's "intranets"[7].

A reference process for ontology engineering from scratch is divided into the phases specification, conceptualization, formalization, implementation, and maintenance [PM04]. Accompanying activities include the knowledge acquisition, evaluation, and documentation of the generated ontology.

Of the many different approaches to ontology building (for example [FGPJ97], [HJ02], [Gan05]), the Methontology approach stands out for its close connection to the software development process. Pinto et al. defined an evolutional process model for building ontologies which also fits the Methontology approach. It is described in the following paragraphs [PM04]:

- Requirements specification
  Parameters concerning the intended users and usage of the future ontology are collected as well as its properties like the degree of formality of the ontology, or the degree of completeness.

- Knowledge acquisition
  Using an ever-growing knowledge-acquisition methods body [OR87] [HH99], the existing relevant knowledge is captured.

- Conceptualization of domain knowledge
  The collected knowledge is processed in order to derive concepts and instances and their properties and relations. UML, while not being ideally suited for semantic modeling, is proposed by some researchers, as modeling choice for this phase since the conceptualization of knowledge is not too different from an information model [BCC06]. Additionally, the developers will have good command of UML and therefore will be able to use (and comment on) the semantic model without learning new technologies.

- Formalization of domain knowledge
  In this step, the first formal representation of the knowledge is built. It is not yet tied to a specific language but aims at higher-level concepts like a hierarchy generated by relations like 'is-a' or 'subclassOf' and axioms.

---

[7]Intranets with their manifold uses have not been easy to place in organizations. After a slow start they picked up steam, however, and eventually became quite common in organizations of all sizes despite their complexity.

- Implementation of the formal model
  After picking a knowledge representation language, the model developed in the previous step is encoded into the language.

- Maintenance
  Periodically checking and updating the ontology is an auxiliary task that is not directly executed on its own.

Alongside these steps, the following global steps are additionally carried out:

- Documentation
  In accordance to one of the most important demands that are made towards well-managed software projects, a thorough documentation of the ontology is inevitable.

- Evaluation
  For the ontology to really succeed, it is not only necessary to check the ontology for correctness and update it accordingly but also to carry out thorough evaluation of the results.

10.4.2. The Hybrid Process

Comparing the process of requirements engineering in Figure 10.2 with the Methontology in Figure 10.3 shows similarities that are ideal starting points for merging both process models into a semantically enhanced, hybrid requirements engineering model specifically tailored to SSOAs. In fact, both Figures depict the same basic steps on a slightly different aggregation level. Almost two decades ago, Byrd et al. already once described this close connection but failed to generate adequate follow-up research [BCZ92].

The resulting combination is shown in Figure 10.4 while being explained in more detail in the following paragraphs.

Elicitation

Elicitation methods for requirements (cf. Section 4.2.2.1) and acquisition methods for knowledge (cf. [BCZ92]) use very similar methodologies and can usually be used interchangeably. Combining both activities in this phase has the potential to generate synergies as both tasks are very communicative, with lots of involvement of all user groups.

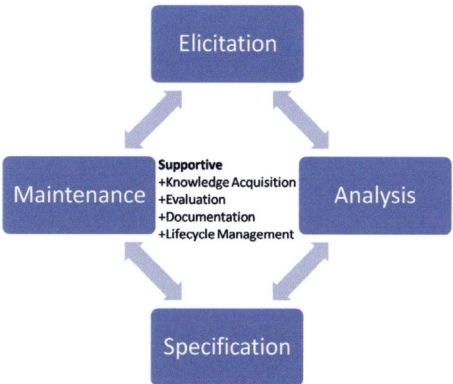

Figure 10.2.: Requirements Engineering Process Model

To facilitate this alliance, at least one of the task leaders of requirements and knowledge engineering has to be trained in the respective other discipline.

Feedback between analysis and conceptualisation in Figure 10.4 can already be initialiased during the elicitation phase when the roles of requirements and knowledge engineers are filled by two different persons.

Design

Requirements Engineering is only divided into two processes (cf. Section 4.2). The analysis phase in such cases implicitly contains documentation and specification of the results. In terms of this hybrid process model, however, a more fine-grained distinction is made by splitting the conventional analysis task into analysis, specification, and documentation subtasks.

Analysis and specification are summarized as design, linking them to the KBT counterparts of conceptualization and formalization. Feedback between KBT and requirements engineering has to commence in this phase at the very latest.

10.4.2.1. Documentation / Implementation

Documenting requirements engineering and knowledge acquisition results is a combined task in this process. Requirements have to use the terminology built into the semantic model that results from the formalization of the acquired knowledge. Requirements additionally have to contain selected provisions for working with knowl-

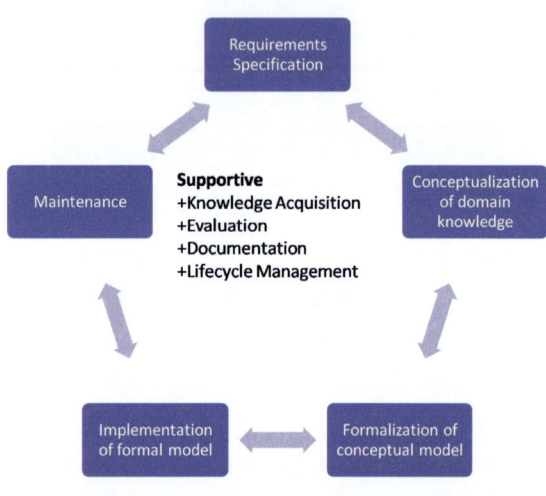

Figure 10.3.: Methontology Process Model

edge, for example quality attributes that describe the actuality of the used knowledge.

Implementation extends documentation by codifying the involved knowledge in a formalism.

10.4.2.2. Evaluation

Evaluation of both activities has to be thorough and ongoing which is represented by the feedback loop. Requirements and the semantic model should not be evaluated independently, but rather through evaluation strategies that take into account both, the specific project settings and the tight integration of semantic model and requirements.

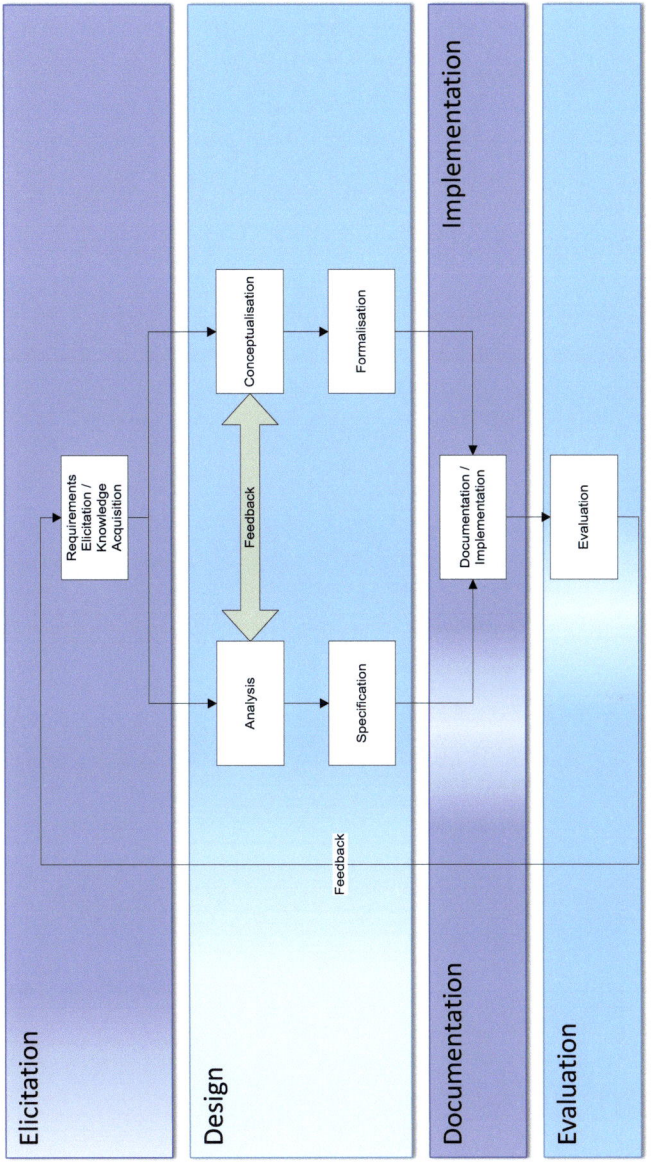

Figure 10.4.: Hybrid Requirements/Ontology Engineering Process

11. Architecture

The design of the GENSOA is no exception to the rule that designing a reference architecture is similar to designing a system architecture (cf. Part I, Section 2.2). Some small deviations of this rule are introduced where appropriate.

Of course, the aim of a reference architecture is not a fully functional prototype, let alone a finished product. Quite to the contrary, a reference architecture process usually finishes after a specification has been created and validated. There is, however, the possibility to fork reference implementations of key concepts of the architecture. It happens quite frequently[1] and generally has a very positive effect on community uptake of the architecture in question.

For the architecture introduced in this chapter no reference implementation of any of its components were part of this work. A number of reference implementations for the constituting parts are named as appropriate.

Specification and documentation of the architecture is done in the format proposed by IEEE-1471 (cf. Section 4.4.2).

11.1. Preliminary Considerations

IEEE-1471 does not state anything about its relation to reference architecture contexts. It is easy to adapt to this situation by selecting a proper set of views, however. The following considerations have to be taken into account:

- Implementation-related views
  While some aspects of the implementation have to be factored into the reference architecture, the most important views are situated on a higher level than implementation related views like the development and deployment views are.

- Strategic views
  Deciding on an underlying (reference) architecture is foremost a matter of inspecting available alternatives and appraising their different technical and

---

[1]Notable examples are the WSMO4J (http://wsmo4j.sourceforge.net) API or the JAXB reference implementation (http://jaxb.dev.java.net), both of which originate in reference architectures.

economical outcomes. A solid judgment of these outcomes is available based on views that look at architectures from a strategic viewpoint. Such decisions are highly dependent on the current environment and have to be left outside a reference architecture.

- KBTs
  KBTs need to be adequately represented within the specification, even if no standard KBT view has emerged so far.

- Perspectives
  Common quality criteria like security or performance could be represented in views. Common current practice is to describe them in individual perspectives [RW06] instead.

Based on Rozinski et al. [RW06] and the previous considerations, the originally proposed six viewpoints are used to construct the corresponding views. All in all, six views have been picked:

- Functional view
  A detailed description of all components and their respective functionalities is contained in this view in order to allow the reader to assess the structure, interconnections, and overall functionality of the system.

- Information view
  Of particular importance in the GENSOA is the information view explaining how KBTs are included in the GENSOA.

- Concurrency view
  This view contains details on concurrency aspects of the architecture.

- Operational view
  Envisioned modes of operation of the architecture are described within the operational view.

- Deployment view
  Different modes of employment of the whole resulting system are described in this view.

- Development view
  Generic hints on implementation and development issues are contained in the deployment view.

The IEEE adds so called extended enterprise architecture viewpoints grouped in economic, legal, ethical, and discretionary views [Sch04]. Based on this work, the following, rather strategic, views are added as was postulated above:

- Benefits vs. costs
  Increasing the complexity of software systems is by no means a desired effect. It has to be tolerated, at best. This view relates the benefits of the GENSOA to a very rough cost estimation.

- Innovation
  Risks and chances of using the highly innovative KBTs are compared in this view.

Cross-cutting concerns are represented as perspectives. The main properties in this category are [Sch04]:

- Security

- Performance, in this thesis extended with scalability concerns

- Availability and resilience

- Internationalization

- Knowledge usage and semantics

After identifying a set of generic user requirements the most important steps of the IEEE 1471 architecture framework description of the GENSOA are presented in the following chapters, using the skeleton laid out here. Sections left out include obvious metadata like revisions, ToC or references. An ubiquitous section on methodology has also been left out after the methodology has been explained in full detail in previous chapters.

11.2. Requirements

In this reference architecture stakeholders are described as abstract user classes while requirements are derived from real-world cases, from information on comparable systems, and from generally accepted design requirements.

Requirements are described in a format closely related to that proposed by Balzert in [Bal09]. A requirement is defined by a unique ID of the form `<Designator>/<Number>/`

where <Designator> conveys the group this requirement belongs to[2] and <Number> is a counter. Thus, L/0010/ is the requirement in the quality group that has the internal counter of 10.

Tables containing those requirements have three columns containing ID, description of the requirement, and its origin.

11.2.1. Theoretical Requirements

Quality criteria for system architectures were already introduced in Chapter 3. Sources of criteria used there can also be used to define the set of generic design requirements that can be found in Table 11.1.

While a large number of other quality criteria exists, many of them do not make sense in a reference architecture setting and thus are omitted. No functional or data requirements are contained because there are no universally accepted generic requirements in these fields.

In this thesis, two internal sources of requirements exist: Access-eGov and SPIKE, both of which are introduced in Part IV and are an ideal source of functional requirements as well as a basis on which a data model can be established. While still possible to distill higher-level functional and data requirements from all of these sources, a scientific value in such an exercise is not identifiable.

---

[2]F for functional requirements, L for quality requirements and D for informational requirements

Quality requirements		
ID	Origin	Description
L/0060/ Communication Security	General software practice	Every communication channel in the platform has to be secured against injection of modified data or eavesdropping.
L/0070/ Privacy	General software practice	The platform has to support privacy throughout its components. The principle of data sparsity has to be obeyed.
L/0080/ Access Control	General software practice	Concise mechanisms have to be designed that act as reference monitor or, in XACML terms, a policy enforcement point.
Non-functional requirements		
ID	Origin	Description
NF/0010/ Maintainability	[ISO01]	The source code of the resulting product has to be easily maintainable.
NF/0020/ Portability	[ISO01]	The degree to which the SSOA is dependent on a specific environment has to be minimized.

Table 11.1.: Generic Design Requirements of the GENSOA

11.2.2. Real-world requirements

Section 10.4 explained a model for requirements engineering that built on semantic technologies, and more specifically on the interactions between conventional requirements engineering and usage of KBTs. As the goal of this thesis is a reference model, this hybrid approach is not useable since a generic architecture does not have any real world users.

Thus, elicitation is reduced to sighting requirements documents of other systems and extract the most important requirements, ultimately summarizing them in a single user requirements table.

The first finding in a survey of requirements documentations was that commercial projects almost never do publish detailed user requirements. Sometimes a one-paragraph summary of the requirements is published in a press release[3] but even this is an exception. Possible reasons for this may include:

- Detailed user requirements allow insights in the future usage of the new software products. If it is very innovative, publishing these details could lessen the competitive edge the user or developing partner has.

- User requirements convey knowledge about processes at the users' premises.

- User requirements, enhanced by semantic information, contain even more data which, used through any kind of inference mechanisms, could leak classified business-related information.

- Once a project is deployed, user requirements are used to evaluate the performance of the system with regard to those requirements. While this is very good for the project partners, competitors suddenly are also brought in the position to evaluate the competitions' success in implementing the new software system.

Other than expected, not even public projects always share their user requirements.

One additional source of requirements, however, are public research projects. EU Framework Programme projects[4] usually have a very promiscuous policy to publish their research findings which includes requirements documentation as well.

---

[3]Often a so-called "'joint press conference"' with user and vendor participating.
[4]The European Union funds research in a multitude of ways. At the time of writing, the umbrella for all these research fundings is called the seventh Framework Programme (http://cordis.europa.eu/fp7/).

Careful examination of GENSOA related projects[5] yielded no additional requirements, however.

Thus, Table 11.2 only lists the requirements that were gathered as part of the SPIKE and Access-eGov projects ([KUW06], [AFG⁺08]).

---

[5]Among the projects examined where SEKT, DIP, S-TEN, SUPER, LUISA, and KNOWL-EDGEWEB. All of them can be conveniently access through the EU website at `http://cordis.europa.eu/ist/`.

Functional requirements

ID	Origin[6]	Description
F/0010/ AAI	A1.4.1, SF-Req.-16, SF-Req.-17	Support for AAIs is especially important in systems with a heterogeneous user base. Identity Management (IdM, F0130) is not always needed but a SSOA should be able to support standards-compliant AAIs and accordingly their issued tokens. The platform itself has to have the concept of a user session of which the state is kept only inside the platform.
F/0020/ Search	A1.5.1, A1.5.2, SF-Req.-6	Support for means of searching other than semantic matching, textual search over a fulltext index for example, has to be implemented because otherwise unstructured data is lost in the content repositories of the platform. The platform cannot guarantee any retrieval results as such a "non-semantic" search suffers from the very same problems that information retrieval suffers since its inception.
F/0030/ User Support	A3.5.1, A3.5.2, A1.8	The platform has to provide enough means to support users in all of the typical usage scenarios by means of a help system.
F/0040/ Information Quality	A1.9.1, A1.9.2, SF-Req.-4, SF-Req.-5, SF-Req.-20	While users of the instantiated architecture are usually responsible for the quality of their data, the platform has to supply means to manage them. Versioning of the data or at least timestamping can be a part of a solution. Reality shows, however, that most problems with information quality are not solvable by software systems but need organizational backing.

---

[6]In order to be consistent, the original requirement IDs have been preserved.

F/0050/ Semantic Matching	A2.3.1, A2.4.1, SF-Req.-17	The users' goals, as expressed through semantic statements, are contrasted with the annotations carrying the capabilities of an individual service offering (cf. Section 8.1.1).
F/0060/ Composition	A2.6.1, A2.4.1, A3.2.1	Processes in a SSOA are not executable on their own but rather acts as guidance for a sequence of services that need to be invoked to fulfill the (higher-level) user goal. Services fitting in the current slot of the workflow are discovered and chained in the correct order. (cf. Section 8.1.2)
F/0070/ Orchestration	A2.4.1, A2.6.1, A3.2.1	Composed or atomic services need to be executed. The multitude of available standards and service types complicates their execution while grounding annotations have to be introduced to hint the platform at details of the execution (cf. Section 8.1.2)
F/0080/ Process Management	A2.6.1, A2.4.1, A2.2, SF-Req.-1	Process management takes up many forms in a SSOA. It is responsible for providing the processes and keeping them up-to-date and in sync on different parts of the platform.
F/0090/ Security	A2.7.1, A2.7.2, SF-Req.-10, SF-Req.-18	cf. Chapter 5.
F/0100/ Ontology Management	A3.1.1, A3.1.2	Like information, the underlying ontologies also have to be managed.

ID	Origin	Description
F/0110/ Semantic Markup	A3.2.1	Means of semantically annotating the offered services have to be provided. Whether this functionality is provided by the platform or external tools is a decision of the individual architect instantiating at the GENSOA. Nonetheless, the architecture has to support this functionality.
F/0120/ Wrapper Technologies	A3.3.1, SF-Req.-32, SF-Req.-33	Traditional services need wrapper technologies in order to communicate with a semantic infrastructure especially considering the currently very low number of available natively electronic services.
F/0130/ Identity Management	SF-Req.-21, SF-Req.-22, SF-Req.-23, SF-Req.-29	Finding ways of integrating large user bases hosted on different systems is especially important in B2B collaborations where provisioning of user accounts is a major annoyance for both the managers and the users.
F/0140/ Inclusion of external sources	SF-Req.-7	"Information management" in enterprises as provided by CMS or DMS technologies.

Informational requirements

ID	Origin	Description
D/0010/ Service information	Access-eGov and SPIKE informational view	All functional and non-functional properties of a specific web service.
D/0020/ User Goals	Access-eGov and SPIKE informational view	Everything needed to represent the goal of a user.

ID	Origin	Description
D/0030/ Processes	Access-eGov and SPIKE informational view	Means to store process definitions. Statically and dynamically combined processes need to coexist.

Quality Requirements

ID	Origin	Description
L/0010/ Security	Both projects	All data in the system has to be kept confidentially. Data leaks must not occur. Access control policies must be obeyed.
L/0020/ Performance	SNF-Req.-1	Reasonable execution times on all supported functionalities have to be guaranteed.
L/0030/ Reliability	SNF-Req.-2	Reliability provisions in the systems have to comply to common best practices.
L/0040/ Extensibility	SNF-Req.-5	Extensibility of the architecture has to be a system property, no add-on.
L/0050/ Usability	SNF-Req.-10	Neither an architecture nor its implementations are directly used. Therefore the property usability does not make sense in this context. The infrastructure nonetheless has to provide all necessary means to support usability in all attached user interfaces. This especially means support for latest usability enhancing technologies.

Table 11.2.: Real World Requirements of the SSOA.

11.3. The Generic Semantic Service-Oriented Architecture at a Glance

The aim of this reference architecture is to design a generic software system extending the existing SOA patterns. Considerable deficiencies of traditional SOAs, especially in the areas of service discovery and composition (cf. Section 8.1.2), leave no other option than to improve the description of the offered web services as well as the representation of the current task[7] by addition of semantic technologies.

11.3.1. Scope of the System

In accordance with the generic user requirements devised in Section 11.2, the following textual use cases present a concise overview of this architecture's envisioned functionalities.

- Storing web service-related functional and non-functional properties efficiently and securely.

- Expressing a stakeholder's intention (user goal, cf. Section 4.2.2) as a task which can be further divided into sub-tasks and, finally on the lowest level, atomic tasks.

- Semantically matching user goals with web service properties.

- Inclusion of advanced security features offering Single-Sign-On (SSO) and different backends for attribute storage.

- Wrapping non-semantic web services and legacy (not web service-enabled) software artifacts.

- Possible inclusion of human (offline) services into the system.

Additionally, the following system properties have to be observed:

- Optional message routing capabilities.

- Usage of open standards wherever possible.

- Provisions for reliability enhancements.

---

[7]The current task can be a generalized objective of a user or a - possibly atomic - subprocess of such a user objective.

11.3.2. System Context

Clements et al. suggest using UML use-case diagrams as a high level context diagram in order to facilitate a conceptual view on the system [CGB+02]. Figure 11.1 uses an use-case diagram to identify the main actors as explained in the following paragraphs.

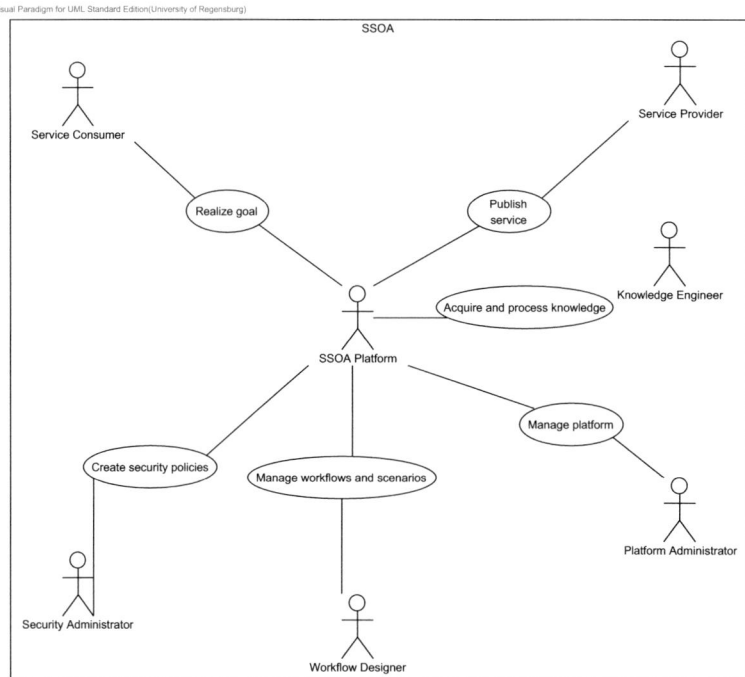

Figure 11.1.: Context Diagram of the Proposed SSOA Platform

One group of them are *Service Consumers*, denoting entities having a specific goal they want to accomplish by using services in the SSOA. Depending on the level of abstraction this group is looked at, it might either be a human platform user[8] or an agent contemplating execution of lower level services.

Service Providers are the counterpart, offering services that fulfill the consumers' goals. In order to make those services discoverable, annotations of the services' ca-

---

[8]This kind of user is usually wanting or needing to execute a chain of services, not one specific or atomic service. Services for human users can also include offline services like attending a certain government office.

pabilities and Non-Functional Properties (NFP)s as introduced in Section 8.1.1 have to be added by the provider. Using graphical utilities improves general usability.

In order to annotate services semantically, at first some sort of common vocabulary has to be created by eliciting and sorting all the available knowledge. A *knowledge engineer* is tasked with this assignment.

Three distinct groups of administrators also have to exist. Firstly, a *Platform Administrator* responsible for configuration, tuning and monitoring of the platform. This role does not neccessarily have any permissions to work with the data contained in the platform no matter if read-only or read-write access. Later in this document (cf. Section 14.2), applications will be shown where exactly this behavior is desirable and implemented. *Security administrators*, on the other hand, do have permissions to create and modify contained data as the security policies they generate are highly dependent on the individual services. Very important from a business roles point of view is the *Workflow Designer*. Heacquires all information on the expected processes and models them into an artefact that can either be imported into the SSOA or directly used by it.

11.4. Architectural Views

After having identified requirements of the system and its stakeholders, the previously announced architectural views are the next elements of this IEEE-1471 specification instance.

11.4.1. Functional View

Firstly, the system's decomposition into modules and their corresponding functionalities will be shown in this section.

11.4.1.1. Components

Components making up the GENSOA can be divided into four internal assemblies and the GENSOA client landscape, all of which are going to be explained in the following and are depicted in Figure 11.2.

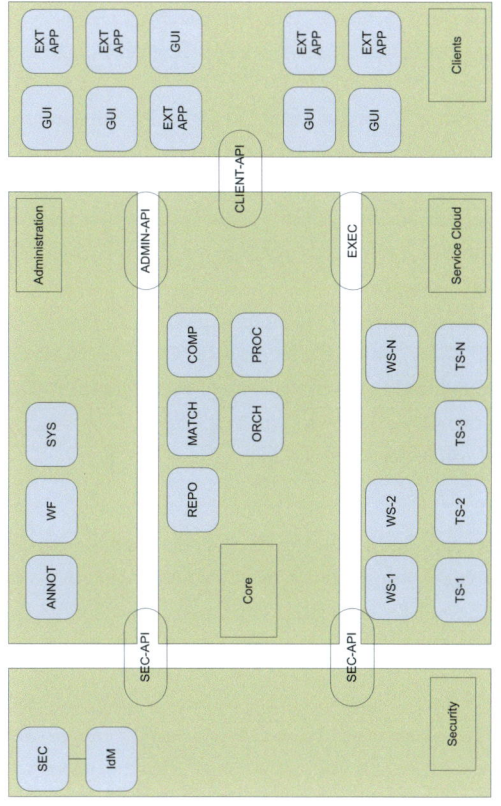

Figure 11.2.: Overview of the SSOA Architecture

Core

At the heart of the GENSOA core modules for low level functionality reside. While they are allowed to communicate among each other, the components themselves are not exposed to the outside world themselves but instead through distinct interfaces.

A *REPO* (Repository) component is responsible for effective storage of all system relevant information (D/0010/, D/0020/, D/0030/[9], F/0040/). Data present in the system is expected to vary greatly in type and quantity, making it mandatory to have a truly generic storage management system. In general, approaches involving a static data dictionary will not be able to solve the challenges presented in SSOAs (L/0040/). When looking at the individual real-world-requirements of the validation cases AeG and SPIKE, this issue becomes evident: expected data types range from ontologies and semantic service descriptions to workflows and physical documents. Equally important as storing data is a fast and complete retrieval mechanism (F/0050/). The expected search facility relying on fulltext indices (F/0020/) will be supported in REPO as well.

The management of the previously mentioned generic processes is handled in the workflow component *PROC* which also employs the execution component *EXEC* to execute the services and store the current state of execution (F/0080/).

SEM, the most innovative component in the GENSOA, is concerned with the following knowledge processing tasks:

- Reasoning
  Based on ontologies and especially on the contained axioms and their constraints it is - to a certain extent at best- possible to infer previously unknown knowledge and use it for subsequent processing steps (F/0050/).

- Mediation
  Open platforms can not guarantee that all data is described based on a single set of ontologies. These mismatches can be solved in an automated fashion if the gap between source and destination objects is small enough. Manual hints on mediation[10] can always be given and considerably simplify the process. Limited automated approaches are subject of current research (F/0050/).

- Matching or selection
  Contrasting actors' goals, and services' offerings in an automated fashion is

---

[9] Other data elements introduced later are the consequence of a design capable of storing these information elements effectively.

[10] Possibly as simple as a straight forward mapping between ontology elements.

one of the main goals of each SSOA. This task can only succeed if the system is supported by knowledge contained in semantic service annotations and underlying ontologies (F/0060/).

Accessing both, REPO and SEM, the *COMP* component builds chains of services starting with a description of a generic process (F/0060/). This process can be imagined as carrying typed slots, each of which able to link in one instance of a service. Resolving in this context means the activity of populating these slots with real service instances.

A resolved process, however, is not executable since the grounding (cf. Section 8.1.3) is still missing. *ORCH*, the Orchestration component, takes care of grounding by identifying all necessary information to allow service execution (F/0070/).

Management of the generic processes is handled within the workflow component *PROC* (F/0080/).

Administration

All functionalities concerned with managing the whole platform are subsumed under the Administration assembly which in turn consists of three further components.

By far the most important component concerned with administration of semantic addons, *ADM-SEM* (F/0100/, F/0110/). Here, selected administration roles have the possibility to:

- Annotate services

- Mediation

- Ontology management

Closely connected to the semantic side of the GENSOA, the processes are important enough to warrant their own specific administration component: the *ADM-PROC*. Mainly lifecycle management of the processes is envisioned since powerful standards and accompanying graphical tools for editing the processes are already available in the workflow world (F/0080/).

Concerned with all runtime configuration possibilities, *ADM-SYS* finally is the component that system administrators use to track key performance data and status messages and act accordingly (L/0020/, L/0030/).

169

Security

Security in GENSOA is not confined to a credential-based login procedure. In fact, management of credentials is not even in the scope of the security subassembly. The Identity Management Component *IdM* provisions ways to include already available credential storage mechanisms (F/0130/). *SEC* itself acts as large scale distributed AAI (L/0010/, F/0010/, F/0090/).

The security API (SEC-API) allows components to request security and identity management related functions.

Service Cloud

The service cloud is no longer part of the GENSOA internal system and connected to the outside world via an execution component called *EXEC*. Its sole responsibility is to execute services in ways specified by *PROC* (F/0120/).

Clients

Using a so-called Client API, clients can connect to the core of the GENSOA through standardized XML-based interfaces.

11.4.1.2. Relations and Communication Flows Between Components

Figure 11.3 visualizes the relations between the components of the GENSOA. According to the design considerations previously laid out, the interfaces have been tailored to maximize cohesion inside the modules while minimizing coupling between them.

Core components therefore are unreachable with one exception: The repositories implementation exports a generic interface called the *External Repository Interface (ERI)* for CRUD operations on all contained physical bits of information. The necessary integration of access control creates a circular statement: Components of the SEC need to retrieve[11] from REPO via the interface but this retrieval operation has to be secured, too. Instantiations of this design will therefore have to ensure that only trusted callers can use the ERI by introducing appropriate technologies.

Equally sensitive, the Admin API (ADAPI) has to be secured identically to the ERI as, according to the admin roles involved, most of the important data can be read and written from there.

---

[11]Mainly the PIP. It uses REPO to retrieve policies on initialisation. Attributes of users and services are handled through a PAP which resides in the Core and is exposed through the SECAPI.

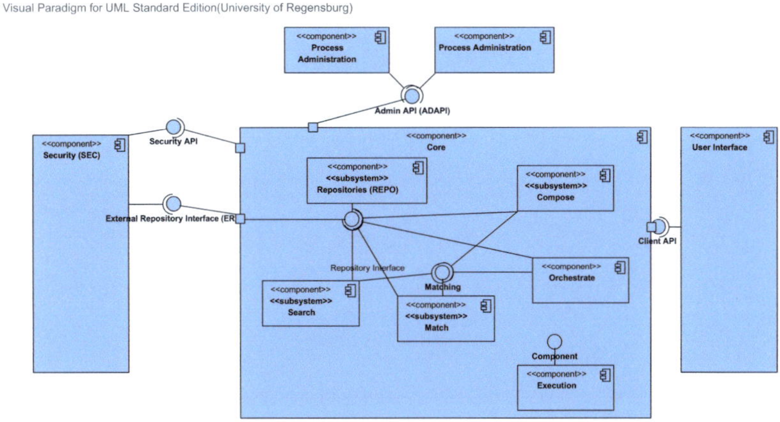

Figure 11.3.: Decomposition of the SSOA

The Client API (CLAPI) is the main entry into the Core and thus into the GEN-SOA. Clients, mostly different kinds of user interfaces, talk to this API directly.

Execution of atomic services is handled directly between the Core and the called services through EXEC. It is also home to any possible implementation of a service bus (cf. ESB in SPIKE in Section 14.3.1.2).

11.4.2. Information View

A SSOA strongly depends on a usable and concise data model. In this information view, the data model of the GENSOA is introduced in detail.

11.4.2.1. Overview of Data Objects and Relations

Figure 11.5 describes all information elements of the GENSOA. Closely following the WSMO structure of *WebService, Goal, Mediator* and *Ontology*, the GENSOA's data model revolves around these basic concepts.

Security-related information data elements are not explicitly specified in the model as recursively using the platform as envisioned in Chapter 5 waivers the need for additional data elements[12].

A *Process* is the basic data structure for holding information on the general sequence and structure of the task at hand. *Users* do not interact with a process

---

[12]This information model already contains an User object with a flexible set of attributes. PDP and PIP do not have to have seperate datastores in order to evaluate access control decisions.

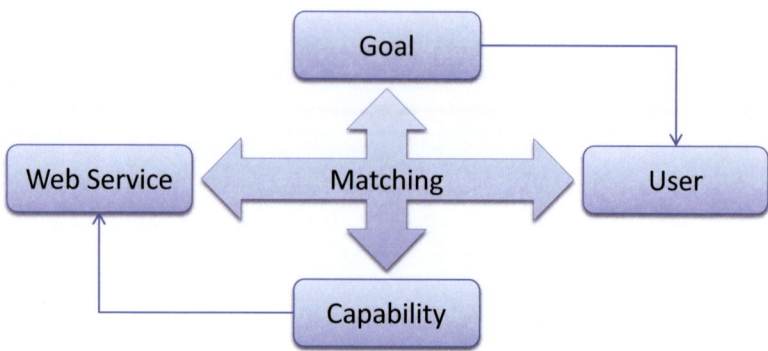

Figure 11.4.: Users and Web Services Connected Through Goals and Capabilities

directly but rather are represented by their *Goal* or set of *Goals*. They are the representation of what a user wants to achieve and are realized through following the process model from start to end. A *Process* is not directly executable itself on the other hand, but rather can be depicted as a data structure holding different slots with attached *Goals*[13].

Users with their flexible set of attributes have the only constraint that attribute identifiers have to be known inside the knowledge store. *Users* usually are interested in the execution of a very specific task and therefore always operate on upper levels of the process hierarchy.

Capabilities are the link between *Goals* and *WebServices*. *Goals* ask for matching capabilities while *WebServices* fulfill *Goals* (Figure 11.4 illustrates this connection).

WebServices occur in two different shapes, one representing an electronic service[14], the other representing a traditional service, subsuming all services that are not available as electronic service. A further property of *WebServices* is its recursiveness. Only atomic services can be executed and to facilitate that, a *Process* has to be resolved to services. In cases where sub-goals cannot be mapped directly to a *WebService* but those *WebServices* are goals or sub-goals themselves instead, another iteration of the resolving task is invoked.

---

[13]Some researchers call these types of goals sub-goals but this distinction is not warranted in the case of a fully recursive platform: Goals on every level of recursion can be a new starting point for a new process. N.B.: The Access-eGov platform differs from this description in that recursion is not allowed for processes.

[14]In its most desirable form a service adhering to the SOAP or REST standard. Otherwise some effort has to be made to implement wrapper technologies.

All information needed for the correct actual execution of electronic services is stored in *Grounding* data objects.

Once *Processes* enter the execution state, some of them will generate requests for user inputs or will want to output informational messages to the user. Depending on the type of service the input can sometimes be directly fetched from within a GUI if the whole process is executed in a single transaction. If the process is taking extended periods of time and the possibility of a user intermittently logging off increases, the process execution stalls during the time in which no input is received. In any case, there has to be the possibility to emit and receive notifications which are represented by the type *NotificationEvent*.

Semantic technologies, at this point of time, are reliant on the corresponding ontologies which are described in *Ontology* objects. The accompanying mediators are both a software component which is of no concern for the information view and a list of mapping rules which are stored inside repositories.

SemanticAnnotations, created by annotators using *ADM-SEM*, link ontology elements, their instances, and concepts to *Goals* and *WebServices*.

Different additional kinds of artefacts also need to be stored in the GENSOA which usually is a challenge for implementors of this design because the physical, file-based storage breaks the object-oriented paradigm and cannot be integrated with standard Object Relational Mapper (ORM)s like JPA[15] or Hibernate[16].

---

[15]Java Persistence API, a standardization effort for object relational persistence in Java.
[16]Both, an implementor of the JPA standard and at the same time extending it with own concepts.

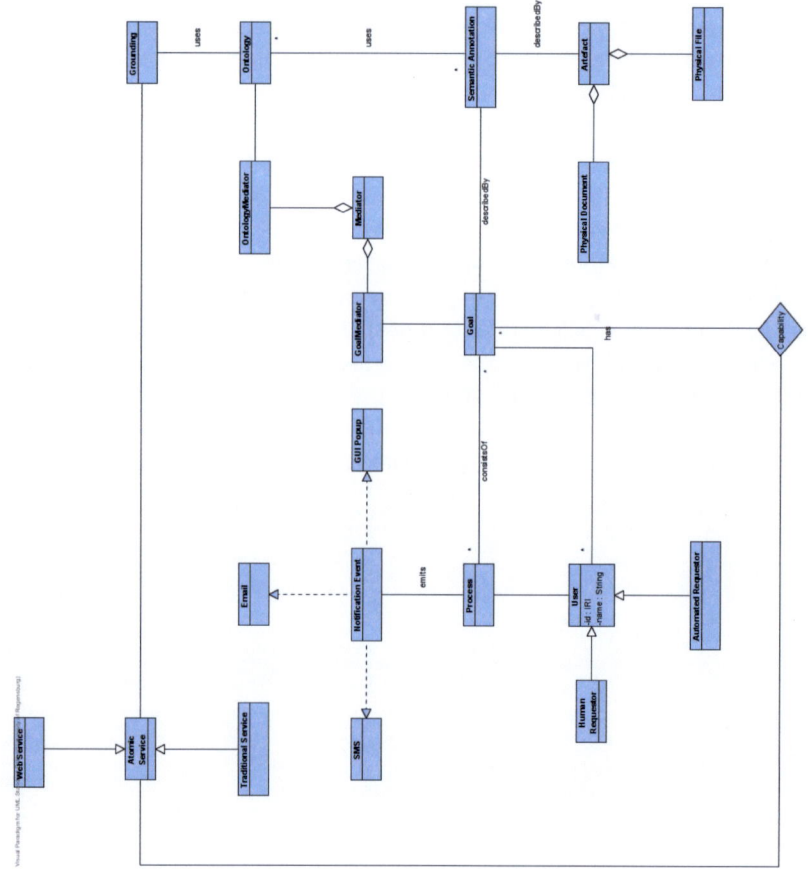

Figure 11.5.: UML Diagram Depicting the Information Model of the GENSOA

11.4.3. Concurrency View

Concurrency issues are important in large software systems. In the case of the GENSOA, however, concurrency issues are limited and can be identified in the following areas:

Data Objects

Data objects are susceptible to concurrency issues to a varying degree. Notification Events, for example, do not exhibit problematic concurrency behavior. They exist from the point of creation until the message has been sent to a recipient regardless of the transport. No possibility of altering them in transit exists and once created, they cannot be deleted until sent, with eventual error conditions being the only - nonetheless unrelated to concurrency - exception that has to be taken care of.

Goals and capabilities are an auxiliary construct originating in ontologies. Thus, they do not add extra concurrency constraints.

Process definitions consisting of goals and NFPs, on the other hand, are problematic from a concurrency point of view. They form the backbone of all service composition and execution and thus inconsistencies may have unpredictable consequences. Processes, however, do change only infrequently, generating the possibility to put the system in a maintenance mode while updating definitions.

The most problematic part of the data model with regard to concurrency are the semantic annotations interconnecting services and capabilities. These interconnections frequently vary when for example existing services gain new capabilities. There is no need however, for multiple users to update these annotations at the same time. A pessimistic locking strategy just blocking all but one concurrent access at a time and failing the remaining attempts, is sufficient.

Artifacts need even better concurrency control methods since, depending on the application case, many people at once work with instances of those artifacts. In principle, two different approaches exist that can be merged if needed. One way to ensure data integrity during concurrent modifications is to use versioning, effectively increasing the version identifier for each instance of an artifact that was returned by a client after a modification while returning a new copy of the artifact. Source control systems like CVS use another approach, by automatically merging the different versions as far as possible. In cases where portions of data were modified independently, the platform creates an exception. Merging does not work reliably with certain types of binary files.

Process Execution

During execution, the concurrency aspect is of utmost priority. Unexpected or false results can occur if a process is executed and generates unexpected side effects. Due to the parallelism of involved processes and workflows, implementations of the GENSOA use a workflow engine adhering to a specific workflow standard[17]. Related workflow languages usually provide means to eliminate some concurrency issues by making available advanced control constructs like a statement to wait until another process has finished its execution.

11.4.4. Development View

Giving a complete development view is not feasible in a reference architecture because too many questions remain unanswered in this phase. Nonetheless there are a number of important design considerations that every implementor of the GENSOA should follow in order to limit possible problems during the implementation phase of their specific instances. In the following, important guidelines for developers basing their systems on the GENSOA are described. It is assumed that any software development project follows generic quality criteria like maintainability, or portability (NP/0010/, NF/0020/) and also takes usability of the resulting system into account (L/0050/).

11.4.4.1. Pluggable Components Support

All components communicate through strict and well defined interfaces. While some of the components are already finished[18] with regard to their functionality across GENSOA instances, other components are highly individual. The main example is a service bus, which in some cases is an Enterprise Service Bus (ESB) while in others it is just a simple message router.

11.4.4.2. Revision Control

Revision Control should be one of the foundations of each software project. A carefully designed revision control scheme is especially important in SSOAs as, in addition to common assets like source code, information on and representations of ontologies and knowledge in general have to be managed.

---

[17]Which workflow engine is used is up to the architects creating the specific instance of the GEN-SOA. A BPEL engine is envisioned as the default components, however.

[18]The REPO component, for example, is projected to be reusable among all instances of the GENSOA. A possible scenario would be the case of an open source implementation of REPO.

11.4.4.3. Communication Facilities

Communication facilities should exist and be used regularly in every software project. They are, however, of added importance in the GENSOA case as with the group of knowledge engineers / knowledge staff, a second developers group joins the development effort.

11.4.5. Deployment View

Each of the GENSOA components identified in the functional view can be placed anywhere in a network, providing that the following constraints are kept in mind:

- Performance
  While it is perfectly possible and reasonable to place all components on a single server, performance issues have to be taken into account. For all but sparsely loaded sites, a recommended option is to install the repositories on their own physical node and all other components on another node. In addition, REPO implementations shall be designed to facilitate load-balancing either through partitioning of the data[19] or through replication of underlying databases.

- Security
  It might be useful to place certain components in different physical network segments or even in different physical premises, according to the specifics of the project. An administration component, for example, does not have to be reachable outside certain, limited IP networks. The REPO component does not have to be placed in the open in most cases as well. Another example is shown in Chapter 5 which describes a distributed access control scenario. It quite obviously can benefit from distribution of its components across multiple providers.

- Organizational regulations
  Especially large organisations have their own set of regulations and policies that need to be implemented. Many corporations for example govern the possible storage locations for sensitive user data. A possibly resulting requirement might be that the REPO is placed under direct control of the specific organization. This can further be complicated if two corporations are sharing data[20]

---

[19]The partitioning schema is decided on at implementation time. Possibilities include a partitioning by type of the stored resource or - useful in supra-regional settings - by their geographical distribution.

[20]SPIKE as introduced in Chapter 14 is one example that features this problem since organisations within SPIKE are part of short term collaborations.

which can mean that some common (physical and/or organizational) ground for hosting the components has to be established that is under control of all involved parties. While trivial from a technical point of view, some legally binding regulations have to be devised that allow an appropriate relationship between all involved parties.

- Law
  State and country laws additionally influence the possible physical distribution of components. Privacy laws might govern that certain data may only be stored in the originating country, calling for distributed REPOs with effective partitioning by geographical origin of certain data elements, for instance.

Figures 11.6 and 11.7 show two opposing variations of the GENSOA deployment. The former example has all components placed on only two different computers, spanning one single regulatory space. The complex example in the latter case shows involvement of four companies and possibilities to distribute the components.

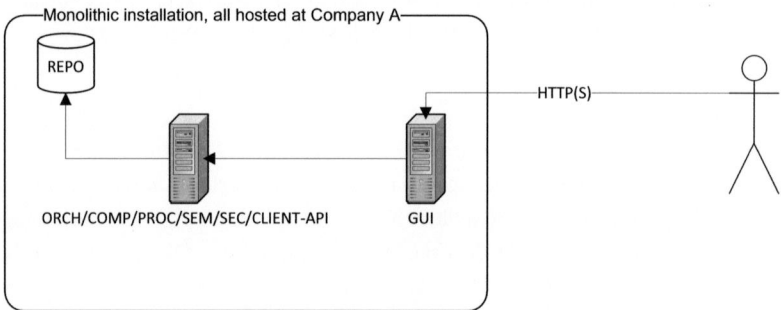

Figure 11.6.: Simple GENSOA Deployment

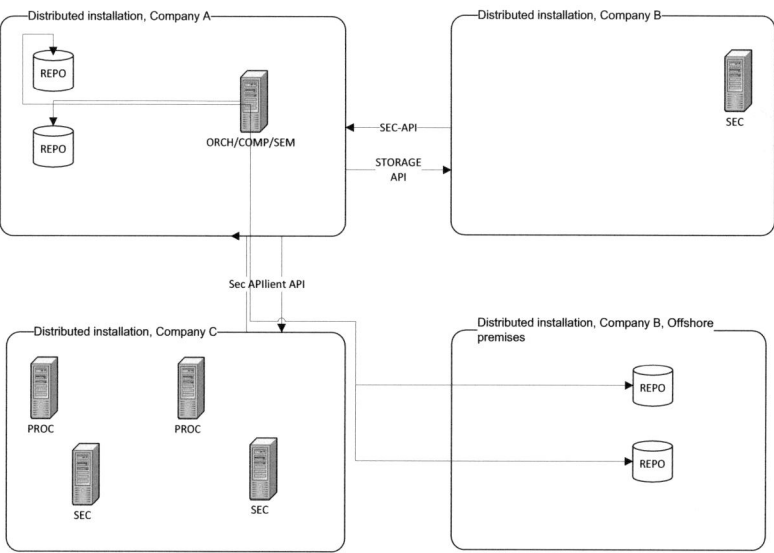

Figure 11.7.: Complex, Distributed Deployment of the GENSOA

11.4.6. Operational View

Operating the implemented GENSOA involves a number of activities which are explained in the following paragraphs:

11.4.6.1. Installation

Components of the GENSOA instance shall be packaged into modules representing the component structure and should be deployable in any servlet container.

Installation of a GENSOA is no frequent task and requires extensive configuration and performance tuning. Therefore, ease-of-use of the platform, for example through providing an installer, is not a very pressing issue. Supporting administrators of the system by providing them with a complete list of required software versions in conjunction with a concise installation guide is sufficient.

11.4.6.2. Administration

The three administration components introduced in the functional view call for at least as many administrative roles. In addition, a role able to administer the ontologies has to be added:

- Annotator (ADM-SEM)
  Responsible for annotation of the services. Needs to be a domain expert but may be a beginner in semantic technologies. Every service provider has to assign one or – depending on the number and complexity of involved domain fields – more annotators.

- Process administrator (ADM-PROC)
  The ideal process administrator is a knowledge engineer. Creating and keeping process definitions up to date is a challenging task with a multitude of contact points to semantic technologies and used knowledge representation languages after all. Depending on the number of active processes in the system, one process administrator is usually enough for a whole GENSOA.

- System administrator (ADM-SYS)
  This role does not necessarily need to be able to write to any of the data stored in the platform. Since administrative accounts also are in charge of backups, one possible solution is to introduce a Separation of Duty (SoD) methodology, at least for restoring backups. System administration is usually done by a team

located on site at the installation premises. In case of distributed installation, several System Administrators from different organizations share this task.

- Ontology Administrator
  An ontology administrator has to be a very good knowledge engineer with a minimum expertise in the specific domain. If domain knowledge is lacking, cooperation with domain experts is necessary.

11.4.6.3. Monitoring

In addition to general system administration activities, the ADM-SYS is also tasked with monitoring the platform. Probes in performance-sensitive parts of the platform, statistics on CPU load, network usage or disk I/O, and other metrics all have to be carefully analyzed in order to instantly learn about performance bottlenecks and problems with sparse resources.

Another activity attributable to monitoring is auditing of system logs in order to find and identify breaches of security policies.

Audit logs are useful also with regard to compliance to certain regulations[21].

11.4.6.4. Support

Here the initiator of the GENSOA instance is authoritative. Apart from providing a working infrastructure for an online help system, this blueprint architecture cannot give any guidelines for its envisioned usage. Company or system policies have to be instantiated that provide both, human and IT resources to establish a helpdesk.

11.4.6.5. Migration

Due to its modularized architecture, migration is not a problem in the GENSOA environment. Important data is versioned, the software itself extremely loosely coupled. Thus, even smallest parts (cf. Deployment View) are working on their own and can be replaced by other versions of the components, even at other physical locations.

---

[21]In Europe, most notably the Basel II accord (http://www.bis.org/publ/bcbsca.htm), in the USA the Sarbanes-Oxley act (http://www.sarbanes-oxley.com/), postulate varying degrees of auditing within systems.

11.5. Architectural Perspectives

Perspectives are orthogonal to views as they can encompass more than one view while describing only one specific property of the set of views in detail. In the following paragraphs, a number of important perspectives on certain properties of the GENSOA are described.

11.5.1. Security Perspective

The first in this series of perspectives is one of the most important qualities of software systems, security.

11.5.1.1. Threats

An adversary model shows the main characteristics of an assumed attacker by first describing whether its role is a passive (only eavesdropping) or an active (attacker also has the ability to actively modify data) one. In addition to that, the adversary model classifies prototypical attackers according to their resources:

- Computing resources
  Does the attacker have state-of-the art computing power? Future state-of-the-art computing power? Often an only hypothetic variation is included: What if the attacker has unlimited computing resources? While at first glance attackers will always be constrained by computing resources, masking this constraint helps to explore attacks that are unreasonable today, yet may be possible as soon as computing resources increase by an order of magnitude.

- Time resources
  Does the attacker have any time constraints?

- Diffusion
  How deeply can the attacker penetrate the system? (Which network components and links can he monitor/eavesdrop on? Can he place his own nodes in the network at will?)

- Financial resources
  Which monetary limits does the attacker have?

- Location of the attacker
  Is the attacker an insider to the organization? Is he an external adversary?

External attackers can only use the external interfaces of the GENSOA, which usually excludes the external storage API. it includes, however, all possible sorts of bugs in the code between the attacker and the platform, which is not limited to GENSOA code but extends to firewall code and code in application servers on which the GENSOA is deployed on. External attackers additionally are able to misuse other vulnerable services not directly connected to the GENSOA (e.g. SSH which is almost always needed for administration). He cannot eavesdrop on any GENSOA-internal connections because he cannot wiretap the network traffic.

An internal attacker has the same paths as has the external one, but additionally can eavesdrop on all communication links between the internal components. He is also able to at least contact the external storage API and SEC components and request an access control decision.

It is evident that internal attackers are more dangerous adversaries. Overall security measures, however, have to be high since an external attacker already has a number of possibilities at hand to exploit system vulnerabilities.

In this light, the Access-eGov project team [DSK07] identified main generic security requirements for a semantic SOA as follows:

11.5.1.2. Communication Security

Every communication channel has to be encrypted throughout the platform (L/0060/). One solution for this endeavor is to use the WS-SECURITY set of standards [NKMHB06a] that utilizes XML Encrpytion [ERI$^+$02] and XML Signature [RSY$^+$09] in order to ensure data integrity and privacy. It was introduced in great detail in Section 5.5.1.

WS-Security, however, is only concerned with SOAP messages on which most of the platform is based. Communications between clients and the GUI component have to be secured as well. Using the standard HTTPS protocol instead of the unencrypted HTTP protocol takes care of this task.

11.5.1.3. Trust

Trust between nodes is especially important in widely distributed systems like the GENSOA. There has been frequent research contributions in this field over the past years (cf. [JIB07]) but trust inside the GENSOA is limited. Identity / Authentication trust, trusting verifiable properties like a CA-signed certificate identify or authenticate a user, is the only form of trust the GENSOA architecture supports.

In addition, implementations of the GENSOA could offer reputation-based systems allowing trust in different services. Such a system, however, will not be part of the backend but an addon and as such has to be specified individually. The main reason for this decision is that such reputation systems fit nicely into already existing websites and therefore might be better implemented as an add-on to them instead of an add-on to the GENSOA, especially considering the fact that they are more of an organizational information system than a technical tool.

11.5.1.4. Privacy

In addition to communication security, which hides every bit of information from eavesdroppers, privacy-aware applications also hide information from service providers or other legitimate communication partners by only disclosing the absolute minimum set of attributes needed to verify a specific request (L/0070/). Kolter et al. ([KSP07b]) devises a schema which was elaborated on in Chapter 5.

11.5.1.5. Access Control

More concerned with the operations side of the platform, access control takes care of protecting the individual services (L/0080/). The XACML platform [M+05] is able to support access control in the GENSOA and in connection with SAML also supports Single Sign On [AL05] (cf. Section 5.5.2).

11.5.2. Performance & Scalability

Performance concerns are another key factor for the success of any software system. Increasing response times induce a drop in user satisfaction. This is especially important for systems as complex as the GENSOA, and particularly interesting when semantic functionality is involved. Reasoning is very resource hungry and is added on top of conventional SOA technologies which already generate a considerable overhead.

11.5.2.1. Response Times

For 14% of users, 10 seconds is the maximum amount of time they are willing to wait for a web application, and waiting one minute is the maximum for 68% as is reported in [Kus09]. Those numbers will all but drop as users are increasingly spoiled by very fast services and high-speed internet links.

Thus, for the GENSOA, the acceptable response time shall not be more than 5 seconds.

11.5.2.2. Scalability

Scalability in our setting is measured in three dimensions: space, network throughput, and computing resources. Space is only an issue for the REPO component and can be handled easily. Either space is added through hardware means, like extending a disk array or moving the REPO databases to a different location with more space, or through distributing the REPO component over different nodes as already described in the deployment view.

Network throughput[22], possibly a huge factor in limiting response times, also can be improved through hardware measures. Depending on the bottleneck, this usually means upgrading existing network infrastructures to new technologies. Switching from Fast Ethernet to Gigabit Ethernet boosts throughput by 1000%. If this is not possible for certain reasons[23], modifications of the general networking structure might yield the desired benefits. A thorough planning of the physical network topology is standard network operations practise and is not further described in this thesis.

Computing resources are very hard to project before the system is deployed in its normal surroundings. Scalability of computing resources is achieved either again through hardware upgrades or through improvements of the software. While algorithm improvements, especially of semantic components, appear possible they cannot be predicted and therefore cannot be factored in. Especially problematic is the fact that load-balancing is not as helpful because in the GENSOA, resources are not consumed by the number of simultaneous requests (which could easily be distributed across nodes), but by the complexity of each single interaction which always will run on one specific node until completed.

11.5.3. Availability and Resilience

Just like response times, availability of systems is a major quality property. Stability of software systems, which reached an absolute low point in the mid 1990s, has rebounded by orders of magnitudes since then and is among the top priorities of

---

[22]The throughput between the different GENSOA components as opposed to the throughput between GENSOA and its clients.

[23]The network might already be Gigabit Ethernet and a switch to 10-gigabit Ethernet is impossible for financial reasons.

both managers and users. Therefore it is vital for the GENSOA to support a high uptime by design.

Firstly, however, the scope of availability has to be clarified. In the GENSOA, availability extends to three levels:

- Hardware

  The most basic demand for highly-available systems is the availability of the underlying hardware. Currently every part of modern hardware is covered by strategies for assuring its availability. Storage systems may use RAIDs, many other components are also configured redundantly. Other cases of hardware failures can be mitigated through the usage of failover aware combinations of hardware and software which, in case of a hardware failure in one system, directly continue processing on a backup system. Today, major operating systems vendors offer specialized high availability solutions like IBM's PowerHA for AIX[24] or Vmware's vSphere[25] for virtualized environments.

  Ultimately, the GENSOA architect has to determine an appropriate level of hardware availability measures and indicators.

- Software

  The best way of improving and securing availability of software is not always through the use of supportive tools but also through making sure that the software source code and design are of highest possible quality. Tools exist to measure certain quality metrics (cf. the seminal work of Chidamber et al. who developed a set of six different metrics for object oriented design [CK94]) but the quest for best quality software starts even earlier: at the programming language level.

  Programming languages are not equally secure. Two contradictory examples are the C language, giving its user remarkable flexibility at the cost of many issues with buffer overflows and general problems with pointers and memory allocation, and the Java language which does not cut the users' freedom in noteworthy ways, yet eliminating many of the problematic peculiarities of the C language. Another key issue to factor in is the availability of experts in the used language and framework. A GENSOA architect has to take care of a proper selection process involving all of these issues.

---

[24]http://www-03.ibm.com/systems/power/software/availability/
[25]http://www.vmware.com/de/products/vsphere/

- Process level

  Each GENSOA is also a broker between (possibly) externally offered services which are out of control of the GENSOA administration team. Depending on the layout of a process, the GENSOA might be able to route around service outages by just filling the specific slot with another service. If no other service fulfilling the needed capability exists, the process will fail no matter what the status of the overall GENSOA is.

As important as availability, disaster recovery also has to be planned. A concise and tested backup concept is mandatory. All standard tools and techniques apply also for the GENSOA case. A suitable backup concept has to take into account the typology of data within the GENSOA. While no necessity exists to backup the ontologies every day (they are not changing that frequently), service data should be backed up daily. Process data, changing even more frequently, might benefit from a backup schedule that executes multiple times a day.

The information view in Section 11.4.2 already explained strategies for keeping the contained data concise, where one of the solutions, used for ontologies, was to restart the platform. It is a valid and feasible proposal but limits uptime. Therefore, occasions of data updates should be scheduled to coincide with other mandatory downtimes[26].

11.5.4. Internationalization

Integration solutions - the GENSOA undoubtedly is one - need to be designed with internationalization support in mind. While the implementation details lie in the hands of the GENSOA architect, the following items have to be considered beforehand:

11.5.4.1. Character Sets

Ever since invention of computers, data interchangeability was hampered by incompatibilities in character sets. To rid the GENSOA of these problems, the design must only understand one characterset[27]. At the time of this writing, the global encoding standard is Unicode[28] in its various occurences and since almost every known character can be mapped into it, the GENSOA shall be based on it as well.

---

[26]Security updates to the application server or OS updates may result in the requirement to restart the platform or the whole node as well.

[27]In very urgent circumstances, this rule can be relaxed by allowing other charactersets to be included in the GENSOA by means of character set translation.

[28]http://unicode.org

11.5.4.2. Application Localization

Strings, help files, and other textual resources have to be localized to support the mother tongue of the many different user groups. Nowadays, every programming language or paradigm has its own concept of internationalization helpers. Java for example uses ResourceBundles which do not contain a single line of program code and therefore can easily be translated by domain and/or language experts.

11.5.4.3. Dates and Numbers

Internationalization / Localization does not stop at the textual level. Dates are another very complex issue that varies from region to region. The system should be able to automatically choose the best fitting representation[29]. Number formats differ in different cultures as well.

11.5.4.4. Presentation Layer

If the whole system is based on UTF, there is no immediate problem in displaying the characters to a client application which usually will run as a server side web application in a browser. Languages with a different orientation, however, pose problems as designs common in European (and many other western) countries usually are not geared towards both, left-to-right and right-to-left texts.

11.5.4.5. Input Problems

Depending on the client and language, inputing characters in languages with complex charactersets[30] is a challenge. The GENSOA does not have a lever to simplify this process, but the GENSOA architect has to take care that only a client technology is chosen that can cope with all current and important projected future charactersets and languages.

11.5.5. Knowledge and Semantics Perspective

One of the most important points of improvement that the GENSOA wants to introduce is the extensive usage of knowledge and semantics. Since perspectives explain cross cutting concerns and knowledge and KBTs are indeed situated in every

---

[29]Here again, all major programming languages have the concept of Locales that govern the output of dates in a region-specific format.
[30]All forms of Chinese require an additional tool, for example.

subsystem of the architecture, their usage is described in this perspective instead of a view.

KBTs have to be viewed as an overall process. Knowledge usage has a number of unique advantages with certain disadvantages, of which the single most important one is the great deal of energy an organization has to put into semantic/knowledge modeling. As explained earlier (cf. Section 10.2), the best moment for inclusion of the semantic technologies and therefore for building and integrating the system-wide knowledgebase is the early requirements process. Consequently, a knowledge engineer[31] has to be paid from project onset until late in the implementation phase and probably will be employed for consulting later on: unsurprisingly as the problem domain of a relatively small and self-contained project like the marriage scenario of Access-eGov (cf. Chapter 13) already produced a core resource ontology with 55 concepts. Ontologies describing services on a metadata level are considerably larger.

Another drawback is the added resource consumption, already partially addressed in the deployment view. Comparing a semantically enabled SSOA to a traditional SOA already shows considerable, mostly organizational[32], overhead but for reasons explained in Chapter 1, conventional SOAs do not offer enough advantages over Client/Server or other distributed architecture styles. The comparison between Client/Server and the GENSOA, however, is clearly favoring the Client/Server design as long as only resource consumption is viewed.

Still, SSOAs are a promising approach as they exhibit a number of advantages which were explained in great detail in previous chapters and are summarized as follows:

- Common vocabulary

  If instantiated at the very beginning, the common vocabulary built by the ontology is of benefit for the whole development effort. Where exactly the borders of the discourse world are drawn has to be carefully considered, but in the usual case, every important aspect of the domain in which the system is located in is modeled into the semantic model. Naturally, this is the best case for any large-scale project. Developers have formalized knowledge at hand, which they can use to lookup and define critical requirements engineering concepts. Documentation writers share and reuse the same vocabulary again, making

---

[31]There is no formal, standardized job title of a "knowledge engineer", however its functions are clear. He has to design, update, and maintain the conceptual model of the whole problem domain.

[32]Almost only through the adoption of KBTs that are both complex and most often new to organizations.

them fully integrated even in the case of a fully outsourced documentation process.

- Automated or semi-automated means of mediation
  Concepts divergently defined in different parts of the considered domain can be mapped through knowledge conveyed in the ontologies. If this mapping is done manually by setting up mapping rules, or even totally automated by reasoning, in any case it is adding value to the system, even if the usability of reasoning approaches is disputed (cf. Section 8.1.4).

- Alleviation of the information retrieval problem
  Not only automated processes (composition, orchestration) but also manual retrieval is considerably improved by the use of semantic information. Metadata that is added to the genuine pieces of information is - at least in theory - unambiguous. Compared with conventional information retrieval, none of the common makeshift tools[33] have to be used in order to find best matching results.

Finally, another important matter that has not been discussed so far is the quality of the semantic annotations. Different methods to generate them exist, ranging from automated approaches [DEG+03], [HSC+02] to manual annotation of the whole content. Reality shows that in usual projects the result is always a hybrid approach which lets automated tools create an initial set of metadata and have a knowledge engineer check and improve the annotations.

---

[33]Like word frequency or link counting.

12. Security Infrastructure (SEC)

Security, as an integral part of each software system is of utmost importance especially in the GENSOA case. Thus, special care has been taken to design a flexible integrated security component for the GENSOA that fulfills key requirements compiled in Section 5.4.5. SEC uses all components introduced so far in order to be able to treat the different security services (cf. Section 5.3.1) as GENSOA processes.

Using this technology, all standard security services are composed of their atomic building blocks at runtime. SSOA-inherent methodologies to use semantic metadata support building individual instances of those security processes, tailored to the users' specific needs.

Outside of the formally defined requirements introduced earlier, prototypical use of SEC with a small set of test users in Access-eGov has shown, that the following attributes may influence this automated process:

- Jurisdictional location of user
  Depending on the location of the user, different laws or other reglementations may be effective. Some might prohibit certain kinds of encryption while others might even mandate minimum security standards.

- Geographical location of user
  Network topology of the system and current geographical position of the user in relation to network nodes also influences decisions on which the atomic building blocks are combined.

- Privacy concerns
  Both, users and service providers have privacy concerns. Both groups also offer different facilities for protecting privacy sensitive data. Semantic matchmaking can balance concerns of both sides to instantiate a process ideal for both parties.

In the following paragraphs, this security architecture is introduced in detail.

12.1. Architecture

The goal of SEC is not only protecting the infrastructure and information content but also acting as the basis for building mutual trust in the platform. Users have to trust the service providers which in turn have to trust the users.

While there is no problem proofing an identity (cf. Section 5.3.1), approving properties is the main concern. Usual approaches require a trusted third party or some other form of provider-approved authority. Once the provider verifies the attributes, access control decisions can be positively evaluated. Problematic for service providers is that they have to convey lots of details on their access policies.

Exactly how much trust the consumer has to put into the trusted third party is a different question. The most simple approach from a trusted third party point of view is to just fetch all attributes from the client and attest the currently requested ones to the provider. Privacy issues quickly arise, however as in an average request, only a minority of all available attributes will be required to evaluate the request.

Thus, a consumer has yet another point of view. He probably does not trust the provider and also might not trust the third party to full extent. The less attributes he has to give away, the better protected is his privacy.

These considerations show the main focus of SEC as first introduced in [KSP07a]: to bring together these three, partially conflicting points of view in one distributed, semantically enriched, and flexible security infrastructure.

We already laid out the security requirements in Section 11.5.1.1 and grouped them into two classes. One set of requirements is purely technical (like communication security or non-repudiation) and not in the scope of SEC. Every major platform has ways of securing communication for example.

The remaining set of requirements was tackled in the research leading up to the SEC component.

Our approach is based on ABAC since this generalization of Role-Based Access Control (RBAC) is able to achieve all postulated security requirements. Priebe et al. even show that ontologies can easily be integrated into the ABAC approach [PDK06]. ABAC additionally is flexible enough to handle access control for millions of resources; unlike in DAC-based approaches, ABAC does not require every relation between subject and object to be recorded beforehand. Subject and object attributes simplify administration of even the biggest data stores since already existing sets of files can automatically be tagged with object attributes and only a handful of policies is enough to cover most access control decisions in the system.

Already proven technologies for distributing the attribute certification exist in the X.509 world, together with further-reaching implementations like XACML (cf. Section 5.5.3).

12.2. Overview

Figure 12.1 shows a rudimentary sketch of the distributed, semantic-aware security architecture as initially proposed within the Access-eGov project . The first important deviation from the approach standardized in [M+05] and explained in Section 5.5.2 is that the context handler is missing and all components are web services.

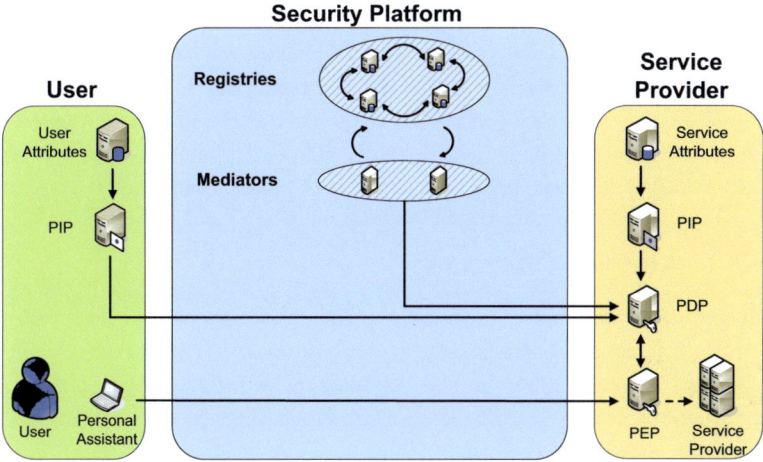

Figure 12.1.: Overview of the GENSOA Security Component [KSP07a]

The sequence of an access control event is roughly the following: an agent discovers a matching service or builds an orchestration of executable services. Subsequently, the EXEC component starts to execute the orchestration, service after service. Once a service is encountered that requires access control, the PEP is involved, in turn relaying the access decision to a PDP. Calling the relevant data repositories and required PIPs, the PDP collects user and service attributes.

In the worst case, these attributes do not originate in one domain but have different vocabulary roots. Thus, a mapping has to take place between the different vocabularies. This mapping is not trivial, however. A very useful approach was

introduced by Priebe et al., namely using an inference engine to resolve disambigui-
ties [PDMP05]. They envisioned using OWL for putting security-related attributes
in an ontological context but their main considerations can be transfered to any
knowledge-representation formalism. Especially large-scale SSOAs can benefit from
added flexibility. In addition, the fact that the GENSOA is based on WSMO adds
WSMO's strong mediation concepts to further the flexibility of the attributing process.

Once the PDP has calculated the result of the policy or policies in action, the PEP
enforces the access control decision and also takes care of any possible obligations.

12.3. Trust and Privacy

The previous chapter showed a security architecture that was built on the XACML
standard and differed only through the simplifications made to the standard and
small hints on possible inclusion of KBTs. Considering the amount of - possibly
very private - data and resources processed[1], additional modifications have to be
made in order to fulfill additional privacy and trust quality metrics.

12.3.1. Attribute Disclosure

A first starting point is the disclosure of attributes. Users need to have better
control over their valuable data in order to maximize their privacy. So-called *Privacy
Preferences* support the user in administrating his/her own set of attributes by
allowing him to control which attribute can be transfered under which circumstances.
Depending on the user interface, attributes can be selected on an attribute level,
or grouped into certain classes. These circumstances are also defined in the user
interface, with one possible circumstance being the context of transmission: Users
may be prepared to transfer their credit card details to a well-known shopping
site like amazon.com while being reluctant to transfer their details to an unknown
online shop. Technical aspects may also be important to the customer, making it a
mandatory possibility to restrict transfer of attributes through unsecure channels.
Lots of research has been undertaken in this field, with [Kol10] being a very concise
work that sums up the research state-of-the-art and introduces new ideas to the
community.

---

[1]This term signalizes that credentials and other private attributes are not necessarily stored inside
the platform by the GENSOA. A PIP is a good abstraction mechanism allowing for flexible
storage locations for all types of data.

12.3.2. Placement of the PDP

Giving users full control over attributes disclosure may not be enough, however. What if they do not trust the service provider? What if they do not trust one of the intermediaries? In any case, if an online business wants to stay competitive, it has to offer as many choices (for example choices of payment methods) as possible. Having a PDP in the service provider's area of control is unacceptable for many customers. Obviously, providers that reached a certain market share may overlook these issues more easily. Small providers, however, cannot as they are usually fighting for each customer. The same is true for sites that are not aiming at e-Commerce but at participation. E-Government is one of those problematic domains. Service provider usually is a state or some local or regional, state-related institution in which not all citizens unconditionally confide in.

Due to the possibility of combining / recombining services along GENSOA processes, it is feasible to run systems without a fixed configuration of their security providers. Each new access control decision can trigger a new resolving of the process, constrained by a set of environmental attributes like the current users' privacy preferences. Thus, moving the PDP inside the overall system is a noteworthy relaxation of usually very strict bindings between services and access control modules.

The concept of placing the PDP flexibly adds a new degree of freedom to access control considerations.

Figure 12.2 illustrates this proposal. To further elaborate on this topic, three of those potential PDP placements are detailed, each representing a specific class.

12.3.2.1. At the Service Provider

Placing the PDP in the provider's domain of control is currently the most frequently seen mode of operations. It is an approach with numerous advantages for service providers. One of them is the full control over the complete deployment of the PDP, making it possible to update or change the software at their own discretion.

Another important advantage is that the provider of the PDP can easily specify and guarantee the physical location of data, which is especially important for many data privacy settings. Ideally, there should be no sensitive data stored in the platform, however, which considerably decreases the importance of this advantage.

For service consumers, on the other hand, this approach has a number of disadvantages. A PDP is a black box, no customer or any representative thereof will be able to gain access to one of the PDP installations at big service providers in

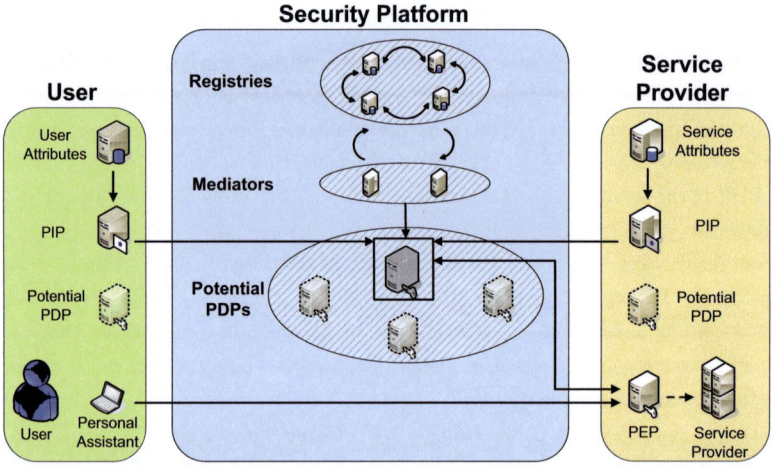

Figure 12.2.: Variation of SEC with the Possibility to Flexibly Place the PDP [KSP07a]

order to verify that they are hosted according to current best-practices of computer security. Obtaining the source code to these installations usually is impossible.

The same holds true even for users' personal data on which no information on location and storage environment are usually published. The important question whether providers keep their privacy promises is not answerable by consumers at all. A consumer has to put great amounts of trust in the platform and the organizations running it. If he is able to confide in it, depends on his own idea of privacy. If he simply does not want his attributes disclosed, he is protected by German and European law and as long as the data is hosted in Germany, these assurances can be legally enforced[2].

In general, data travels through a number of devices across different networks before reaching the recipient. All these nodes are potential leaks of transfered data[3].

---

[2]Once the unapproved disclosure of private data has happened, however, these considerations are not important anymore. The harm is done and cannot be reversed. While certain possibilities for revocation exist, they are not nearly powerful and integrated enough to initiate the deletion of attributes on different platforms, usually not even if they otherwise cooperate.

[3]Obviously depending on the exact protocol and surroundings.

12.3.2.2. In the Security Infrastructure

Neither consumer nor provider have sole control over the PDP when a third party offers the PDP service. Users' agents have to select a PDP matching the users' privacy preferences first before continuing to publish their attributes.

Attributes are only disclosed to trusted third parties and cannot easily reach providers[4].

12.3.2.3. On the Client Side

A very novel approach is to outsource the PDP task to the client that was responsible for creating the initial access request. Guaranteeing maximum user-friendliness, this approach is a provider's nightmare. No attributes leave the client and with it, the service consumers' premises. Trust is reversed in relation to the first solution as the service provider in this setting has to trust the service consumer's infrastructure to correctly execute uncompromised code.

This, very trustworthy, execution environment on the client side is the biggest challenge in this approach. Apart from the obvious protection of attributes and their correct evaluation, the service provider has to be reassured that his policies are not exposed, as well.

At the time of generating first ideas for this section, the impression was that Trusted Computing technologies would be widely available by 2009. In reality, the TCPA/TGM[5] failed to gain substantial ground and, connected to that, market share for their product. While Trusted Computing chips are embedded in many devices today, they are usually turned off by default and no prolific software application building on them has evolved so far.

Without trusted computing hardware, many providers will not be wanting to allow PDPs running on their client PCs and other parts of their infrastructures. As a consequence, this idea has not been worked on further.

12.4. Implementation Considerations

The implementation is based on the XACML (cf. Section 5.5.2) standard and associated reference architecture. Once geared towards a specific use case, some of the features of XACML can be tuned in order to achieve better performance.

---

[4]Or other possibly interested parties like marketing companies or the like.
[5]Open group of trusted computing hardware manufacturers.

12.4.1. Deviations from the XACML Architecture

Some deviations from the standard XACML architecture had to be made, however, and are explained in the following.

12.4.1.1. Context Handler

The context handler is a suitable concept if the security infrastructure has to be very generic as it completely decouples the security subsystem from the rest of the architecture.

However, this concept has some drawbacks. One is the number of format conversions needed at the context handler in certain cases [Fri08]. If, for example, the PEP has its own protocol, messages have to be converted from the native protocol to XACML messages and back for each invocation.

Yet another drawback is its centrality. All messages, obviously including all attributes and their values, have to pass through it. This is not only a grave security and privacy problem, it also creates a single point of failure for the whole security infrastructure. Considering the fact, that many service invocations brokered by the platform rely on it, the single point of failure extends to the whole GENSOA.

While all of the above mentioned issues can be explained and indeed do make sense in some contexts, careful consideration has led to the decision to drop the context handler ([Fri08]) which is easily possible in the GENSOA case: the "director" functionality inherent in it can easily be incurred by the GENSOA's workflow components as later described.

12.4.1.2. Role of the Access Requester and PEP

In the original XACML standard, the access requester and the PEP were decoupled. Again, this only makes sense for generic software systems, but not for SEC as the requirements for SEC and the environment in which it is to be instantiated are clear, making the strict division between PEP and requester unnecessary [Fri08].

As a consequence, the access requester and PEP are combined and the amalgam takes over the following functionalities:

- Protection of resources
  A core PEP functionality which at the same time is the most critical functionality of SEC. Breaches of the PEP cause immediate privilege escalation.

- Obligations
  After the access request has been answered, related to its result some obliga-

tions may have to be fulfilled by SEC. A prominent obligation in any access control setting are logging successful and - usually even more importantly - failed logon attempts.

- Inducing User Authorization
  XACML 2.0 features a complex interaction scenario between access requester and PEP where the PEP is the originator of the access request, not the access requester. As a consequence, the PEP may receive highly confidential data that could be unknown to the PIP and consequently be of dubious origin. Once an attacker manages to inject its own set of data, control over the whole GENSOA is reachable. Limiting the impact of this and other possible attack scenarios, SEC disposes of this possibility but instead adds the constraint that all attributes have to be directly handed out by a PIP.

This component is a typical candidate for the adapter design pattern: its part connected to the backend SEC is generic while the component that is to be integrated into the protected resource is individual. Additional support to alleviate implementation and integration problems is given by the fact that SEC is only geared towards SSOAs that have standard SOA technology roots.

Figure 12.3 summarizes these considerations.

12.4.1.3. PDP Selector

In the preliminaries section it was already shown that the advanced privacy preferences concept inherent in SEC is a useful extension to conservative access control systems.

Supporting it requires an additional and innovative component with a main task of locating a PDP suitable for a specific access control decision. This selection process is further constrained by a set of privacy preferences. Different matching algorithms with varying degrees of support for semantics exist and are further detailed in Section 12.4.3.

12.4.1.4. Inference Engine

An inference engine was also added to the design with one main goal: Having an entity that is able to broker between different labels of attributes with equal semantics. In first prototypical implementations, this inference engine did in fact exist as its own entity. Nowadays, however, the GENSOA platform's capabilities are reused and the inference engine is therefore no longer explicitly mentioned.

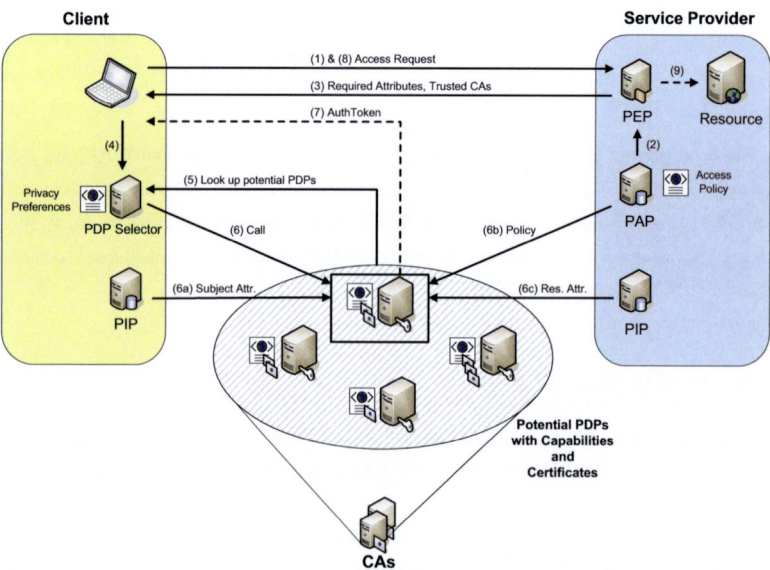

Figure 12.3.: Advanced, Privacy Aware, Distributed Access Control [KSP07b]

12.4.2. Semantic Technologies

Integrating knowledge into the process of securing the GENSOA is a logical consequence. After all, a complete semantic infrastructure is at hand. The designer of a GENSOA instance has a number of possibilities to integrate knowledge and knowledge-related tasks as Figure 12.4 illustrates for an exemplary subtask of Access-eGov's marriage scenario.

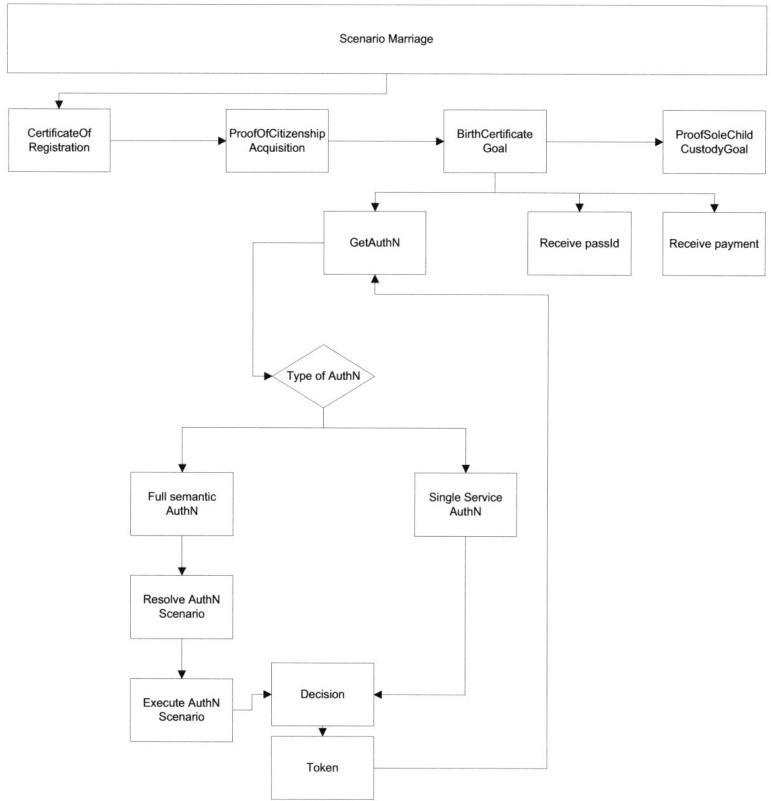

Figure 12.4.: Different Integration Possibilities of Semantic Technologies in SEC

The top-level process is marriage, and one step in this process (also called a sub-goal), namely acquiring a birth certificate, requires authentication. Shown are two important, opposed possibilities:

- Full Semantic Authentication
  Authentication is a sub-goal and is evaluated by means of the included KBTs. A resolved authentication process, itself possibly containing sub-goals, is executed in the EXEC component. Results are relayed to the calling process and used therein.

- Single Service Authentication
  In this variant, the process of Authentication is a self-contained service. No sub-goals are resolved as this authentication step is already executable directly by EXEC.

12.4.3. PDP Selector

SEC so far is a powerful and flexible authentication framework which fulfills all functional requirements. Privacy as a quality requirement remains problematic, however. The often observed behavior of people freely giving out their details may not be their own free will after all. Surveys found out that such decisions are heavily influenced by the service provider [EB03]. Well-known sites and brands have a much better chance of actually receiving the users' attributes than sites that are relatively unknown to the user. A sharp contrast to the openness of the Internet and handicapping business opportunities of smaller or entrepreneurial shops. In order to change the authentication landscape for the better, it is necessary to equip users with ways to stay in control of their private attributes. A variable placement of the PDP, as already described previously, is a good solution to this problem.

PDPs that are moved from the provider to a third party or even to the customer can guarantee better protection of user attributes but raise another problem, the assertion of PDPs' trustworthiness. A PDP Selector component is supporting these assertions by providing functionalities to find a suitable PDP matching constraints of both, users and providers.

Kolter et al. list two groups of functionalities that are executed sequentially [KSP07b]:

- Browse
  Contemplates a semantic search over all service definitions in the system in order to find services with the Capability PDP. Certain constraints[6] can be placed to filter the search results before retrieval.

---

[6]While these constraints can be arbitrarily complex, restricting the search results too much decreases the flexibility of the PDP selector.

- Match

  Matching the browsed results to find the ideal PDP is not different to other applications of semantic matching (cf. Section 8.1.1). The bottom line is the comparison between capabilities and requirements. Capabilities are advertised by the service provider while the requirements define under which circumstances a user is willing to share a given attribute.

Standard XACML-2.0 does not provide proper means to represent this data flow. WS-XACML (cf. Section 5.5.3), however, does so by introducing the XACML-AssertionAbstractType and two derived objects, a XACMLAuthZAssertion and a XACMLPrivacyAssertion.

12.4.4. Administration

The resulting framework is apparently very complex but complexity is never helpful when building and administering complex systems. While not attestable through original research, experience in the field of computer security shows that especially security components benefit from simple user interfaces. Thus, the main goal of the administration component for SEC is its ease-of-use.

All those thoughts combined have led to development of a specialized GUI to administer the Access-eGov SEC component. This administration tool was designed from scratch, employing a strong user interface design background. All relevant standards have been adhered to, and the Java-based implementation of Security Information Administration Tool (SIAT) produced an impressive tool to simulate and manage the network of XACML components, their interrelations, and relevant attributes, as can be seen in Figure 12.5.

12.5. Implementation

Both, SEC and SIAT have been implemented in a prototypical fashion. Problematic in their implementation phase was that despite originally postulated in user requirements, no use case for SEC and SIAT could be found in Access-eGov, mostly due to lack of unified legislature. A prototype, however, has been implemented and successfully tested.

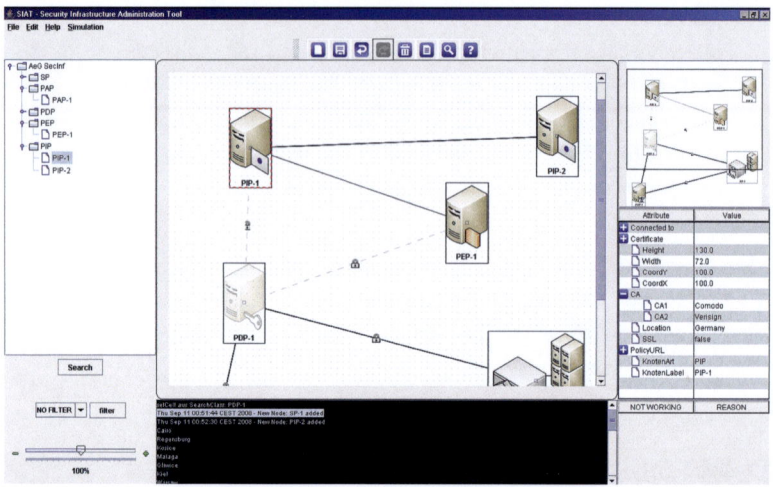

Figure 12.5.: Screenshot of SIAT in Action

12.5.1. Modified Data Flow

At the very heart of SEC is the simple notion that no context handler is needed in SEC to contact the PDP in order to retrieve an access control decision. The return value of these access control decisions rather can be viewed as access tokens that can be verified by downstream components. Figure 12.6 presents a conceptual overview over the final implementation of SEC. The necessary steps for an access control decision are described in the next paragraphs.

(0) Access Request

A user wants to execute a web service[7].

(1) A **XACMLPolicyQuery** trying to retrieve the policy related to the resource (the web service in this case) is issued.

(2) The PAP retrieves the policy matching the requested resource. If no direct match is produced, the PAP uses standard XACML algorithms to combine policies. Sometimes a default policy for undefined results is a good choice

---

[7]Authentication and attribute storage in users' profiles are not part of SEC. There are, however, multiple possibilities offering such functionalities, like X.509 attribute certificates [FH02] or components like REPO in the GENSOA. Due to the generic nature of REPO, it is also feasible to combine those approaches and store X.509 certificates therein.

while in other implementations a NULL reference to a policy object should be returned instead, leaving the PDP in total control of the situation.

(3) The access requester evaluates the **XACMLPolicyStatement** returned by (2) in order to arrive at a set of attributes mandatory for authorization and queries the PIP(s) via a **SAMLAttributeQuery**.

(4) PIP creates a **SAMLAttributeStatement** by querying all its data sources for the requested attributes.

(5,6) The PDP selector is called. It constitutes a component that has a reference to all partaking PDPs and picks a suitable one as has been explained in Section 12.4.3.

(7) Access requester posts a **XACMLAuthZDecisionQuery** to a PDP.

(8-12) In order for the PDP to evaluate the access request, the PAP is queried again to retrieve the policy in use for the requested resource, while the PIP is queried for the required user attributes. This step has further room for improvement as asking for the policy twice is not effective and even not necessary at all. Additionally, the PEP gets access to the policies which is not allowable in all circumstances. Ultimately, a **XACMLAuthZDecisionStatement**, conveying the access decision, is returned.

(13a,b) The returned **XACMLAuthZDecisionStatement** is used as access token to the downstream services. A technically appealing solution to this task is to slipstream the token into the SOAP header where it directly fits into the WS-Security (cf. Section 5.5.1) model.

(14) The resource finally can be used if the access control check was positive.

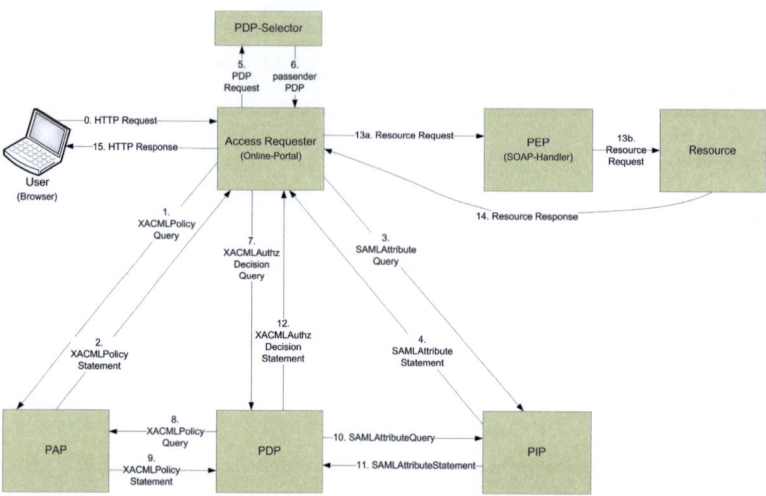

Figure 12.6.: Conceptual overview of the SEC [Fri08]

12.5.2. Integration of Semantic Authorization in the GENSOA

A number of possibilities for integrating SEC into the GENSOA employing semantics exist and are described in the following paragraphs, elaborating on the previously introduced marriage scenario. The LoveBoatService in this case is a fictitious skipper offering transportation services to newly-wed couples.

A semantic annotation could look like Listing 12.1.

```
 1 webService LoveBoatService
 2 [...]
 3 interface LoveBoatServiceInterface
 4 choreography LoveBoatServiceChoreography
 5    sharedVariables { ?input, ?output}
 6    transitionRules
 7    perform receive ?input memberOf LoveBoatServiceInput.
 8       nfp
 9       aeg#endpointGrounding hasValue
10          _grounding("http://localhost:9998/alb/LoveBoatService?wsdl")
11       sawsdl#loweringSchemaMapping hasValue
12          _iri("http://localhost:8080/LoveBoatService_Lowering.xslt")
13       sawsdl#liftingSchemaMapping hasValue
14          _iri("http://localhost:8080/LoveBoatService__Lifting.xslt")
15       endnfp
16    perform send ?output memberOf LoveBoatServiceOutput.
17       nfp
18       endnfp
```

Listing 12.1: WSML code of an example web service

This listing contains two groups of information. Firstly, variables are described as being shared during execution. They are named `?input` and `?output`[8]. Additionally, the choreography of the service is described.

A `perform receive` instructs the platform to accept an instance of the concept `LoveBoatServiceInput` as an input to the service. It also exports the callable URI of the web service and the lifting and lowering schemes of SAWSDL origin (cf. Section 8.1.3).

The `perform send` portion binds the variable `?output` to an instance of the concept `LoveBoatServiceOutput`.

12.5.2.1. Static Service Authorization

The most basic form of semantic integration is contributed by the so-called static service authorization. Semantic annotations are added only for a single service exporting the authorization functionality. Since there is no direct route between services and all exchanged data has to be passed through the platform, an additional variable has also got to be added to carry the authorization token obtained from the authorization web service. The following sequence of events is carried out in order to realize the described functionality:

- Lowering (Authorization)
  An instance of LoveBoatInput is created and bound to the variable `?input`. From this point on this instance variable is the representation of the semantic content. The web service side does not know how to handle semantic objects and therefore has got to be called with non-semantic data. In order to link the semantic instance to a data structure that can be used to call a web service, lowering transactions have to be carried out using XSLT transformations.

- Lifting (Authorization)
  Once the authorization web service is executed with the lowered data, an access control decision will be computed. This, again non-semantic, data structure is converted to an instance of LoveBoatOutput by means of another XSLT transformation.

- Lowering (Requesting Service)
  The previous step produced an access token (usually a SAML token) which is injected into the SOAP header. Standard web service security mechanisms apply now.

---

[8]WSMO variables are denoted through a prefixed "?".

- Lifting (Requesting Service)
  Another invocation of XSLT extracts the web service output and stores the result in an instance variable of the requested type.

12.5.2.2. Full Semantic Authorization through Usage of a Subgoal

The previously introduced approach is not flexible enough for the GENSOA, however. In an ideal world, the exact location and call semantics of the authorization web service have to be retrieved by the platform itself.

Standard process modeling features can be used for exactly this goal. At first, a new *Capability* is introduced that can aptly be named "Authorization". Once services are registered that implement the capability "Authorization", the GENSOA retrieval process is able to find suitable services for the callers' authorization needs.

Adding authorization is simplified to add another *perform achieveGoal*[9]. Listing 12.2 illustrates the simplicity of this approach.

```
1 perform achieveGoal AegAuthZ
2 nfp
3    dc#title hasValue ("en_EN#Authorization Goal")
4 endnfp
5 usesMediator ppMediator
6       dataFlow
7       ?authToken <= ?AegAuthNOutput
```

Listing 12.2: Modeling authorization as a subgoal

12.5.2.3. Full Semantic Authorization Through Usage of a Goal

Instead of working on the level of subgoals, entities on higher levels of aggregation can also be annotated with a request for the "Authorization" capability.

The general principle is the same as previously explained. Implementation, however, is more complex. Gathered security tokens have to be injected in the corresponding handler chains, each needing one shared variable. Nonetheless, this solution can readily be implemented in the GENSOA.

---

[9]This terminology has been taken over from Access-eGov's process model. If different process models are used, the names and semantics of the annotations may be different, not the general approach, though.

12.5.2.4. Full Semantic Authorization Through Semantic Modeling of the XACML Architecture

Not using any composite web service at all for offering security-related functionality is the last presented approach. Instead, XACML and its standard process are broken up into specific components (cf. Section 5.5.2) which are all implemented as their own web service.

Goals, sub-goals or even life events can now be modeled to provide a capability that might be called "XACML", acting as a frontend to a XACML chain of component calls. If the process modeler for some reason cannot choose this approach, it is also easy to add a `perform achieveGoal` for each of the components and pass the results on through using shared variables. Despite its complexity, the approach has indisputable advantages:

- Redundancy and Load Balancing
  Redundancy is built in. The more components capable of providing XACML component functionalities exist, the more redundant nodes are in the system. These redundant components can also be used to offer load-balancing capabilities.

- Choice and Privacy
  Interconnections between services and the platform are standardized; extra flexibility caused by the platform resolving the services at runtime, in connection with standardization, opens up the possibility that many service providers can easily join[10] a system or a federation of systems without having to reconfigure their software.

  Privacy also profits as this approach supports the above mentioned privacy-aware security concepts out-of-the-box.

---

[10]At least technically. Organizational issues may still evolve and are not part of this work.

Part IV.

Application Cases

Finding a testbed for research efforts usually is a daunting task involving extensive paper trails, applications, hearings, and other assorted bureaucratic tasks if the testbed needs to be financed by a third party. European Union research framework programmes are no exception. Compared to the benefits, however, these initial bureaucratic hurdles are minimal as an EU financed research project has a number of advantages:

- Wide range of research topics
  As long as the project proposal is kept inline with research topics currently of interest to the EU, creating a sound proposal within these topics can be done without much limitations.

- Project Plan
  A project plan consisting of workpackages, tasks and milestones is a good tool to monitor feedback of own research efforts in any case and is not just to be implemented because it is mandatory.

- Platforms
  European platforms for sharing research results and for networking between researchers exist and are actively promoted by the EU.

- Financing
  Once approved, the financing is only tied to the project plan, not to any research outcome or even worse: to company interests.

Both EU projects referenced in this thesis, Access-eGov and SPIKE, are introduced in the following sections.

13. Access-eGov

Access-eGov was the first of two projects and contributed valuable feedback into the design of the GENSOA. Under the coordination of the Technical University of Kosice[1], eleven partners in five countries established this project with the title "Access to e-Government services Employing Semantic Technologies" (Access-eGov)[2].

13.1. Project Overview

The main goal of Access-eGov is to simplify access to public administration services for every citizen by supporting extended interoperability between both, electronic services, and services without any ICT interaction[3]. Although more had been planned, Access-eGov could only use one real-world electronic service[4] and one artificially constructed security service in the end. Nonetheless, the final prototype incorporated hundreds of service definitions for each of its main use cases.

In the 38 months between January 2006 and February 2009, the project partners were able to meet their initial project goals by achieving the following scientific and technological objectives as laid out in the proposal:

- Identification of services
  Live events are the core description of a process in Access-eGov. Life events just contain a set of goals and sub-goals that have to be fulfilled in order to (successfully) finish the process in question. The term life event is widely used within the e-Government communities and therefore was chosen to not alienate users with a different terminology than the one they are used to.

- Scenario creation
  Starting from identified services, the Access-eGov platform arranges them in a meaningful sequence and executes them in the correct order to fulfill the life

---

[1]http://tuke.sk
[2]http://www.access-egov.org
[3]"Traditional Services" in Access-eGov terminology.
[4]Slovakian land use planning service.

events. The user can control the current state of service execution in every phase.

- e-Inclusion
Disadvantaged users can particularly benefit from a system like Access-eGov. It is therefore vital that special care is taken to ensure that the EU e-Inclusion criteria[5] are closely followed.

In addition to these general objectives, a number of purely technical objectives have been derived from the above set, containing the following items:

- Reference ontologies and their management

- Semantic markup components

- Semantic infrastructure including reasoning, choreography, and orchestration

The phases of the project are detailed in the following sections.

13.2. Requirements Engineering Approach in Access-eGov

Just like any other software project, Access-eGov started life in the requirements engineering phase. It did not, however, follow a strict and process-oriented approach during the requirements engineering phase. Instead, the lead contractors of the user requirements' deliverable carefully chose different instruments to gather the following set of requirements:

13.2.1. Pilot Projects

Three pilot projects were agreed upon in the initial project phase, each of them carried out under the responsibility of a specific group of user partners and all of the development partners. A first step in describing each one of them was the creation of activity scenarios by the user partners under careful guidance of the German University of Cairo. Each of the pilots produced an activity scenario. An additional activity scenario, describing the process of annotating a web site, has been created by one of the user partners but is a basic feature needed for all pilot projects.

---

[5]http://ec.europa.eu/information_society/activities/einclusion/index_en.htm.

Obtaining a building permission

Kosice Self Governing Region and the city of Michalovce[6] described a scenario to help citizens build a new family home. Prior to Access-eGov, this task was lengthy and not straight forward, spanning a number of governmental bodies in a very complex and error-prone process. Post-Access-eGov, the user is guided by his very own personal assistant, an agent system that is able to tailor a workflow especially to his current and individual needs. Public administration officials' wish list included the following ICT technologies: electronic correspondence, online forms provisioning, online tracking of the process' progress, online (and therefore correct and up-to-date) information on the pricing and a list of all involved institutions [KUW06].

Establishing an enterprise

In Poland, the local government of Gliwice envisioned a scenario guiding the user through the necessary steps to register an enterprise. Four processes are customized and combined to an executable, meaningful workflow by the Access-eGov system:

- Registration in the city hall

- Registration in the statistical office

- Registration in the tax office

- Registration at the social insurance agency

While legacy systems exist for parts of the process, it is up to Access-eGov to unite them all under a single user interface, giving the user the impression that he never has left the Access-eGov platform.

Obtaining information about marriages

The biggest trial in terms of resources spent took place at the Schleswig-Holstein Ministry of Finance. The first instance of this scenario foresaw a generic responsibility finder, an idea which was taken up by the Access-eGov consortium and refined to support only one life event, "marriage", which is complex enough in German law to act as theoretical basis for a full-featured prototype. Supporting a user by presenting him with all information needed on the process of getting married and on the actors involved is this scenario's main goal. The Access-eGov platform acts as

---

[6]A neighboring district of Kosice.

an integrating force in this context as it combines process information from different sources to a new, executable process.

These three scenarios are all described from an information consumer perspective in [KDM$^+$06]. While being concerned with three independent application cases, some features of the platform are universally important in Access-eGov as all of the three trials build on them:

- The system should be able to ask the user meaningful questions in a meaningful context and a reasonable sequence.

- A list of questions has to be generated at runtime from semantic annotations and semantic processing.

- The accompanying user interface has to be able to provide an end-user with a uniform user interface acting as a frontend to all combined services. Additionally, it must have the capability to visualize the current state of the process.

One last scenario was created from the point of view of an information provider:

Web Site Annotation

This scenario mainly describes tools required for semantically annotating existing resources according to the rules governed by the Access-eGov resource ontologies [KUF$^+$07]. The tasks of "Complete annotation of the existing communal website", "Creation and annotation of a single new web page", and "Annotation of a new element on an existing page" have been identified as being representative in the Access-eGov setting.

13.2.2. Questionaire

Another important tool for requirements gathering was a specially crafted questionnaire. The German university of Cairo prepared a list of visions for future e-Government applications which the user partners had to label according to their perceived importance of the presented issues. These visions ranged from the overall Access-eGov vision of implementing a system that can be used to lookup information on marriages to rather specialized visions involving full-featured, semantic web-enabled web sites at user partners' premises.

The results of these questionnaires unearthed a number of cultural differences between Eastern European partners on one side and German partakers on the other.

Germans, for example, were more concerned with the privacy of their data than any of the other partners in the project. They also want to keep a firm control over the process: While Slovaks and Poles want the personal assistant to make appointments with public administration officials, Germans dislike the idea and rather plan their appointments on their own.

13.2.3. Interview

A number of interviews with user partners and developers have been conducted in the first five project months (January to May 2006). Interviewer and interviewee elaborated on a set of topics in the form of guided interviews. Among the discussed aspects were organizational and technical aspects of the Access-eGov vision, the problems Access-eGov tries to solve, and the solutions Access-eGov offers.

13.2.4. Round Tables and Workshops

Round tables were used in several stages of the requirements gathering phase, mainly as internal tool for partaking partners to agree on their requirements, to exchange their ideas, and reach consensus on the scope of their projects. A workshop involving all the partners was used to discuss results of the requirements gathering among user partners and developers.

13.2.5. State-of-the-art Report

In contrast to above mentioned instruments that require involvement of users and/or developers, an extensive state-of-the-art report [KDM$^+$06], surveying e-Government projects in 14 countries was carried out. The authors of this report, in order to aid in comparing different e-Government projects in different countries, established the following set of criteria:

- Accessibility

- Multi channel support

- AAI support

- Search facilities

- Interoperability / Openness to external partners

- Standardization / Uniqueness of the solution

- Quality of service

- User support

- Usage guides

- Web services / Usage of XML-based middleware

As a side note, lining up different European countries alongside these criteria reveals that Germany is not nearly as advanced as it wants (and claims) to be with regard to e-Government.

13.2.6. Resulting Requirements

The resulting requirements coming from this approach were the most important result of the report and consisted of a total of 42 requirements grouped into three broad categories, namely General e-Government Requirements[7], Access-eGov specific requirements, and administration's requirements. Except for a tiny fraction[8], the requirements do not add much to the content, their main use is as a good and concise summary of activities/functionalities that have to be implemented in order for the pilot application to be successful.

13.3. The Access-eGov Architecture

To effectively introduce the Access-eGov architecture, only the most important views are presented in the following paragraphs before aligning this design with the GENSOA. Figure 13.1 shows the main physical architecture of the Access-eGov system broken down into components.

13.3.1. WS connection (WSC)

Designed with a clear separation of frontend and backend functionality in mind, the resulting architecture is to a certain extent independent from the user interface[9]. The WSC component is the interface to the outside world and – as currently implemented – exports interfaces in two categories.

---

[7]These requirements were structured according to the criteria elaborated in [KUW06].

[8]E.g. many accessibility requirements did not originate at the user partners but rather in a consulting process through partner E-ISOTIS who is a distinguished accessibility experts.

[9]The resulting prototype still has got too much functionality in the frontend components. The WSC interface only caters for a minimal subset of all possibilities the architecture is offering.

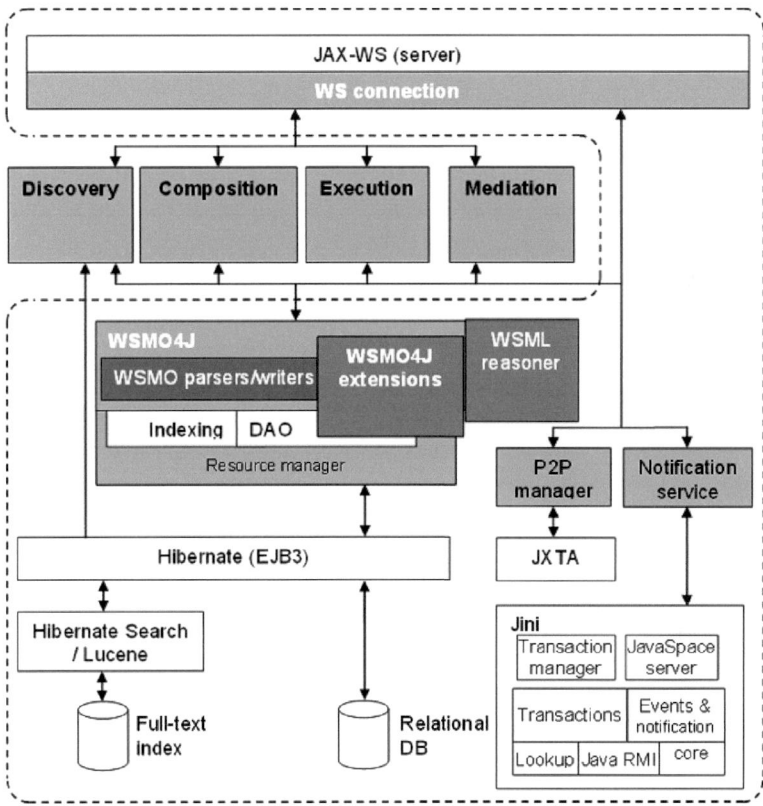

Figure 13.1.: Access-eGov Physical Architecture as proposed in developers' documentation

Interfacing to the repository:

- Locating any ontology element (usually used for goals and services)

- Saving and updating ontology elements

- Removing ontology elements

- Listing all services in the repository

- Listing all goals in the repository

Interfacing to the **Resolver** is less complex as only one method has to be exported through the WSC. It resolves a LifeEvent into goals, subgoals, and services.

Input to the WSC currently has to be given in XML-serialized Web Service Modeling Language (WSML).

13.3.2. Discovery

One of the biggest and most important modules is the discovery module. It is split up in the following set of components.

Matching Component

Matches goals and capabilities (cf. Section 8.1.1) according to either a simple or a rich semantic evaluation. After processing, this component returns a WebService that matches a given goal and optionally constraining NFPs.

Filtering Component

In addition to matching done by the previous component, a filtering facility for a given list of already matched services is realized in this component.

Full-text Search

Even with fully functional semantic matching in place, the conducted trials showed that many users expect some sort of full-text search. It appears as if a majority of users currently is accustomed to search engines and textual retrieval to an extent that makes a complete abandonment of such a feature unrealistic.

Reasoning Component

Usage of reasoning is limited to few simple cases in this prototype, simply for the reason that requirements did not ask for more complicated reasoning scenarios.

Mediation Component

Mediating between data or knowledge present in different ontologies is the task of this component. It is only used for reasons inherent in the underlying WSMO framework and not visible to any user (not even knowledge engineers).

13.3.3. Composition

The composition module aims at providing dynamic service composition. Fully automated service composition as envisioned in Section 8.1.2 is not implemented in the prototype. Instead, an indirection involving generic scenarios[10] is implemented. The main exported function is resolving a goal into an executable workflow. In order to achieve this, any sub-goals have to be recursively resolved. If, for a given service, the pre-conditions are not met, they have to be decomposed and turned into a new and additional set of sub-goals recursively.

The Composition module consists of a Resolving and a Chaining component. It has strong ties to the mediation component. Figure 13.2 shows the interactions of Resolver, Chaining and Discovery, once a composition event is started.

13.3.4. Execution

Execution is split into two components with largely unrelated functionalities:

Goal and scenario Execution component

This component either directly (through the use of the Web Service Invocation component) contacts a web service or first uses Discovery to resolve the scenario or the goals to atomic services which in turn are passed to Web Service Invocation for execution.

In the requirement section it was already explained that Access-eGov puts a strong focus on so-called traditional services which are not electronically accessible, a fact

---

[10]A knowledge engineer manually creates a workflow with generic goals which are later resolvable to an executable workflow if enough registered services exist.

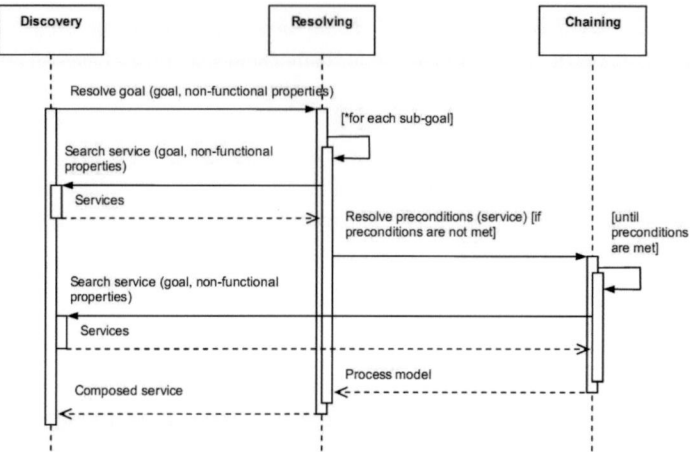

Figure 13.2.: Composition in Access-eGov (taken from internal developers' documentation)

with obvious consequences on the Execution component: Rather than only forwarding service after service to the invocation component, Execution keeps track of the invoked processes and supplies active tracking of their execution through the use of a timer and a periodical check of service results.

Web Service Invoker component

The Web Service Invoker component is the low-level thread that communicates with the resolved atomic web services and imports their results back into the system. In this context, lifting and lowering as explained in Section 9.2.3 are used to bridge the gap between non-semantic and semantically enabled web services.

13.3.5. WSMO4J and Extensions

WSMO4J[11] is an implementation of WSML in Java. Due to the differing process model (cf. Section 8.2), the original WSMO4J distribution could not be used directly. Instead it had to be modified to accomodate the new process model. Another reason for own extensions and some simplifications was very poor performance in

---

[11]http://wsmo4j.sourceforge.net

the initially used distribution, mainly caused by excessive inheritance relationships due to a very clean and structured design which, however, proved not to be effective enough in real-world settings that use ORM facilities.

13.3.6. WSML Reasoner

The only functionality implemented in this prototypical reasoning component is the evaluation of grounded logical expressions. Reasoning requirements of the security subsystem can be fulfilled by external reasoners since a number of already implemented, pluggable alternatives already exist.

13.3.7. Resource Manager

The very central Resource Manager provides repository functionalities.

DAO

DAO[12] acts as a central point of contact to the different types of repositories. After getting a reference to the corresponding repository, the caller can store any data in an effective and well-performing way, without needing to know details about the underlying storage engines.

Indexing

Since full-text indexing ended up as a requirement, one of the better points in the system for hooking up the indexer is found inside the repositories where indexer callback functions are registered to fire on CRUD operations. Thus, in addition to handling those CRUD calls, the index automatically gets updated and later can be used for effective full-text information retrieval.

13.3.8. Notification Service

Passing messages between all components internally and between the platform and external services is the main task of this component. It is not just blindly forwarding messages to components, however. It implements a message queue, catering for the likely events that senders or receivers are unavailable for a certain period of time.

---

[12]The Access-eGov DAO is not linked to Microsoft's Data Access Objects even if the acronym translates to the same name. Both share the general goal of being abstractions of database access.

13.3.8.1. P2P Manager

The P2P manager was expected to keep track of different Access-eGov platform nodes communicating in a peer-to-peer network. For project internal reasons, this mode of operations has not been implemented in the project's lifespan, even if it would have been a very interesting addition. P2P technologies and their potential to share large sets of data have already been discussed in Section 3.3.8.

13.4. Security in Access-eGov

Security issues in Access-eGov were initially given elevated priority. In the progress of the project it turned out that an extensive and innovative security solution is not required by any of the pilot projects and also not required by any of the user partners. As a result, Access-eGov acquired two different security systems with extremely different requirements and implementations.

13.4.1. Initial Approach

Access-eGov's initial plans for the security subsystem were promising as security had its own objective in the original project proposal:

> "A distributed security infrastructure providing multiple security services for authenticating users and protection of data and enabling easy administration of complex security policies."

Requirements engineering saw many security requirements surface. Table 13.1 extracts all security-related requirements from the relevant document [KUW06] and also lists their initial priorization.

Req. Nr.	Security Requirement	Priority[13]
1.4.1	Security subsystems shall be usable without additional modules so that it is also usable in public terminal settings	D
1.4.2	Secure authentication & authorization is based on qualified electronic signature	E
2.7.1	Support for user profiles that can be created by end users	E

---

[13]E - essential, D - desirable, O - optional

2.7.2	Secure information exchange	E
2.7.3	Privacy compliance according to certain laws	E
3.4.1	Digital Rights Management (DRM) for annotated content[14]	O

Table 13.1.: Access-eGov Security Requirements

Over the course of the first few project months, however, it turned out that the only requirement left to implement was user profile support. User partners did not require any of the proposed advanced functionalities after finalizing their respective pilot projects.

Thus, two security systems resulted, "practical security", and "extended security". The extended security subsystem of Access-eGov is the prototype of what was described in Section 13.4. SEC in the GENSOA is able to fulfill all of the requirements in Table 13.1, and many more.

What was finally implemented as part of the overall platform prototype was a user profile system with few added functionalities making it fit in a SSOA. Of note are necessary hooks for integrating it into SEC where it can serve as a provider of user attributes and the possibility to have arbitrary numbers of attributes in each user profile.

Users, however, only see a well-known user profile pattern with the following standard functionalities:

- Register Account
  By providing a minimal set of personal data, the user creates a profile with an account name and password, both of which he picked himself.

- Change password
  Users can later change their password.

- Password recovery
  In the event of a forgotten password, a function exists to set a new random password and mail it to the account's email address.

- Add attributes
  The user can gradually convey more information on him.

---

[14]Mainly a demand of consultants external to a specific user partner. Spending resources on a semantically accessible system was out of question for them as long as the annotated data could later be reused by other, not directly involved, parties.

227

- Delete attributes

  The user is also free to delete any attribute at any time, even if it has implications on the services he wants to use.

- Delete account

  Access-eGov had some very privacy-aware user partners. Therefore the project guarantees that all data associated with user accounts are deleted once the particular user account is deleted. No restrictions at all exist as to when an account may be deleted.

14. SPIKE

Key project partners of the Access-eGov consortium rejoined to take SSOAs one step further. A new EU research framework programme project, dubbed a Secure Process-oriented Integrative Service Infrastructure for Networked Enterprises (SPIKE), was commenced at the start of 2008 and features numerous improvements of both the design and the scope of the SSOA that is the heart of the system. Key design decisions, most prominently the central message passing bus, can be found in the GENSOA as well.

14.1. Project Overview

Lead by the University of Regensburg, SPIKE in addition to the core research team of Access-eGov[1] links in another university[2] and several interesting user partners.

The settings in which SPIKE operates are quite different from Access-eGov's e-Government centric world. Here, the focus is on short-term business alliances, a subtopic of the more broadly defined business alliance theme which the EU Commission explicitly advocates in order to boost EU-wide fitness for the "digital economy" with a strong focus on Small to medium-sized Enterprise (SME)s. And indeed, systems allowing technologically guided assembling and operating of alliances can offer benefits to SMEs. A group of specialized SMEs can undoubtedly compete with much larger corporations if, and only if, they manage to build a working alliance in a very short timeframe, enabling them to act as one single consortium.

To fully understand the impact of SPIKE, a look at its objectives is helpful. Organizational objectives as laid out in the technical annex to the project grant agreement include:

- Outsourcing and offering of parts of the value chain to business alliance partners.

- Simplified collaboration supported through technology.

---

[1] The University of Regensburg, Technical University of Kosice, and Intersoft, also from Kosice.
[2] University of Malaga in Spain.

- Interoperability and integration in heterogeneous environments.

- Generic solutions to interoperability and integration between organizations in the form of reference processes.

Even more important in research projects, SPIKE also aims at achieving the following Science and Technology[3] objectives:

- Inclusion of a Semantic Service Bus (SSB) as extension of the SSOA concept which has the ability to not only use KBTs for message routing but to semantically transform the messages themselves.

- BPM extended to use KBTs.

- Extended security subsystem with functionalities to filter messages at the service bus level, a complete attribute management, authentication and authorization, and auditing.

- High performance storage for semantically enriched objects.

- Integration of portal technology as frontend of choice.

14.2. Requirements Engineering in SPIKE

Requirements of SPIKE are described by means of market research and the following three application cases.

Intra and interorganisational Offering of Technical Documentation Services

One of the project partners, a technical documentation company, contributes this use case which is concerned with creation of technical documentation, requiring close collaboration of a multitude of different stakeholders. They range from sales and procurement departments to engineering and operations of a specific technological product. In the course of this use case, a software pilot will be staged that has the following functionalities:

- Setup of a business alliance which is accessible through a portal-based frontend.

---

[3]Science and Technology (S&T) in the context of project proposals is a term coined by the European Commission. Its meaning is almost identical to Research and Development (R&D) albeit with a focus that is more on the research side where R&D shares its focus between Research and Development.

- Identity Management in a virtual alliance.

- Support of the documentation process, initially intra-organizational, then extended to the inter-organizational case.

An already established communication process within this particular user partner is still lacking technological support beyond the already existent Content Management Systems (CMS). An advanced project management tool is required in order to meet the required functionality. The main advantages expected from implementation of a SPIKE-based system are increased business opportunities for SMEs[4], optimized cost-efficiency, and improved time to market.

Business Alliances and Identity Management

Another user partner contributes a case which is rooted in the design and manufacturing of semiconductors where joining alliances is vital under certain circumstances. To simulate such an alliance, the user partner together with its technology partner (also in the SPIKE consortium) provide access to a legacy application[5] to arbitrary external users.

Integrating legacy applications into the newly created workflows also is technically ambitious and presents its own challenges. Even more so if the application in question does not communicate to outside entities via standardized and text-based interfaces[6] but requires the usage of a GUI that adheres to non-text-based standards like X11.

Identity Federations

In addition to already mentioned functionalities, it is necessary to not only model and implement the root process of sharing that application but also to provide end users as well as administrators with a federated identity management system.

14.2.1. Use Cases

Use cases describe the previously mentioned application cases in great detail. In contrast to the requirements process in Access-eGov, SPIKE's requirements engi-

---

[4]That particular user partner shares the assessment of the EU with regard to digital economies and SMEs to full extent.

[5]The application in question is a web based customs information system which is deployed at the technology partners' premises.

[6]In such situations, the full potential of XML as a data transfer language can be seen. While it creates lots of processing overhead, interfacing XML sources and sinks to any other software system is trivial.

neering team used a more formal approach by using a template use case description form as shown in Figure 14.1.

USE CASE#	<the name as a short active verb phrase>	
Context of Use	<a longer statement of the context is needed>	
Scope	<what is the scope of this use case>	
Level	<one of summary, primary task, sub-function>	
Primary Actor	<a role name for the primary actor, or a description>	
User group and Interest	**User group**	**Interest**
	<name of the user group>	<put here the interests of the user group>
	<name of the user group>	<put here the interests of the user group>
Preconditions	<what we expect as being the state of the world already>	
Description	**Step**	Action
	1	<put here the steps of the scenario from trigger to goal delivery
	2	<...>
	3	
	1	<list of variations>

Figure 14.1.: Use Case Template (SPIKE Requirements Engineering Process)

14.2.2. Questionaires

As an additional source of requirements, a carefully selected[7] group of IT companies was asked to provide answers to a questionnaire involving a set of questions in the following topics:

- Requested functionality of the SPIKE portal system

- Usage of collaboration software, participation in collaboration projects

- Security

- Relevance of SOA and Business Process Modelling

- Voluntary company details

14.2.3. Interviews

While being very informative, certain aspects in several questionnaires remained inadequately answered. Therefore, the same user partner identified a subset of participants of the questionnaire and interviewed them.

The outcome of these interviews serve as further inputs to SPIKE's implementations.

14.2.4. Round Tables and Workshops

This instrument has been extensively used in order to facilitate a shared understanding of the problem domains of the application cases. A hierarchical layout of the participants of these workshops helped gradually elicit requirements and find a common approach. A final roundtable was subsequently used to assemble the final set of requirements, taking into account aforementioned strategies as well as input from current research and related projects.

14.2.5. Resulting requirements

Classification of the resulting requirements is essential in any project. SPIKE's documentation used the well-known distinction between functional and non-functional requirements and named 35 functional and 24 non-functional requirements [AFG+08].

---

[7]One of the partners' main area of expertise is the promotion and advancement of regional IT activities. Thus, the partner has lots of valuable links to different IT companies.

14.3. The SPIKE Architecture

SPIKE used the ISO/OSI standard 1471 (cf. Section 4.4.2) to describe the architecture in the typical semi-standardized form. The most important findings of the architecture design phase are described in the following, while the detailed specification is available in a project report [ABF⁺08]. The whole specification document revolves around the initially defined set of key functionalities[8] needed in order to build a successful SPIKE prototype:

- Workflow definition, execution and control

- Incorporation of external services as workflow elements

- Security concepts

- Portal-based GUI

- Portal-based administration GUI

- Supportive semantic technologies

- ESB-like component amended with KBTs

- Identity federations

14.3.1. Physical Architecture

SPIKE is a considerably more complex project than Access-eGov, which is directly represented in its architecture. The SPIKE GUI is an integral part of the whole architecture as a so called SPIKE Portal Instance (SPI) and an equal one of four main components. Additionally, a SPIKE System Core (SSC) subsumes all core functionality of a SSOA while the SPIKE Service Bus (SSB) is a central component that intelligently forwards and transforms messages. Housekeeping activities are handled by the SPIKE Administration, Monitoring & Reporting (SAMR) component. Figure 14.2 illustrates the relationship of these four components.

These central modules are further described in the following paragraphs.

---

[8]Comparing this list with the requirements yields a first indicator of the quality of the architecture since all requirements present in [AFG⁺08] are present in the architecture design document as well.

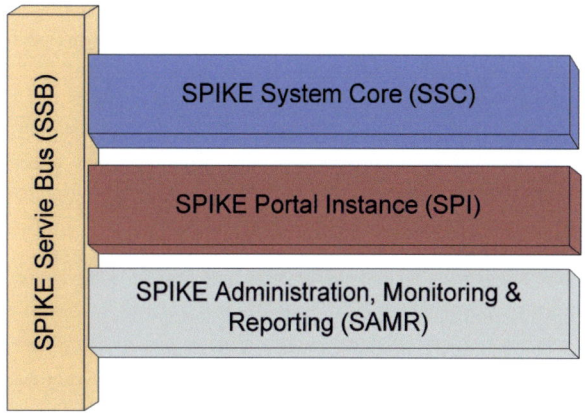

Figure 14.2.: Main SPIKE Building Blocks and their Relationship [ABF+08]

14.3.1.1. SPIKE System Core

An SSC consists of eight modules, in SPIKE terminology called managers:

- Content Manager
  Basic storage component of SPIKE. Storing any data element is done through passing it to this component. Also offers high performance retrieval of data for the Search Manager.

- Security Manager
  Central point of contact for security functionalities (including but not limited to authorization and authentication of content).

- Semantic Manager
  Provides stand-alone semantic functionalities (Reasoning, Mediation, Matching in conjunction with the Search Manager) which work like the corresponding components in Access-eGov (cf. Section 13.3).

- Process Manager
  Main component for all workflow-related functionality. Enables the platform to directly execute standardized workflows[9].

---

[9]A very probable candidate for this standardized formalization is BPEL (cf. Section 4.2.2).

- Search Manager
  Allows searching the SPIKE information stores by different means ranging from full-text querying and metadata-based search to complete semantic matching.

- Service Manager
  Service discovery and execution are handled by the Service Manager.

- Notification Manager
  Global and service- or user-specific alerts and notifications are broadcast or transmitted to a specific receiver. In addition, this component provides functionality to set triggers. Triggers make sure that new messages are generated after specific events have happened. This way, also timers can be set as special form of events.

- Identity Manager
  Federated identity management is important as SPIKE will not be run inside one company but between many different actors taking part in an alliance. Facilitating this and easing the pain of administration of such systems is the goal of this component.

14.3.1.2. SPIKE Service Bus

An ESB in general can be pictured as a very intelligent switch in a network. After inspecting each message, it decides whether it will be forwarded at all and, if yes, to which recipient. Additionally, the SSB has the ability to transform messages between different applications, a task which can massively benefit from the usage of KBTs. Two components make up the SSB:

- Communication Manager
  Receives each transmitted message and inspects it according to certain predefined rules. In a semantically enabled environment the rules can be extended or altered by the KBT subsystem. Translating messages between two different applications which usually involves a mismatch of terms is accomplished here as well, either through the use of KBTs or just through a static mapping.

- Interface Manager
  Subsumes all functionality to include external services. In the case of SOAP services, this endeavor is simple. If, however, legacy applications have to be included, this task's difficulty increases. Everything, whether legacy or not,

that has no direct SOAP interface has to be connected to SPIKE[10] through wrappers.

Figure 14.3 illustrates the interdependencies of the SSB and SSC.

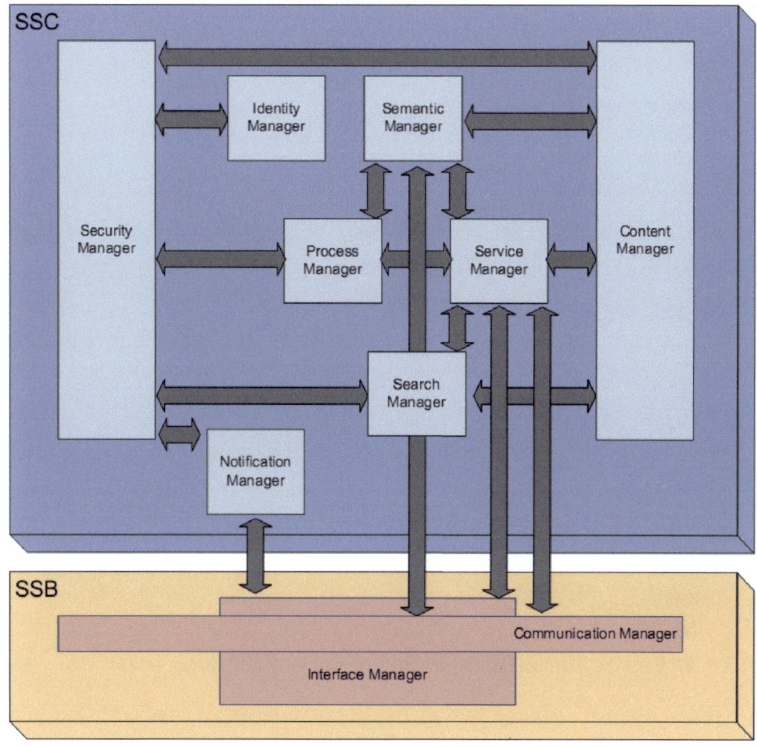

Figure 14.3.: SPIKE Service Bus and SPIKE System Core Interdependencies and Contained Modules [ABF+08]

14.3.1.3. SPIKE Portal Instance

SPIKE defines a GUI as an integral part of the system, called SPI. It supports two main tasks within SPIKE, namely acting as a GUI for web applications, and taking

---

[10] Actually this is not only a problem of SPIKE but also a problem in the generic GENSOA. Even SOAs need the wrapper concept in such situations.

care of interportlet communication. To satisfy the GUI part of the functionality, support for X11[11]- and RDP[12]-based applications is planned. Both X11, and RDP do currently not support native web-based clients at all and are binary protocols.

Extending interportlet communication, SPIKE does not only capture the users' current context within a session but brings the captured context into the perspective of the whole workflow.

The SPI is composed of the following components:

- Session Manager
  Component used to track data and context information related to user sessions.

- Intra Portlet Manager
  Communication among and between portlets and the notification subsystem are handled by this component.

- Display Manager
  Component to render the current session which usually amounts to providing a GUI representation of a specific application in turn represented by a portlet.

- Wrapper Manager
  External applications are included through the Wrapper Manager. It is realized through adapter patterns. Adapters are application-specific and therefore have to be rewritten and rebuilt for every new external application.

The internal structure of the SPI is shown in Figure 14.4 together with important links to other components.

14.3.1.4. SPIKE Administration, Monitoring & Reporting

The last subsystem of the SPIKE architecture takes care of administration (managing whole alliances with the Alliance Manager, managing the execution platform with the Platform Manager) and creating all sorts of reports and statistics (the most important one being the accounting statistics using the Report Manager).

14.4. Security in SPIKE

SPIKE's security subsystem is very straightforward, yet powerful. Figure 14.5 illustrates the possible modes of operation of the SPIKE Authorization and Authentica-

---

[11]X11 is a Client / Server graphical user interface framework commonly used in Unix systems.

[12]The Remote Desktop Protocol is the Microsoft Windows way of displaying graphical applications' outputs on remote computers.

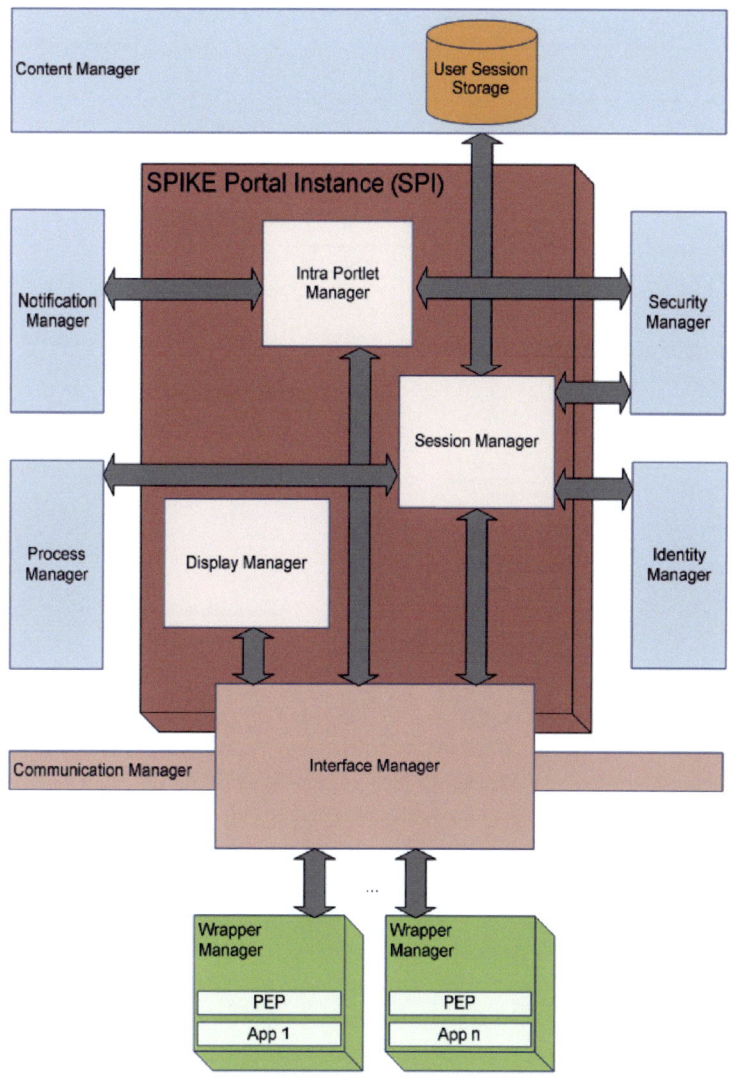

Figure 14.4.: Internal Structure of the SPI with some Important Links to other Components [ABF+08]

tion Infrastructure (AAI). The two cases that need to be discerned are companies

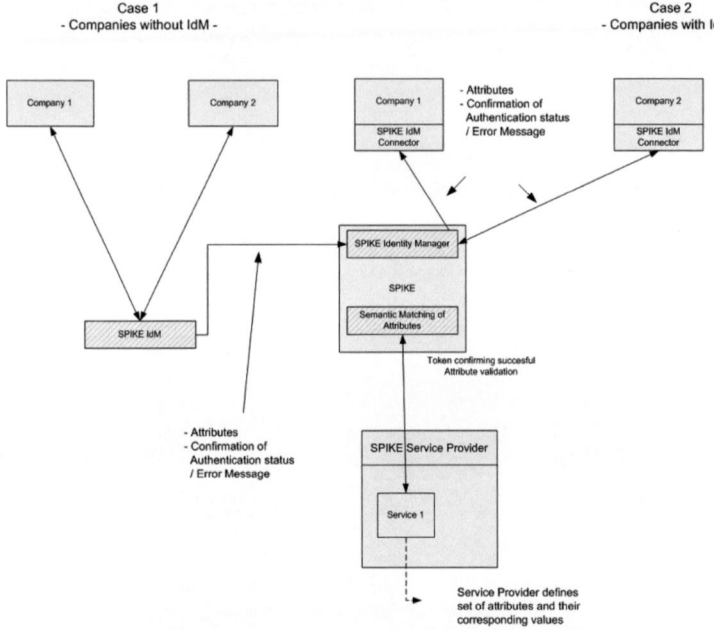

Figure 14.5.: SPIKE Authorization and Authentication Infrastructure (taken from internal developers' documentation)

that have implemented their own Identity Management (IdM) and companies that did not. The core process of the whole security subsystem is the interaction between the subsystem and service providers who define attributes and values of those attributes that need to be matched by the client.

Attributes are input into the system either by SPIKE's own IdM, forming the basic case. No attribute conversion or semantic matching of attributes is needed in this constellation as all attributes and their respective range of values are known to the subsystem. Considering the case of companies with their own IdM systems, however, the situation changes. Semantic matching of attributes is necessary now in most of the cases since almost all of these attributes will not be known to the SPIKE platform.

Part V.

Comparative Evaluation

15. Real-World Implementations of the GENSOA

15.1. Access-eGov System

All of the previously described components (cf. Chapter 13) have been implemented to a working state within the project duration of Access-eGov.

15.1.1. Main Implemented Components

While the main building blocks developed in Section 13.3 are clearly visible in the prototype code, implemented module boundaries do not always align with module boundaries in the architecture. In the following paragraphs, top-level modules of the implementation are introduced and described to some detail. Subversion (SVN) module names were chosen as labels.

While obvious problems exist with Source Lines of Code (SLOC) metric, it at least can give a rough estimation on the effort involved in software projects. Thus, each of the following subsections is ended with a short summary of SLOC statistics for the particular unit. Those statistics have been generated using David A. Wheeler's 'SLOCCOUNT'[1].

15.1.1.1. aeg-annotation-tool

Called the Access-eGov Annotation Tool (AT), this component is the central user interface for service providers. Specifically trained members of the service providers' institutions use it in order to modify data describing involved services. Provided are typical CRUD functionalities for services and attached concepts and instances.

If an annotation of a service contains a member of an ontology-defined type, the AT dynamically creates and displays a form that is specific to that type by looking

---
[1] http://www.dwheeler.com/sloccount/

up its representation in the ontology and transforming all of the type's properties into renderable HTML elements.

A hypothetical example: A specific service called ServiceX contains a reference to a PointOfContact, which in turn contains properties of a string type (Name, Street, City, ...). The AT, once having parsed the ServiceX specification, follows the reference to PointOfContact, reads all properties and proceeds to render a textfield for every string-typed property it parses. Direct transformation from ontology concept to rendered HTML is possible for all basic types of XML Schema. Other types require some hints as to the user interface best suitable to them.

Important for service providers providing content on web pages, the AT gained grabber functionality for web pages in the course of the pilots. Using it, administrators are able to quickly import existing metadata and content of a webpage into the AT.

Technically the AT is straight forward, especially since it is not thoroughly integrated with the rest of the platform. It even has its own user management, consisting of user accounts in one of several roles[2]. This - Java Server Faces based - component also offers the possibility to import and export the underlying ontologies from and to text files.

Comprising of 15 java and 1 jsp file, this unit counts 9505 SLOC.

15.1.1.2. aeg-client2

A so called "Personal Assistant", later in the project phase renamed to Personal Assistant Client (PAC)[3] in this svn module is the main frontend for users of this prototype. It is completely detached from the Acces-eGov core through the use of facades that encapsulate all the functionality needed in the frontend[4].

Three main groups of views in this client are implemented and all of them are using Java Server Faces (JSF) technologies:

---

[2]Roles extend from an annotator, only able to alter annotations for his own domain, to a superadmin role that can alter anything in any domain and also create and delete users.

[3]Reasons for this rebranding were rather technical. In the course of the project it turned out that not all partners were equally suited for building semantic applications, especially not from the early outset. Therefore the "Personal Assistant" was redesigned to be a virtual application splitting its functionality between the backend (aeg-core) and the GUI as implemented by aeg-client2.

[4]This additional layer of indirection proved very complex to be implemented and maintained, quite the opposite of what was to be achieved by introducing it in the first place. Nonetheless the GUI development could be completely decoupled from core development efforts which in certain phases of the development cycle was very important.

- User and profile management
  Views used for logging in with an existing profile, for creating a new profile, and for modifying personal attributes.

- Goal selection
  Presents the user with a list of possibly filtered Goals that either are LifeEvents or are already resolved subgoals of a LifeEvent.

- Visualization and data entry
  Main point of interaction with the platform. These views display and let the user manipulate the current status of a workflow's execution.

For performance reasons, the initially planned connection to the core system through the Web Service XML-based API was dropped in favor of directly including the core as a jar. Sharing data between different instances is still possible because the underlying repository structure takes care of multi-user specific consistency issues. The core itself acts as a proxy to the database, lifting database content into the object-oriented domain.

Figure 15.1 illustrates the interconnection between the core and the PAC.

A typical user session involving the PAC is shown in Figure 15.2. It depicts a fully resolved life event (Marriage), listing all possible steps in the correct order.

157 java and 77 jsp(x) source files total a SLOC count of 12.385.

15.1.1.3. aeg-ontologies

Every pilot installation has its own set of ontologies in its specific subdirectory. All of those ontology distributions are structured alike, having a core ontology describing Access-eGov's core concepts like Organisation, Service, or Area. Additionally, every goal in the system is placed in its own WSML file as well. One last group of files are service descriptions. Goals and services are directly exported by the AT. In the latest versions, the indirection via exporting and importing is not necessary anymore since the AT talks to the core repositories directly.

Ontologies for all pilot projects combined sum up to the impressive number of 554 WSML files with a count of 109413 lines of WSML code.

15.1.1.4. aeg-rdf

Access-eGov is a Semantic Web project. One of the most interesting bits of its implementation is the actual support for the Semantic Web as envisioned in Part II.

In order to be part of this effort, the whole information contained in the repositories was exported as RDF triples forming a graph of contained concepts and instances. Implementing this addition was very easy through the use of a RDF library originating in the Jena[5] semantic web framework, resulting in a very slim codebase of only 107 SLOC.

A different picture emerges when looking at the client side of the Semantic Web. Semantic Web-enabled browsers[6] do exist, they are, however, dependent on the quality of the data. The generated RDF graphs suffer from one much larger drawback, however: while the data contained therein is correct and sound, each graph is a closed world as no links to outside entities exist yet.

Other RDF providers equally suffer from the same problem as can be seen even when starting to browse the Semantic Web from the RDF-enabled home of Sir Tim Berners-Lee[7]. After two or three links, the borders of the Semantic Web are visible when the user hits the border of the closed semantic web world.

15.1.1.5. aeg-security

Already theoretically introduced in Section 13.4, the security architecture uses a differently grained source code layout. It consists of six top-level svn modules, each of which implements one specific component (aeg-security-pip, aeg-security-pdp, etc.) of the security subsystem. Employing Sun's XACML implementation, these modules exist in 46 files and 3483 SLOC.

15.1.1.6. aeg-web-services

Using Sun's JAXWS[8], exporting a number of core (CRUD) functionalities is a straight forward task requiring no more than 7 files with a total of 298 SLOC.

15.1.1.7. aeg-wsmo4j2

All core components of Access-eGov are summarized in the aeg-wsmo4j2 module. Previous versions were dependent on the official wsmo4j source tree but this dependency was dropped when performance reasons required a leaner object model mostly for that part of wsmo4j that implemented WSML. With the advent of the present wsmo4j2, the dependencies on wsmo4j were minimized and all previously

---

[5]http://jena.sourceforge.net/

[6]Tests were done with a Firefox plugin available at http://dig.csail.mit.edu/2007/tab/ which worked quite well

[7]http://www.w3.org/People/Berners-Lee/

[8]https://jax-ws.dev.java.net/

scattered components[9] were joined to one big svn module containing the following components.

composition

Service composition takes place by resolving a life event to sub-goals. Sharing data between the processes representing the sub-goals is realized through shared variables which have to be attached to process contexts. They usually have both, a sending, and a receiving role which are filled by parent and child processes, respectively. Directly linking those process contexts is neither supported dynamically nor statically due to design reasons[10]. A PPMediator[11] is the most elegant solution for the task as it can be implemented to take into account semantic differences of source and target processes [CM06].

core

SVN Module containing a factory that is able to generate WSML parsers and serializers, Configuration-, Execution-, Invoker-, Reasoner-, Resolving-, and Resource-Manager instantiations.

execution

Execution is solely concerned with process creation and updating. On creation of a process, a so-called ProcessContext, a datastructure representing important properties of a running process is returned.

invoker

The Invoker provides the ability to directly communicate with web services, including potentially necessary lifting and lowering operations.

reasoning

Straight-forward implementation of the envisioned functionality in Section 13.3.6.

---

[9]The code was structured with a different granularity. Every core component (Execution, Chaining, ...) resided in its own svn module.
[10]The semantic of a direct link between processes and therefore between services is too straight forward and developers would expect these links to have properties that they cannot have. After all, diverse processes cannot easily be linked.
[11]Process to Process Mediator.

repository

Every data type has its own repository implementation:

- DataRepository

- GoalRepository

- OntologyRepository

- ProcessRepository

- ServiceRepository

- UserRepository

The underlying storage technology is based on Java Persistence API[12] and has been tested with several different databases (MySQL, PostgreSQL, and MS SQL).

resolving

A management module that subsumes tasks in different modules that are needed in order to transform a generic process into an executable service chain.

usermanagement

Management of user profiles, from their creation to securely deleting them, happens in this module.

wsmo

The last package contains all classes and interfaces needed in order to implement the WSML language in a well performing way.

911 source files in this unit contain 99036 SLOC, making aeg-wsmo4j2 the biggest unit in the whole project.

15.1.2. Crosschecking With Requirements

Since the project is already finished, the best documentation of achieving all requirements are the quality assurance procedures within the project. A project publication on the second and last pilot phase within the project's lifetime assess this property [SKH+09]: it identifies no areas where the project would be missing any key requirements.

---

[12]http://java.sun.com/developer/technicalArticles/J2EE/jpa/

15.1.3. Evaluation

The Access-eGov consortium also provides extensive evaluation results in [SKH+09], attesting the finished platform a high usability and efficiency. Even the high user expectations prevalent in sensitive eGovernment environments could be fulfilled with one notable exception: the annotation client. While all frontend[13] functionality received very good marks, the domain experts' user interface "Annotation Tool" did not fare so well. Performance and usability reasons were among the most often cited problems.

From a technical point of view, the last version of the platform components featured significant improvements over prior versions, both in objective performance figures and in the subjective quality of implementation.

All in all, the evaluations showed that a SSOA can act as a central service broker in that specific setting and can do so in a well-performing way while providing a very good user experience.

15.1.4. Improving the Design

Despite the thorough evaluation in [SKH+09], no new requirements or change requests arose that related directly to the architecture.

15.2. SPIKE System

At the time of writing of this thesis, SPIKE is just in its initial pilot phase. Thus, all of the following statements should be considered as preliminary.

15.2.1. Main Implemented Components

Most of the main components have already been implemented and integrated in preliminary versions. Implementation closely follows the architecture laid out in Section 14.3, while further details are not part of this thesis but will be published on the project's website[14].

---

[13]The backend has not been evaluated directly but only through properties that were visible to users (e.g. information quality).

[14]http://spike-project.eu

15.2.2. Crosschecking with Requirements

SPIKE's development team validated architectural components in relation to the user requirements early in the development process in [ABF+08] with the result that the SPIKE architecture can fully support all user requirements.

15.2.3. Evaluation

SPIKE also features an ambitious evaluation schema that initializes after the end of the first trials. If, however, components are implemented as planned, the evaluation result, at least for the architecture itself, will be positive.

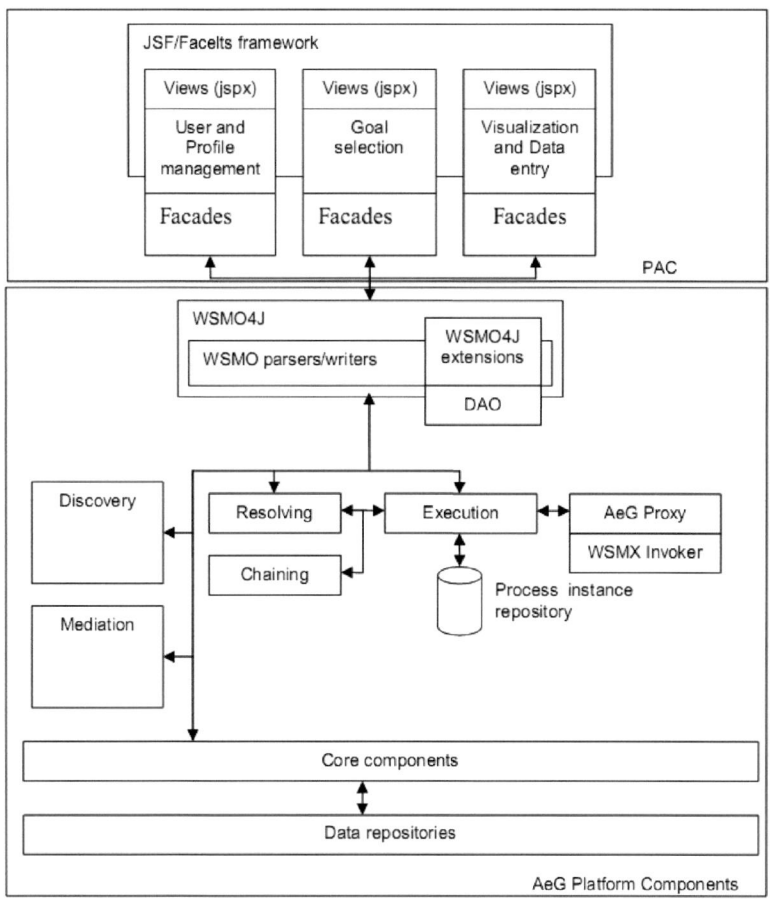

Figure 15.1.: Interconnection of Access-eGov's Personal Assistant Client and Backend (taken from internal developers' documentation)

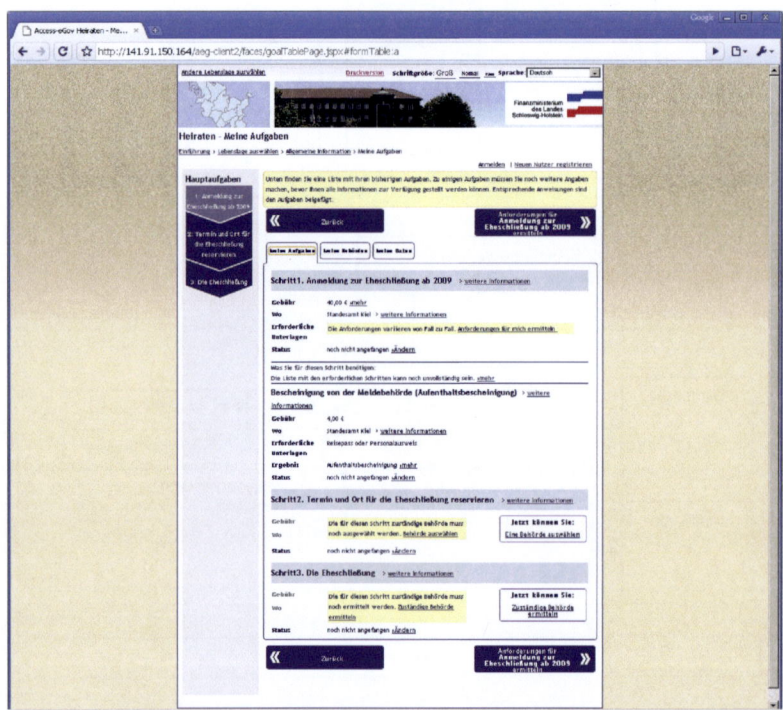

Figure 15.2.: Screenshot of the Personal Assistant Client

16. Alternative Client / Server-based Implementation

So far, this thesis has shown that SSOAs can efficiently be implemented using today's technologies. Another important finding is, however, that they are complex and require rethinking and rebuilding of processes within the involved entities. Simply judging from the requirements, implementing a competitor to the GENSOA does not require KBTs nor the underlying SOA-foundations in all cases. To assess whether the added complexity of introducing those technologies is worth the effort, the GENSOA has to be put in relation to implementations built using traditional technologies.

The following sections introduce a different architecture attempt which does not use KBTs and is based on the Client / Server architectural style. In order to have tangible requirements to discuss, a system with Access-eGov-like functionality (cf. Section 13.2) is the goal. Since an actual implementation is not envisioned, the description of the alternative does not follow IEEE-1471 or any other formalized structure, but only briefly lays out the basic concepts behind the design.

16.1. Design

Client / Server systems as introduced in Section 3.3.1 can act as the central hub in a service brokering software system. Figure 16.1 is one of many possible solutions that can fulfill most, and with some indirections even all, requirements of Access-eGov.

Although the components seem familiar, they have particularly different areas of usage and are arranged in varying ways as is explained in the following paragraphs.

Server Component

Typical of Client / Server systems, the server component encompasses the majority of functional components and contains the following subcomponents:

- Service Registry
  Focal point for registering all services through service-related metadata. Since

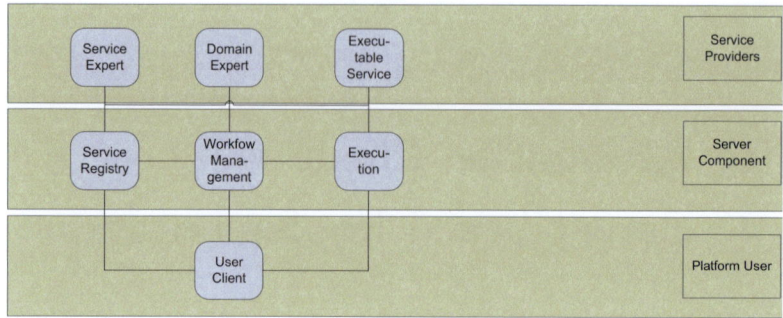

Figure 16.1.: Client / Server Implementation of a Service Brokering Infrastructure

all KBTs are missing in this approach, metadata cannot be standardized across user groups and other means of standardizing on metadata have to be chosen. An effective approach to limit the degrees of freedom in descriptive metadata is the usage of a wizard asking questions with a very narrow set of expected answers. Utilizing standard UI widgets, particular steps of the wizard will leave the user with a fixed set of choices and no possibility to input textual descriptions. Other types of metadata may contain random text but on a very selective facet of the service descriptions. All of these widgets are hardwired in general, thus lacking flexibility.

- Workflow Management
  Similar in functionality to workflow components in the GENSOA (cf. Section 11.4.1.1), workflow management takes place in totally different circumstances in a Client / Server world. Service's metadata is potentially unreliable and not formally standardized. If measures as introduced in the previous item are not taken, reliable resolving of scenarios to executable services cannot succeed.

  In any case, resolving can only happen on a static level; even if services are described along a fixed set of terms, mediation between the terms is not even remotely possible as no information on semantics of the used terminology exists.

- Execution
  Executing the resolved chain of services can quickly become impossible. Since no standard way of talking to services exists in this approach, service-interactions

might have to be implemented for each involved service. If no such implementation exists, the resolved service chain comes to a halt and exits with a failure.

Service Providers

Service providers are located outside the core server component and consist of the core concept `Executable Service` and two administrative roles:

- Executable Service
  An entity that is executed after successful scenario resolving. While the service might be reachable via a rather common SOAP interaction, the Client / Server case does not put any constraints on the nature of services. This leads to the already mentioned problems of unstandardized interfaces.

- Domain Expert
  Equal to domain experts in the SSOA case, a domain expert here has to provide the scenarios. Additionally, he has to be involved in creating the wizards as they define available metadata per service.

- Service Expert
  A service expert role is not present in SSOA approaches for the simple reason that all communication is standardized through using the SOAP protocol. His task is to provide technical details on the services' communication parameters.

Platform Users

A user client has to contact all three components of the server core in order to realize the goal he has in mind when operating the platform. The usual sequence of events is:

1. Client discloses his goal/scenario to the Workflow Management.

2. Workflow Management resolves the goal/scenario to an executable service chain.

3. Client fetches first service reference from Workflow Management's return value.

4. Client asks Service Registry for protocol information on the current service.

5. Client interacts with the service, temporarily storing any returned data.

6. Client fetches next service and continues at step 3.

16.2. Crosschecking with Requirements

Evaluating this architecture sketch in relation to its capabilities can be done by applying the requirements established for the GENSOA in Section 11.2. Table 16.1 explains the mechanisms by which the aimed at functional requirements are supported in this alternative approach.

Functional Requirements	
Requirement	Counterpart in the Client / Server system
F/0010/ AAI	Supporting AAIs in this setting is possible but difficult due to the lack of any centralized security system (cf. F/0070/).
F/0020/ Search	Implemented in the Service Registry.
F/0030/ User Support	Separately implemented in any component that has a need for it.
F/0040/ Information Quality	Similar to the GENSOA case, this requirement can only be supported by software to a certain degree and is mostly an organizational effort.
F/0050/ Semantic Matching	–
F/0060/ Composition	Only possible manually.
F/0070/ Orchestration	Only possible through specific guidelines. Lacking standardization, these guidelines have to be concise and all-embracing. Thus, storing them as meta data is not feasible and the best the platform can offer is a reference to this description from within the service registry. Every user client has to have a working implementation of the specific orchestration data structures.
F/0080/ Process Management	Solved in the workflow management component.
F/0090/ Security	Lack of standardization and global data models makes it impossible to equip the system with a security component as far-reaching as the one introduced in Chapter 12. Thus, the platform is missing ABAC and SSO functionalities.

F/0100/ On-tology Management	–
F/0110/ Semantic Markup	–
F/0120/ Wrapper Technologies	Lack of standard communication protocols shifts wrappers from being a singular case to being the norm.
F/0130/ Identity Management	–
F/0140/ Inclusion of external sources	–
Quality Requirements	
Requirement	Counterpart in the Client / Server system
L/0010/ Security	Cf. F/0070/.
L/0020/ Performance	Client / Server systems are easily tunable; standard methodologies exist today. They also lack the overhead of semantic processing. Thus, Client / Server Systems have less performance constraints than SSOAs put on the infrastructure.
L/0030/ Reliability	Usage of common practices for boosting reliability is mandatory.
L/0040/ Extensibility	A Client / Server system used in the task at hand fails this requirement. Any extension involves implementation efforts and every service has to be described according to parameters important to the current system. No service metadata is reusable between systems.
L/0050/ Usability	No additional usability constraints arise from using Client / Server systems.

L/0060/Communi-cation Security	Implementable in protocols used between communica-tion partners. Each communication relation, however, has to take care of these issues itself, thus providing their own security implementations for each protocol used[1].
L/0070/ Privacy	Since a centralized security subsystem is missing in this case (cf. F/0090/), supporting privacy is a huge effort. Too many partakers of the system do have to know most users' complete set of attributes.
L/0080/ Access Control	Implemented between Server Core and User Client as well as between User Client and Service.
Non functional requirements	
Requirement	Counterpart in the Client / Server system
NF/0010/ Main-tainability	Not Client / Server specific, this requirement is taken care of by adherence to well-established software engineering methods.
NF/0020/ Portability	Not Client / Server specific, this requirement is taken care of by adherence to well-established software engineering methods.
Informational Requirements	
Requirement	Counterpart in the Client / Server system
D/0010/ Service information	Kept in the service registry.
D/0020/ User Goals	Kept in the workflow management.
D/0030/ Pro-cesses	Kept in the workflow management.

Table 16.1.: Generic Design Requirements of the GENSOA

[1]Protocols in this context are application specific protocols in the application layer of the network stack.

16.3. Evaluation

These considerations show that a Client / Server system in the place of a GENSOA can fulfill the purpose of the system. It has a number of distinctive drawbacks, however.

One main problem with this design is its problematic extensibility. Due to KBT usage, SSOAs, unlike the Client / Server design, can respond to service additions without any human interaction. Any reconfiguration of this system on the other hand at least requires tedious human configuration work. In many scenarios completely new communication protocols have to be implemented from scratch.

Lack of a common vocabulary for user-related attribute sets is another major problem as it makes impossible the inception of a central security system. Without it, and consequently without SSO facilities, user administration cannot rely on ABAC for access control but has to be manually configured. The resulting system will most likely adhere to the RBAC standard with all its problems in large-scale distributed systems.

The only source of complexity in this otherwise straight-forward design is the multitude of different communication relations. On the other hand, the system lacks the complexity and overhead of SOAs and SSOAs, resulting in a system that is - once it is setup correctly, and not taking administrative tasks into account - performing well.

16.4. Improving the Design

Alleviating these problems is possible, however. Two modifications to the design considerably improve the design:

- Standard communication protocols
  Using standardized communication protocols like SOAP limits implementation and configuration effort when new services are added to the platform.

- Introduction of KBTs
  If some sort of KBT is additionally introduced, the effort for administration tasks is lessened as those technologies offer support for more or less automated lifting and lowering transformations, enabling seamless communications between otherwise not directly compatible services. KBTs also support SSO and are basis for an ABAC-enabled security system.

Above all, KBTs are the sole foundation on which automated composition and orchestration functionalities operate on.

The resulting system now closely resembles a SSOA, validating the case made for the SSOA and GENSOA in previous chapters in the first place.

17. Conclusion

The last phase in the Design Research cycle laid out in Chapter 1 is the conclusion of the research effort. As already addressed in the motivational Section 1.1, it is of utmost importance to unearth and explain weaknesses of the more and more prevailing SOAs. Offering corrective measures that finally lead to the SSOA concept is one of the most important research outcomes of this thesis. In order to reach this goal, a generic architecture for SSOAs has been proposed together with extensive discussions of theoretical foundations and practical building blocks.

In order to determine whether this thesis produced successful end results, the following paragraphs will summarize the answers to the research questions posed in Section 1.2.4 and provide links to detailed answers in corresponding chapters of this work.

- What is a possible design for a large scale, extensible, service brokering infrastructure like the Access-eGov system?

  Applying a common software development process to two real-world projects has shown that for service brokering infrastructures a SSOA currently is the best solution even if very complex, mostly because SSOAs have great advantages over many other important architectural styles (cf. Section 3.3) and even over similarly complex SOA-based architectures (cf. Section 3.3.5 and especially Section 3.3.6).

  The initially planned SSOA (Access-eGov), together with theoretical requirements, also served as foundations for the design of a generic reference model and architecture for SSOAs, called the GENSOA, which is the main matter of Part III.

  Experience gained within Access-eGov lead to evolution processes as can be seen by the addition of an ESB-like component to the GENSOA and SPIKE architectures (cf. Sections 11.4.1.1, 14.3.1.2).

- Are standard security services applicable in a SSOA? If not, can they be modified?

After having analysed standard security services in Section 5.3 and security requirements of a technical and theoretical nature in Section 5.4, the most important finding is that standard security services are still sufficient in SSOA-based approaches.

Within the design of the GENSOA reference architecture, a security subsystem has been designed that uses standard security services applied to SSOAs (cf. Chapter 12).

- Based on a XACML architecture, can a flexible placement of a PDP help boost privacy in a SSOA?
  In addition to answering the previous question, the security subsystem introduced in Chapter 12 also features the possibility of flexibly placing the PDP in locations along the service consumer / service provider axis. It can be shown that such a flexible placement indeed boosts privacy of partaking users.

- What will an implementation look like?
  Implementations of SSOAs are explained in the form of two real-world projects of which one has already been fully implemented while the other is in its initial implementation phase. Part IV describes both implementations.

- Are SSOAs already usable? Do they introduce value added?
  A comparative evaluation in Chapter 15 contrasts GENSOA-derived implementations with less complex Client / Server-based architectures and comes to the conclusion that SSOAs are not only usable yet (proven by the fact that Access-eGov finished quite successfully) but do indeed introduce added value as especially the comparison with the Client / Server approach in Chapter 16 shows.

- Can semantic / knowledge-based technologies effectively be used in the requirements engineering phase of an architecture definition?
  Semantics indeed are an interesting solution when it comes to building a shared vocabulary over development and requirements teams. Section 10.2 examines the suitability of this approach.

Bibliography

[ABC+97] G. Abowd, L. Bass, P. Clements, R. Kazman, and L. Northrop. Recommended best industrial practice for software architecture evaluation. Technical report, Carnegie Mellon University Software Engineering Institute, 1997.

[ABDM01] A. Abran, P. Bourque, R. Dupuis, and J.W. Moore. Guide to the Software Engineering Body of Knowledge-SWEBOK. Technical report, IEEE and ACM, 2001.

[ABF+08] I. Agudio, C. Broser, C. Fritsch, K. Furdik, C. Fernández Gago, O. Gmelch, M. Mach, and R. Schillinger. D3.1 spike system architecture. Technical report, SPIKE Consortium, 2008.

[ABFG+08] I. Agudo, C. Broser, C. Fernàndez Gago, C. Fritsch, K. Furdik, O. Gmelch, M. Mach, A. Possegger, T. Sabol, and R. Schillinger. D2.1 State-of-the-art report. Technical report, SPIKE Consortium, 2008.

[AD01] K. Aberer and Z. Despotovic. Managing trust in a peer-2-peer information system. In *Proceedings of the tenth international conference on Information and knowledge management*, pages 310–317. ACM New York, NY, USA, 2001.

[AFG+08] S. Alonka, C. Fritsch, O. Gmelch, U. Kantojarvi, W. Ogris, I. Palola, A. Possegger, A. Stopper, H. Vogler, and S. Wiesbeck. D2.2 user requirement analysis & development / test recommendations. Technical report, SPIKE Consortium, 2008.

[AFG+09] M. Armbrust, A. Fox, R. Griffith, A.D. Joseph, R.H. Katz, A. Konwinski, G. Lee, D.A. Patterson, A. Rabkin, I. Stoica, and M. Zaharia. Above the clouds: A berkeley view of cloud computing. Technical Report UCB/EECS-2009-28, EECS Department, University of California, Berkeley, Feb 2009.

[AFM⁺05] R. Akkiraju, J. Farrell, J. Miller, M. Nagarajan, M.T. Schmidt, A. Sheth, and K. Verma. Web service semantics-WSDL-S. Technical report, University of Georgia and IBM Research, 2005.

[AFO⁺09] S. Alonka, K. Furdik, W. Ogris, I. Palola, A. Possegger, A. Stopper, and Wernig.H. D6.1 guidelines for semantic markup of business services. Technical report, SPIKE Consortium, 2009.

[AL05] A. Anderson and H. Lockhart. SAML 2.0 profile of XACML. Technical report, OASIS, 2005.

[And06] A. Anderson. Web services profile of XACML (WS-XACML) version 1.0. *OASIS Working Draft*, 2006.

[AP94] A. Aamodt and E. Plaza. Case-based reasoning. In *Proc. MLnet Summer School on Machine Learning and Knowledge Acquisition*, pages 1–58, 1994.

[Bal09] H. Balzert. *Lehrbuch der Softwaretechnik: Basiskonzepte und Requirements Engineering*. Spektrum Akademischer Verlag, Heidelberg, Neckar, 3. edition, 2009.

[BBC⁺06] S. Bajaj, D. Box, D. Chappell, F. Curbera, G. Daniels, P. Hallam-Baker, M. Hondo, C. Kaler, D. Langworthy, A. Malhotra, et al. Web Services Policy Framework (WS-Policy). Technical report, World Wide Web Consortium, 2006.

[BCC92] V.R. Basili, G. Caldiera, and G. Cantone. A reference architecture for the component factory. *ACM Transactions on Software Engineering and Methodology (TOSEM)*, 1(1):53–80, 1992.

[BCC06] G. Brusa, M.L. Caliusco, and O. Chiotti. A process for building a domain ontology: an experience in developing a government budgetary ontology. In *AOW '06: Proceedings of the second Australasian workshop on Advances in ontologies*, pages 7–15, Darlinghurst, Australia, 2006. Australian Computer Society, Inc.

[BCDG⁺03] D. Berardi, D. Calvanese, G. De Giacomo, M. Lenzerini, and M. Mecella. Automatic composition of e-services that export their behavior. *Lecture notes in computer science*, pages 43–58, 2003.

[BCE+02] T. Bellwood, L. Clement, D. Ehnebuske, A. Hately, M. Hondo, Y.L. Husband, K. Januszewski, S. Lee, B. McKee, J. Munter, et al. UDDI version 3.0. Technical report, OASIS, 2002.

[BCK03] L. Bass, P. Clements, and R. Kazman. *Software architecture in practice*. Addison-Wesley Professional, 2003.

[BCZ92] T.A. Byrd, K.L. Cossick, and R.W. Zmud. A synthesis of research on requirements analysis and knowledge acquisition techniques. *Management Information Systems Quarterly*, pages 117–138, 1992.

[BDO06] A. Barros, M. Dumas, and P. Oaks. Standards for web service choreography and orchestration: Status and perspectives. *Lecture Notes in Computer Science*, 3812:61, 2006.

[BG04] D. Brickley and R.V. Guha. RDF vocabulary description language 1.0: RDF schema. Technical report, World Wide Web Consortium, 2004.

[BHM+04] D. Booth, H. Haas, F. McCabe, E. Newcomer, M. Champion, C. Ferris, and D. Orchard. Web services architecture. Technical report, 2004.

[Bis03] M. Bishop. *Computer Security: Art and Science*. Addison-Wesley, 2003.

[BL98] T. Berners-Lee. Semantic Web road map. Technical report, World Wide Web Consortium, 1998.

[BLFM05] T. Berners-Lee, R. Fielding, and L. Masinter. RFC 3986: Uniform resource identifier (URI): Generic syntax. Technical report, ISOC, 2005.

[BLHL01] T. Berners-Lee, J. Hendler, and O. Lassila. The semantic Web. *Scientific American*, 284(5):34–43, 2001.

[BME+07] G. Booch, R. Maksimchuk, M. Engle, B. Young, J. Conallen, and K. Houston. *Object-oriented analysis and design with applications, third edition*. Addison-Wesley Professional, 2007.

[BN96] P. Bernus and L. Nemes. A framework to define a generic enterprise reference architecture and methodology. *Computer Integrated Manufacturing Systems*, 9(3):179–191, 1996.

[Boe98] B.W. Boehm. A spiral model of software development and enhancement. *Computer*, May 1998.

[BP98] S. Brin and L. Page. The anatomy of a large-scale hypertextual web search engine. *Comput. Netw. ISDN Syst.*, 30(1-7):107–117, 1998.

[BS07] R. Bhagwat and M.K Sharma. Information system architecture: a framework for a cluster of small-and medium-sized enterprises (SMEs). *Production Planning and Control*, 18(4):283–296, 2007.

[BSW07] T.J. Blevins, J. Spencer, and F. Waskiewicz. TOGAF ADM and MDA®. *Revision 1.1. http://www. opengroup. org/cio/MDA-ADM*, 2007.

[Bus03] C. Bussler. *B2B integration: concepts and architecture*. Springer-Verlag New York Inc, 2003.

[BYRN99] R.A. Baeza-Yates and B. Ribeiro-Neto. *Modern Information Retrieval*. Addison-Wesley Longman Publishing Co., Inc., Boston, MA, USA, 1999.

[CGB+02] P. Clements, D. Garlan, L. Bass, J. Stafford, R. Nord, J. Ivers, and R. Little. *Documenting software architectures: views and beyond*. Pearson Education, 2002.

[Che90] B. Cheswick. An evening with berferd in which a cracker is lured, endured, and studied. In *USENIX proceedings*, volume 20, page 1990. Citeseer, January 1990.

[CK94] S.R. Chidamber and C.F. Kemerer. A metrics suite for object oriented design. *IEEE Transactions on Software Engineering*, 20(6):476–493, 1994.

[CKK02] P. Clements, R. Kazman, and M. Klein. *Evaluating software architectures: methods and case studies*. Addison-Wesley Professional, 2002.

[Cle08]   P. Clements. Origins of software architecture study. Technical report, Carnegie Mellon University Software Engineering Institute, 2008.

[CM02]   A. Chakrabarti and G. Manimaran. Internet infrastructure security: A taxonomy. *IEEE network*, 16(6):13–21, 2002.

[CM06]   E. Cimpian and A. Mocan. WSMX process mediation based on choreographies. *Lecture notes in computer science*, 3812:130, 2006.

[CS93]   D.E. Comer and D.L. Stevens. *Internetworking with TCP/IP. Vol. 3: Client-server programming and applications for the BSD socket version.* Prentice-Hall, 1993.

[CW00]   S. Chaudhuri and G. Weikum. Rethinking database system architecture: Towards a self-tuning RISC-style database system. *The VLDB Journal*, pages 1–10, 2000.

[dB08]   J. de Bruijn. WSML abstract syntax and semantics. Technical report, ESSI WSMO Working Group, 2008.

[dBBD+05]   J. de Bruijn, C. Bussler, J. Domingue, D. Fensel, M. Hepp, U. Keller, M. Kifer, B. Konig-Ries, J. Kopecky, R. Lara, et al. Web service modeling ontology (WSMO). Technical report, ESSI WSMO Working Group, 2005.

[DCvH+02]   M. Dean, D. Connolly, F. van Harmelen, J. Hendler, I. Horrocks, D.L. McGuinness, P.F. Patel-Schneider, and L.A. Stein. Web ontology language (OWL) reference version 1.0. Technical report, World Wide Web Consortium, 2002.

[DEG+03]   S. Dill, N. Eiron, D. Gibson, D. Gruhl, R. Guha, A. Jhingran, T. Kanungo, S. Rajagopalan, A. Tomkins, J.A. Tomlin, et al. SemTag and Seeker: Bootstrapping the semantic web via automated semantic annotation. In *Proceedings of the 12th international conference on World Wide Web*, pages 178–186. ACM New York, NY, USA, 2003.

[DFP03]   F. Dridi, M. Fischer, and G. Pernul. CSAP-an adaptable security module for the e-government system WEBOCRAT. In *Security and privacy in the age of uncertainty: IFIP TC11 18th International Conference on Information Security (SEC2003), May 26-28, 2003, Athens, Greece*, page 301. Springer, 2003.

[DOJ+93] A. Davis, S. Overmyer, K. Jordan, J. Caruso, F. Dandashi, A. Dinh, G. Kincaid, G. Ledeboer, P. Reynolds, P. Sitaram, et al. Identifying and measuring quality in a software requirements specification. In *Software Metrics Symposium, 1993. Proceedings., First International*, pages 141–152, 1993.

[DS05] M. Duerst and M. Suignard. RFC 3987. Technical report, ISOC, 2005.

[DSK07] S. Duerbeck, R. Schillinger, and J. Kolter. Security requirements for a semantic service-oriented architecture. In *Proc. of the 2nd International Conference on Availability, Reliability and Security (ARES '07), Vienna, Austria*, April 2007.

[Ear01] M. Earl. Knowledge management strategies: toward a taxonomy. *Journal of Management Information Systems*, 18(1):215–233, 2001.

[EB03] J.B. Earp and D. Baumer. Innovative web use to learn about consumer behavior and online privacy. *Communications of the ACM*, 46(4):81–83, 2003.

[Eck06] C. Eckert. *IT-Sicherheit: Konzepte-Verfahren-Protokolle*. Oldenbourg Wissenschaftsverlag, 2006.

[ERI+02] D. Eastlake, J. Reagle, T. Imamura, B. Dillaway, and E. Simon. XML encryption syntax and processing. Technical report, World Wide Web Consortium, 2002.

[Erl05] T. Erl. *Service-oriented architecture: concepts, technology, and design*. Prentice Hall PTR Upper Saddle River, NJ, USA, 2005.

[FFGL00] F. Fabbrini, M. Fusani, S. Gnesi, and G. Lami. Quality evaluation of software requirement specifications. In *Proc. of Software & Internet Quality Week 2000 Conference, San Francisco, CA*, pages 1–18, May 2000.

[FGJ02] P. Fenkam, H. Gall, and M. Jazayeri. Visual requirements validation: Case study in a corba-supported environment. *IEEE International Conference on Requirements Engineering*, page 81, 2002.

[FGPJ97] M. Fernandez, A. Gomez-Perez, and N. Juristo. Methontology: From ontological art towards ontological engineering. In *Proceedings of the AAAI97 Spring Symposium Series on Ontological Engineering*, pages 33–40, 1997.

[FH02] S. Farrell and R. Housley. RFC 3281 – An internet attribute certificate profile for authorization, 2002.

[Fie00] R.T. Fielding. *Architectural styles and the design of network-based software architectures*. PhD thesis, 2000.

[FL06] P. Fettke and P. Loos. *Reference Modeling for Business Systems Analysis*. IGI Global, 2006.

[FP00] H. Federrath and A. Pfitzmann. Gliederung und Systematisierung von Schutzzielen in IT-Systemen. *Datenschutz und Datensicherheit DuD*, 24(12):704–710, 2000.

[Fri08] C. Fritsch. Implementierung einer verteilten Sicherheitsinfrastuktur in Access-eGov. Diplomarbeit, February 2008.

[FT02] R.T. Fielding and R.N. Taylor. Principled design of the modern web architecture. *ACM Transactions on Internet Technology (TOIT)*, 2(2):115–150, 2002.

[Gal00] B.P. Gallagher. Using the architecture tradeoff analysis methodsm to evaluate a reference architecture: A case study. Technical report, Carnegie Mellon University Software Engineering Institute, 2000.

[Gan05] A. Gangemi. Ontology design patterns for semantic web content. *Lecture notes in computer science*, 3729:262, 2005.

[GHA09] S. Grimm, P. Hitzler, and A. Abecker. Knowledge representation and ontologies. *Semantic Web Services-Concepts, Technologies and Applications*, pages 51–105, 2009.

[GHM+03] M. Gudgin, M. Hadley, N. Mendelsohn, J.J. Moreau, H.F. Nielsen, A. Karmarkar, and Y. Lafon. Simple object access protocol (SOAP) 1.2. Technical report, World Wide Web Consortium, 2003.

[GL93] J.A. Goguen and C. Linde. Techniques for requirements elicitation. *Requirements Engineering*, 93:152–164, 1993.

[GS93] D. Garlan and M. Shaw. An introduction to software architecture. *Advances in Software Engineering and Knowledge Engineering*, 1:1–40, 1993.

[Gua98] N. Guarino. Formal ontology in information systems. In *Formal Ontology in Information Systems: Proceedings of the First International Conference (FOIS'98), June 6-8, Trento, Italy*, page 3, 1998.

[HH99] R.J. Hilderman and H.J. Hamilton. Knowledge discovery and interestingness measures: A survey. Technical report, Department of Computer Science, University of Regina, Saskatchewan, Canada, 1999.

[HJ02] C.W. Holsapple and K.D. Joshi. A collaborative approach to ontology design. *Communications of the ACM*, 45(2), February 2002.

[HMPR04] A.R. Hevner, S.T. March, J. Park, and S. Ram. Design science in information systems research. *Management Information Systems Quarterly*, 28(1):75–106, 2004.

[HNS99] C. Hofmeister, R.L. Nord, and D. Soni. Describing software architecture with UML. In *Proceedings of the First Working IFIP Conference on Software Architecture (WICSA1)*, volume 2, pages 145–159, 1999.

[HNS00] C. Hofmeister, R. Nord, and D. Soni. *Applied software architecture*. Addison-Wesley Professional, 2000.

[HSC+02] S. Handschuh, S. Staab, F. Ciravegna, et al. S-cream-semi-automatic creation of metadata. *Lecture Notes in Computer Science*, pages 358–372, 2002.

[IEE98] IEEE recommended practice for software requirements specifications. Technical report, IEEE Computer Society, 1998.

[IEE00] IEEE Std 1471-2000: Recommended practice for architectural description of software-intensive systems. Technical report, IEEE Computer Society, 2000.

[ISO01] Software engineering – product quality, part 1 (TR9216). Technical report, ISO/IEC, 2001.

[ITU08] Information technology - open sytsems interconnection - the directory: Public-key and attribute certificate frameworks. Technical report, ITU-T, 2008.

[JIB07] A. Jøsang, R. Ismail, and C. Boyd. A survey of trust and reputation systems for online service provision. *Decision Support Systems*, 43(2):618–644, 2007.

[JM90] F. Jay and R. Mayer. IEEE standard glossary of software engineering terminology. Technical report, IEEE, 1990.

[KAK01] R. Kazman, J. Asundi, and M. Klein. Quantifying the costs and benefits of architectural decisions. *International Conference on Software Engineering*, page 0297, 2001.

[KC99] R. Kazman and S.J. Carrière. Playing detective: Reconstructing software architecture from available evidence. *Automated Software Engineering*, 6(2):107–138, 1999.

[KCM04] G. Klyne, J.J. Carroll, and B. McBride. Resource description framework (RDF): Concepts and abstract syntax. Technical report, World Wide Web Consortium, 2004.

[KCSS02] M.M. Kande, V. Crettaz, A. Strohmeier, and S. Sendall. Bridging the gap between IEEE 1471, an architecture description language, and UML. *Software and Systems Modeling*, 1(2):113–129, 2002.

[KDM+06] J. Kolter, S. Duerbeck, M. Mach, P. Bednar, J. Hreno, and M. Skokan. D2.1 state-of-the-art report. Technical report, Access-eGov Consortium, 2006.

[KMRM07] J. Kopecký, M. Moran, D. Roman, and A. Mocan. D24. 2v0. 1. WSMO grounding. Technical report, ESSI WSMO Working Group, 2007.

[KMZ02] S. Kremer, O. Markowitch, and J. Zhou. An intensive survey of fair non-repudiation protocols. *Computer Communications*, 25(17):1606–1621, 2002.

[Kol10] J. Kolter. *User-Centric Privacy - A Usable and Provider-Independent Privacy Infrastructure*. Josef Eul Verlag, Lohmar - Köln, 2010.

[Koo00] P. Koopman. Thoughts on system architecture research and education, 2000.

[Krc90] H. Krcmar. Bedeutung und Ziele von Informationssystem-Architekturen. *Wirtschaftsinformatik*, 32(5):395–402, 1990.

[KRMF06] J. Kopecky, D. Roman, M. Moran, and D. Fensel. Semantic web services grounding. In *AICT-ICIW '06: Proceedings of the Advanced Int'l Conference on Telecommunications and Int'l Conference on Internet and Web Applications and Services*, page 127, Washington, DC, USA, 2006. IEEE Computer Society.

[Kru95] P. Kruchten. Architectural blueprints - The 4 + 1 view model of software architecture. *IEEE Software*, 12(6):42–50, 1995.

[Kru00] P. Kruchten. *The rational unified process: an introduction*. Addison-Wesley Longman Publishing Co., Inc. Boston, MA, USA, 2000.

[KSP07a] J. Kolter, R. Schillinger, and G. Pernul. Building a distributed semantic-aware security architecture. In *Proc. of the 22nd IFIP TC-11 International Information Security Conference (SEC 2007), Sandton, South Africa*, May 2007.

[KSP07b] J. Kolter, R. Schillinger, and G. Pernul. A privacy-enhanced attribute-based access control system. In *Proc. of the 21st Annual IFIP WG 11.3 Working Conference on Data and Application Security (DBSec 2007), Redondo Beach, CA, USA*, July 2007.

[KUF+07] R. Klischewski, S. Ukena, K. Furdik, A. Marciniak, J. Hreno, and M. Skokan. D7.1: Public administration resource ontologies. Technical report, Access-eGov Consortium, 2007.

[Kus09] M. Kussler. "Web-Stress" sorgt für frustrierte Arbeitnehmer und sinkende Produktivität in Unternehmen. http://www.contentmanager.de/magazin/news_h36953_web-stress_sorgt_fuer_frustrierte_arbeitnehmer.html, 2009. Last accessed: 10.01.2009.

[KUW06] R. Klischewski, S. Ukena, and D. Wozniak. D2.2 user requirement analysis & development / test recommendations. Technical report, Access-eGov Consortium, 2006.

[KVBF07] J. Kopecky, T. Vitvar, C. Bournez, and J. Farrell. Sawsdl: Semantic annotations for WSDL and XML schema. *IEEE Internet Computing*, 11(6):60–67, 2007.

[KVG08] J. Kopecky, T. Vitvar, and K. Gomadam. Micro WSMO. Technical report, ESSI WSMO Working Group, 2008.

[KWB03] A.G. Kleppe, J. Warmer, and W. Bast. *MDA explained: the model driven architecture: practice and promise.* Addison-Wesley Longman Publishing Co., Inc. Boston, MA, USA, 2003.

[LG05] S.W. Lee and R.A. Gandhi. Ontology-based active requirements engineering framework. In *APSEC'05. 12th Asia-Pacific Software Engineering Conference*, page 8, 2005.

[LGZ⁺07] J. Li, Z. Guo, Y. Zhao, Z. Zhang, and R. Pang. Towards quantitative evaluation of UML based software architecture. In *Eighth ACIS International Conference onSoftware Engineering, Artificial Intelligence, Networking, and Parallel/Distributed Computing, 2007. SNPD 2007.*, volume 1, 2007.

[Lic94] K. Lichtner. An automated internet resource discovery system. In *CASCON '94: Proceedings of the 1994 conference of the Centre for Advanced Studies on Collaborative research*, page 40. IBM Press, 1994.

[LKN⁺06] K. Lawrence, C. Kaler, A. Nadalin, et al. Web services security kerberos token profile 1.1. Technical report, OASIS, 2006.

[LRL04] J.C. Laprie, B. Randell, and C. Landwehr. Basic concepts and taxonomy of dependable and secure computing. *IEEE Transactions on Dependable Secure Computing*, 1(1):11–33, 2004.

[LTC03] M. Lindvall, R.T. Tvedt, and P. Costa. An empirically-based process for software architecture evaluation. *Empirical Software Engineering*, 8(1):83–108, 2003.

[LY02] K. Lyytinen and Y. Yoo. Issues and challenges in ubiquitous computing. *Communication of the ACM*, 45(12):62–65, 2002.

[M⁺05] T. Moses et al. eXtensible Access Control Markup Language (XACML) version 2.0. Technical report, OASIS, 2005.

[MBH+04] D. Martin, M. Burstein, J. Hobbs, O. Lassila, D. McDermott, S. McIlraith, S. Narayanan, M. Paolucci, B. Parsia, T.R. Payne, et al. OWL-S: Semantic markup for web services. Technical report, World Wide Web Consortium, 2004.

[McC05] D.L. McCuinness. Ontologies come of age. *Spinning the semantic web: bringing the World Wide Web to its full potential*, page 171, 2005.

[Meu95] R. Meunier. *The pipes and filters architecture*, pages 427–440. ACM Press / Addison-Wesley Publishing, New York, NY, USA, 1995.

[MH09] R. Maier and T. Hädrich. *Enterprise knowledge infrastructures.* Springer, 2009.

[MKN+06] R. Monzillo, C. Kaler, A. Nadalin, et al. Web services security: SAML token profile 1.1. Technical report, OASIS, 2006.

[MLM+06] C.M. MacKenzie, K. Laskey, F. McCabe, P.F. Brown, and R. Metz. Reference model for service oriented architecture 1.0. Technical report, OASIS, 2006.

[MMH02] L. Mui, M. Mohtashemi, and A. Halberstadt. A computational model of trust and reputation. In *System Sciences, 2002. HICSS. Proceedings of the 35th Annual Hawaii International Conference on*, pages 2431–2439, 2002.

[MMHR04] J. Matevska-Meyer, W. Hasselbring, and R. Reussner. Software architecture description supporting component deployment and system runtime reconfiguration. In *Proceedings of Workshop on Component-Oriented Programming (WCOP 2004)*. Citeseer, 2004.

[MPG+07] A. Moralis, V. Pouli, M. Grammatikou, S. Papavassiliou, and V. Maglaris. Performance comparison of web services security: Kerberos Token Profile against X. 509 Token Profile. In *Networking and Services, 2007. ICNS. Third International Conference on*, pages 28–28, 2007.

[MR00] M. Maier and E. Rechtin. *The art of systems architecting*. CRC, 2000.

[MSZ01] S. McIlraith, T.C. Son, and H. Zeng. Semantic web services. *IEEE Intelligent Systems*, 16(2):46–53, 2001.

[MT00] N. Medvidovic and R.N. Taylor. A classification and comparison framework for software architecture description languages. *IEEE transactions on Software Engineering*, 26(1):70–93, 2000.

[MVH+04] D.L. McGuinness, F. Van Harmelen, et al. OWL web ontology language overview. Technical report, World Wide Web Consortium, 2004.

[NE00] B. Nuseibeh and S. Easterbrook. Requirements engineering: a roadmap. In *ICSE '00: Proceedings of the Conference on The Future of Software Engineering*, pages 35–46, New York, NY, USA, 2000. ACM.

[Nik97] C. Nikolopoulos. *Expert systems: introduction to first and second generation and hybrid knowledge based systems*. CRC, 1997.

[NKMHB06a] A. Nadalin, C. Kaler, R. Monzillo, and P. Hallam-Baker. Web services security: Soap message security 1.1 (WS-SECURITY 2004). Technical report, OASIS, 2006.

[NKMHB06b] A. Nadalin, C. Kaler, R. Monzillo, and P. Hallam-Baker. WS-security username token profile 1.1. Technical report, OASIS, 2006.

[NKMHB06c] K. Nadalin, C. Kaler, R. Monzillo, and P. Hallam-Baker. X.509 certificate token profile 1.1. Technical report, OASIS, 2006.

[ØAS05] P. Øhrstrøm, J. Andersen, and H. Schärfe. What has happened to ontology. *F. Dau, M.-L. Mugnier & G. Stumme, G.(Eds.): ICCS*, pages 425–438, 2005.

[OBDA08] K. Ostrowski, K. Birman, D. Dolev, and J.H. Ahnn. Programming with live distributed objects. In *ECOOP '08: Proceedings of the 22nd European conference on Object-Oriented Programming*, pages 463–489, Berlin, Heidelberg, 2008. Springer-Verlag.

[OR87] J.R. Olson and H.H. Rueter. Extracting expertise from experts: Methods for knowledge acquisition. *Expert systems*, 4(3):152–168, 1987.

[PBG07] T. Posch, K. Birken, and M. Gerdom. *Basiswissen Softwarearchitektur: Verstehen, entwerfen, bewerten und dokumentieren.* Dpunkt-Verl., 2. edition, 2007.

[PDK06] T. Priebe, W. Dobmeier, and N. Kamprath. Supporting attribute-based access control with ontologies. In *First International Conference on Availability, Reliability and Security (ARES'06)*, pages 465–472. IEEE Computer Society Press, April 2006.

[PDMP05] T. Priebe, W. Dobmeier, B. Muschall, and G. Pernul. ABAC–Ein Referenzmodell für attributbasierte Zugriffskontrolle. In *Proc. 2. Jahrestagung Fachbereich Sicherheit der Gesellschaft für Informatik (Sicherheit 2005)*, 2005.

[Pel03] C. Peltz. Web services orchestration and choreography. *Computer*, 36(10):46–52, 2003.

[PG03] M.P. Papazoglou and D. Georgakopoulos. Service-oriented computing. *Communications of the ACM*, 46(10):25–28, 2003.

[PHS+08] E. Prud Hommeaux, A. Seaborne, et al. SPARQL query language for RDF. Technical report, World Wide Web Consortium, 2008.

[PM04] H.S. Pinto and J.P. Martins. Ontologies: How can they be built? *Knowledge and Information Systems*, 6(4):441–464, 2004.

[PP07] C Pfleeger and S. Pfleeger. *Security in Computing.* Prentice Hall, 2007.

[Pre04] C. Preist. A conceptual architecture for semantic web services. *The Semantic Web–ISWC 2004*, pages 395–409, 2004.

[PSHH04] F. Patel-Schneider, P. Hayes, and I. Horrocks. OWL Web Ontology Language Semantics and Abstract Syntax. Technical report, World Wide Web Consortium, 2004.

[PW92] D.E. Perry and A.L. Wolf. Foundations for the study of software architecture. *SIGSOFT Software Engineering Notes*, 17(4):40–52, 1992.

[Raj98] G.S. Raj. A detailed comparison of CORBA, DCOM and Java/RMI. Whitepaper, 1998.

[RD01] A. Rowstron and P. Druschel. Pastry: Scalable, distributed object location and routing for large-scale peer-to-peer systems. In *IFIP/ACM International Conference on Distributed Systems Platforms (Middleware)*, volume 11, pages 329–350, 2001.

[Ree02] P. Reed. Reference architecture: The best of best practices. http://www.ibm.com/developerworks/rational/library/2774.html, Jun 2002. Last accessed: 23.07.2009.

[RSF+06] D. Roman, J. Scicluna, D. Fensel, A. Polleres, and J. de Bruijn. D14 ontology based choreography of WSMO services. Technical report, ESSI WSMO Working Group, 2006.

[RSY+09] J. Reagle, D. Solo, K. Yiu, M. Bartel, J. Boyer, B. Fox, B. LaMacchia, E. Simon, et al. XML Signature Syntax and Processing Version 1.1. Technical report, World Wide Web Consortium, 2009.

[RW05] N. Rozanski and E. Woods. *Software systems architecture: Working with stakeholders using viewpoints and perspectives.* Addison-Wesley Professional, 2005.

[RW06] N. Rozanski and E. Woods. Applying viewpoints and views to software architecture. http://www.viewpoints-and-perspectives.info/doc/VPandV_WhitePaper.pdf, 2006. Last accessed: 22.09.2009.

[SB07] W. Stallings and L. Brown. *Computer security: principles and practice.* Prentice Hall, 2007.

[SC96] M. Shaw and P. Clements. Toward boxology: preliminary classification of architectural styles. In *Joint proceedings of the second international software architecture workshop (ISAW-2) and international workshop on multiple perspectives in software development (Viewpoints '96) on SIGSOFT '96 workshops*, pages 50–54, New York, NY, USA, 1996. ACM.

[SC97] M. Shaw and P. Clements. A field guide to boxology: preliminary classification of architectural styles for software systems. In *Proceedings of the twenty-First Annual International Computer Software and Applications Conference, 1997. COMPSAC'97.*, pages 6–13, 1997.

[Sch04] J. Schekkerman. Another view at extended enterprise architecture viewpoints. Technical report, Institute for Enterprise Architecture Development, 2004.

[Sem07] The semantic web layer cake. Technical report, The W3C Consortium, Mar 2007.

[SG96] M. Shaw and D. Garlan. *Software architecture: perspectives on an emerging discipline.* Prentice-Hall, Inc. Upper Saddle River, NJ, USA, 1996.

[SGA07] R. Studer, S. Grimm, and A. Abecker. *Semantic web services: concepts, technologies, and applications.* Springer Verlag, 2007.

[Shi00] R. Shirey. RFC2828: Internet security glossary. Technical report, ISOC, 2000.

[Sie05] J. Siedersleben. *Moderne Softwarearchitektur: Umsichtig planen, robust bauen mit Quasar.* dpunkt-Verl., 2005.

[Sim65] R. F. Simmons. Answering english questions by computer: a survey. *Communications of the ACM*, 8(1):53–70, 1965.

[SKH+09] M. Sroga, P. Karasewitz, M. Hajdukova, M. Kmes, T. Bielovsky, M. Kleimann, S. Ukena, P. Bednar, J. Hreno, S. Duerbeck, A. Gizikis, and D. Smogor. D8.4 evaluation of 2nd trial and specification for revision of Access-eGov platform. Technical report, Access-eGov Consortium, 2009.

[SMK+01] I. Stoica, R. Morris, D. Karger, M.F. Kaashoek, and H. Balakrishnan. Chord: A scalable peer-to-peer lookup service for internet applications. In *Proceedings of the 2001 conference on Applications, technologies, architectures, and protocols for computer communications*, pages 149–160. ACM New York, NY, USA, 2001.

[SN96] R.W. Schulte and Y V. Natis. SSA research note SPA-401-068, service oriented architectures, part 1. Technical report, Gartner Group, 1996.

[Som05] S. Some. Use cases based requirements validation with scenarios. *13th IEEE International Conference on Requirements Engineering*, pages 465–466, 2005.

[SR90] M.D Smith and D.J Robson. Object-oriented programming – the problems of validation. In *Proceedings of the Conference onSoftware Maintenance, 1990*, pages 272–281, 1990.

[SSV06] S. Sukumaran, A. Sreenivas, and R. Venkatesh. A rigorous approach to requirements validation. *International Conference on Software Engineering and Formal Methods*, pages 236–245, 2006.

[Sto05] M. Stollberg. Reasoning tasks and mediation on choreography and orchestration in WSMO. In *Proceedings of the 2nd International WSMO Implementation Workshop (WIW 2005), Innsbruck, Austria*, 2005.

[TLH07] T. Tran, H. Lewen, and P. Haase. On the role and application of ontologies in information systems. In *Proc. of 5th IEEE International Conference on Research, Innovation & Vision for the Future (RIVF), Hanoi, Vietnam*, pages 14–21. Citeseer, 2007.

[TVTY90] H. Takeda, P. Veerkamp, T. Tomiyama, and H. Yoshikawa. Modeling design processes. *AI magazine*, 11(4):37–48, 1990.

[VB03] J. Vom Brocke. *Referenzmodellierung*. Jan vom Brocke, 2003.

[VBWV+98] H. Van Brussel, J. Wyns, P. Valckenaers, L. Bongaerts, and P. Peeters. Reference architecture for holonic manufacturing systems: PROSA. *Computers in industry*, 37(3):255–274, 1998.

[VGV93] J. Verschuren, R. Govaerts, and J. Vandewalle. ISO-OSI security architecture. In *Computer Security and Industrial Cryptography - State of the Art and Evolution, ESAT Course*, pages 179–192, London, UK, 1993. Springer-Verlag.

[VK04] V. Vaishnavi and W. Kuechler. Design research in information systems, 2004.

[VKVF08] T. Vitvar, J. Kopecky, J. Viskova, and D. Fensel. WSMO-Lite annotations for web services. *Lecture Notes in Computer Science*, 5021:674, 2008.

[WH07] T. Wilde and T. Hess. Forschungsmethoden der Wirtschaftsinformatik. *Wirtschaftsinformatik*, 49(4):280–287, 2007.

[Wil98] T.J. Williams. *The Purdue Enterprise Reference Architecture and Methodology (PERA)*. Kluwer Academic Pub, 1998.

[WLO97] S.A. White and C. Lemus-Olalde. The software architecture process. *Proceedings of ASME and API Energy Information Management– Incorporating ETCE (ASME–ETCE 97)*, pages 170–175, 1997.

[WSSR06] Y. Wang, Y. Sure, R. Stevens, and A. Rector. Knowledge elicitation plug-in for Protege: Card sorting and laddering. *Lecture Notes in Computer Science*, 4185:552, 2006.

[WVBVB] J. Wyns, H. Van Brussel, P. Valckenaers, and L. Bongaerts. Addendum to "workstation architecture in holonic manufacturing systems". http://www.mech.kuleuven.be/goa/extracts/architec.htm. Last accessed: 23.07.2009.

[WVBVB96] J. Wyns, H. Van Brussel, P. Valckenaers, and L. Bongaerts. Workstation architecture in holonic manufacturing systems. In *28th CIRP International Seminar in Manufacturing Systems*. Technische Rundschau Edition Colibri LTD, 1996.

[YM98] E. Yu and J. Mylopoulos. Why goal-oriented requirements engineering. In *Proceedings of the 4th International Workshop on Requirements Engineering: Foundations of Software Quality*, pages 15–22, 1998.

[Zac87] J.A. Zachman. A framework for information systems architecture. *IBM systems journal*, 28(3):454–470, 1987.

[Zav97] P. Zave. Classification of research efforts in requirements engineering. *ACM Computing Surveys*, 29(4), 1997.